Donated In Memory of

EUGENE CHAMBERS

BY

DON AND PAT TOMS

JANUARY 2009

A FOOT SOLDIER FOR PATTON

A
FOOT SOLDIER
FOR
PATTON

The Story of a "Red Diamond"
Infantryman with the
U.S. Third Army

By
MICHAEL C. BILDER
with
JAMES G. BILDER

CASEMATE
Philadelphia & Newbury

Published in the United States of America in 2008 by
CASEMATE
1016 Warrior Road, Drexel Hill, PA 19026

and in the United Kingdom by
CASEMATE
17 Cheap Street, Newbury, Berkshire, RG14 5DD

ISBN 978-1-932033-91-5

Cataloging-in-publication data is available from the Library of
Congress and from the British Library.

Printed and bound in the United States of America.

10 9 8 7 6 5 4 3 2 1

For a complete list of Casemate titles, please contact

United States of America
Casemate Publishers
Telephone (610) 853-9131, Fax (610) 853-9146
E-mail casemate@casematepublishing.com
Website www.casematepublishing.com

United Kingdom
Casemate-UK
Telephone (01635) 231091, Fax (01635) 41619
E-mail casemate-uk@casematepublishing.co.uk
Website www.casematepublishing.co.uk

CONTENTS

*To my father and all the
members of the Greatest Generation who fought the
Second World War.*

FOREWORD

As an infantryman in the 2d Regiment of the 5th Infantry Division, Michael Bilder crossed the Sauer River on January 18, 1945 and participated in the liberation of my hometown of Diekirch in the Grand-Duchy of Luxembourg. It is thus indeed an honor and a pleasure for me as curator of the National Museum of Military History in Diekirch to write a foreword for his fascinating memoir, *A Foot Soldier For Patton*. Spanning the entirety of his service from 1941 to 1945, this book is more than a personal memoir of World War II: it is a tribute to the countless frontline soldiers who experienced similar events but, for whatever reasons, have remained silent.

More than 60 years ago, hundreds of thousands of American GIs from all walks of life came to Europe to fight in a terrible war. Some were highly educated, others were factory workers and farmers, but all understood that they were being sent to help oppressed nations regain their freedom, liberty, and democratic values. They knew they were risking their lives for this just and noble cause, and thousands gave their last full measure of devotion to reestablish those values, a most precious gift to mankind.

Few veterans, however, have such a record as Michael Bilder. He was, to begin with, a member of one of the first American contingents to go overseas. Arriving in Iceland in early 1942, he served 18 months in an artic landscape as the United States geared up for the great crusade in Western Europe. Shipped to France in July 1944, he then participated in five campaigns. As part of General Patton's Third Army, he and his buddies in the "Red Diamond" Division fought their way all across Western Europe. From the breakout in Normandy to the meat grinder of Metz to the bitter Ardennes, and on into the final battles in Germany and Czechoslovakia, Pfc Bilder was there. Thanks to military skills acquired in long and arduous training, or perhaps to the care of a personal guardian angel, he survived without serious wounds. He went on to serve in the occupation of a defeated Germany before returning to the United States in August 1945.

The liberation of Diekirch was part of one of the bloodiest and cruelest battles of World War II, today known simply as the Battle of the Bulge. I was not yet born when Pfc Bilder and his fellow soldiers fought to free my town, enduring subzero temperatures, knee-deep snow, frozen feet, little sleep, cold food, enemy fire, and the anguish of witnessing friends wounded and killed, all in the terrifying atmosphere of continuous battle. After weeks of unparalleled hardship, the United States Army succeeded in driving back a determined and aggressive enemy. They pierced the Siegfried Line in early February 1945, beginning the invasion of mainland Nazi Germany that ended four months later in total enemy defeat.

All of America's sons and daughters from the Greatest Generation who participated in Europe, the Pacific, or other theaters, and managed to survive the war, were marked by the suffering, death, and destruction they witnessed; frontline infantry soldiers like Pfc Bilder encountered these horrors on a daily basis. Once back home, they tried to adjust to normal life, raise a family, and concentrate on their jobs. All tried to quickly forget the horrors of war, but countless veterans were traumatized, and many are still haunted by nightmares. Some shared their experiences with family members; most were never able to "open up." But all remained proud in the knowledge that they had done their duty and personally contributed to the full victory over the evil of Nazism or other fascist regimes.

Decades after the war, Michael Bilder, now in his retirement, began to reflect in detail on his war experiences. He was spurred on by his son James, who developed a great interest in recording his father's story. Motivated by the desire to preserve his father's wealth of information and a strong love of family history, James Bilder effectively co-authored *A Foot Soldier For Patton*, creating a striking and lively written account based on his father's oral history of the war years. The memoir truly captures not only the experience of his father and countless other American GIs, but also that of an entire nation.

It is a story we especially need to hear now, as America's Greatest Generation is regrettably passing away. The world has fewer and fewer witnesses to the horrors of World War II combat, and memoirs such as the Bilders' are both a valuable source of first-hand information and a key to preserving the collective memory of World War II for future generations. The attention to detail and the personal feelings of a frontline soldier, here captured in an open, frank, and unveiled way, makes for fascinating reading. These qualities also make *A Foot Soldier For Patton* highly recommended for the classroom, or for any reading group interested in history as told by first-person witnesses.

As a fellow student of World War II with a key interest in oral history, I commend James Bilder for this superb account. His father's actions are representative of what thousands of American GIs experienced on the battlefields of World War II. For many American GIs, the Luxembourg-American Cemetery has become the final resting place. Their numbers include some of Michael Bilder's closest friends. I express my eternal gratitude to him and all the other American soldiers who sacrificed so much to liberate my hometown and country during the Battle of the Bulge.

"Lest we forget"
ROLAND J. GAUL
Curator, National Museum of
Military History; Diekirch, Luxembourg
www.nat-military-museum.lu

17 November, 1945

To the Officers and Men of the Fifth Infantry Division:

Nothing I can say can add to the glory which you have achieved.

Throughout the whole advance across France you spearheaded the attack of your Corps. You crossed so many rivers that I am persuaded many of you have web feet and I know that all of you have dauntless spirit. To my mind history does not record incidents of greater valor than your assault crossings of the Sauer and the Rhine.

Concerning the former operation, I showed the scene of your glorious exploit to a civilian for whom I have the highest esteem. After looking at it for some time he said, "I did not believe there was enough courage in the world to achieve such a victory." Knowing the Fifth Infantry Division, I was sure you would achieve it and you did.

Now that peace has been re-established I am sure all of you will continue through the remainder of your lives to stand for those great qualities of America which in war you so magnificently demonstrated.

With affectionate regards and sincere congratulations, I am, as ever,

Your devoted commander,

G. S. PATTON, JR.
General

INTRODUCTION

My father seldom volunteered, but never hesitated when asked, to talk about his various military and combat experiences from the war, and we pleaded with him to do this often as we were growing up. He always had one story or another that would widen our eyes, entertain, or just plain provide us with a good lesson for life. We made him tell them over and over again until, after years of repetition, we had committed many of the incidents to memory.

We kids and our buddies were not the only ones who made it a practice to ask him about his experiences. Friends, relatives, and even strangers wanted to talk with a real GI from Patton's Third Army who had witnessed America's involvement in World War II, and survived the fighting from start to finish, from Normandy all the way to VE Day in Czechoslovakia.

I was then, and remain today, awed by his experiences. None of this is to say that my father was a braggart or even considered himself a hero; in fact, it was quite the opposite. Despite being decorated for valor in combat by no less than three different nations, he always said that when the order to retreat was given, he led the way in running away from the enemy. The only times he discussed his experiences without any prompting from others was in the company of fellow combat vets. He always regarded his actions as typical of everyone who served at the time and as nothing especially noteworthy.

My father was never lacking when it came to a sense of humor, and enjoyed most recounting his countless shenanigans, some of which could have landed him in Leavenworth Prison. He kept this characteristic in civilian life and even had me believing when I was in kindergarten that he had been killed twice during the war.

Born in Chicago to parents who immigrated from Germany, he was drafted into the army eight months before the attack on Pearl Harbor, participated in the famed southern maneuvers of 1941, served 18 months of occupation duty in Iceland, had training in commando tactics and as a combat life guard in England, got additional training in Northern Ireland, and shipped out for France in early July 1944.

As a foot soldier for Patton, he participated in the fierce fighting of all five of the Third Army's bloody campaigns. His experiences in the war often were unusual for an American solider, since he could speak fluent German with a good German accent. This made for many interesting encounters with enemy soldiers as well as frequent calls to serve as an interpreter for American officers interrogating German POWs.

Certified as a life guard by the American Red Cross in October 1943, he was among those who had to jump into French and German rivers when the small assault boats used by American infantrymen overturned under enemy fire and spilled their men into the water. My father would swim to the river bottom, unhook their heavy packs, and push them up to the surface. He would then return to the surface himself to be pulled back into an assault boat by his fellow soldiers and resume his duties as a rifleman.

Finally, when he was in England, my father was recruited to perform an additional duty once the 5th Division got into combat. Since the administrative personnel of the American Red Cross were not combat soldiers, or even part of the U.S. military, they were not allowed to be directly on the frontlines. It became my father's responsibility to travel by jeep from one company to another to deliver Red Cross messages from home (usually bad news) to soldiers at the front all throughout the 2d Regiment. He would then spend a few days temporarily attached to whatever company received his messages.

Like something out of Hollywood, my father's story even concluded with a happy ending. He survived the war, was decorated, came home unscathed, married my mother, and went on to fulfill his ambitions to live the American Dream. It doesn't get any more fascinating than that for those of us who can't get enough of World War II and the generation who fought it.

My father said he could speak freely about his experiences because his actions in combat gave him nothing to be ashamed of. I would listen to these as well as his non-combat tales of military life as I was growing up and even then think to myself, "Somebody really ought to write a book about this."

As I was nearing my mid-forties, having an undergraduate degree in journalism and a love of all things historical, especially military and family history, I decided I should get it done while he was still around. My father and I began with a tape recorder in 1988. At the time, he did not want to spend so much time reliving memories of friends and youth lost. He even feared the army would come back decades later to take away his Good Conduct Medal. Despite these concerns, we accumulated numerous hours of tape, countless letters, and official histories, and read and reviewed numerous books and articles.

Unfortunately, the normal obligations of life sapped most of my attention and energies during the 1990s. It seemed like too big a project to accomplish. It was only after my father turned 85 and my mother died in 2004 that I realized it was now or never and threw things into high gear, devoting virtually all my free time to finishing this project. I truly owe my beautiful wife big time for putting up with this.

This book gives the reader a thorough understanding of how soldiers of the time were trained, fed, clothed, equipped and treated. It provides in detail the horrors of combat and the misery of life on the frontlines. It reveals what most GIs were feeling, and how at least one of them thought. It is also written in layman's terms so that the reader need not have served in the military to understand it.

I hope this book brings some long overdue justice to the 5th Infantry Division. Soldiers with the "Red Diamond" participated in long and bloody campaigns, but get very little mention in contemporary histories about World War II. The desire to help rectify the historical record and give credit to the men of the "Forgotten 5th" were part of the reason I was determined to write this book. I hope my father's memoirs shed additional light on this fascinating and important part of Patton's victories in northern Europe.

I apologize if an incident is off by a week or in fact occurred in another small town nearby, but errors such as these should be relatively rare in this book. It has been thoroughly researched, and my father's memory was very solid when we worked seriously on the tapes and notes in the 1980s. Still, it is important to remember that this is a memoir and not a work of academic research. Dates and statistics are from the official histories of the U.S. Army, 2nd Regiment, and 5th Infantry Division.

If my father is alive when this memoir is published, I would ask that he be spared any phone calls or visits. He is now 89 and feels he has spent enough time reliving bad memories. Also, his ability for names and even incidents has started to slip so I'm glad we were able to bring this work to a timely finish.

This book, this memoir, is a true labor of love. My father consented to tell his story out of love for me and, in turn, I wrote it for love of him, as well as for my passionate for all things historical, and especially for family and military history. In this case, both overlapped.

I sincerely hope that readers enjoy this footnote to history and have as much fun reading it as I did writing it. I hope it does justice to the American soldiers of World War II in general and in particular to the men of the 5th Infantry Division.

JAMES G. BILDER
2008

1

PEACETIME INDUCTION
Just a One-Year Hitch for Preparedness

> "I'm nobody! Who are you?
> Are you—nobody—Too?"
> —Emily Dickinson, "I'm Nobody! Who Are You?"

I didn't know it at the time, but September 16, 1940 was a date that would have a pivotal impact on my life. On that day, Franklin Roosevelt signed the Selective Service Act into law. It was the start of the first peacetime draft in American history.

Induction in the United States had *previously* taken place only as a necessity of war. It first occurred in 1863 at the midpoint of the Civil War, and again in 1917 after the United States entered World War I. Selective Service was thus synonymous with war to most Americans, and it created a considerable amount of apprehension.

Circumstances in 1940 caused a strange, almost schizophrenic, split in our thinking. Much of the globe was embroiled in another world war. Most Americans on the other hand were isolationists at heart and wanted no part in it. Any American who had graduated from grade school was familiar with George Washington's "Farewell Address," in which he warned his countrymen against entangling foreign alliances. Washington's advice seemed horrifically justified after the United States entered World War I and won what appeared to be a meaningless victory in a never-ending line of European struggles and conquests.

As in 1917, interventionists in 1940 wanted "to send every aid short of war" to assist the Allied nations in their struggle. This included the United States President, Franklin Delano Roosevelt, who insisted that the Allies were "fighting our fight," implying that if American aid failed to win the war for the Allies, then America herself should enter the conflict. We wondered, were the interventionists right this time?

This split thinking also spilled into America's foreign policy. Neutrality laws that had on the books as since the mid-1930s were amended so that policies such as "Cash and Carry" and "Lend-Lease" enabled the States to extend armaments to nations that were friendly to democratic values. America could remain officially neutral while still taking sides. The result of war-related manufacturing made America the world's "arsenal of democracy" and produced yet another strange split in our values and thoughts as the very war most Americans wanted to avoid was producing jobs and a potential end to the terrible depression of the 1930s.

Even the presidential election campaign that year split America over an issue that it had never before experienced. An American President was running for a third term of office. The entire campaign centered on foreign policy. Who, Roosevelt the incumbent president, or Wilkie the business and administrative whiz-kid, could best get the country prepared for war without getting us into the fray? This was the two-sided coin of our circumstances in the early war years.

We all saw the ominous events occurring throughout the world in 1940. By September, the war had been underway for a year and the Nazis and Soviets had already overrun most of Europe, while the Japanese did much the same in Asia. This was disconcerting, but it occurred across the oceans, on continents far from our own. The attack on Pearl Harbor was more than fifteen months away. Meanwhile, we enjoyed America's neutrality.

My generation was young and largely oblivious to many of the details related to all these happenings. We were busy getting on with our lives. Things were far from perfect, but I had good things to enjoy in the big city of Chicago where I lived. On a hot summer's night we went to plush movie houses like the Avalon Theater to sit in the comfort of "air conditioning" and watch Hollywood's best on a huge silver screen. We went horseback riding in Washington Park, rented rowboats in Jackson Park, and went to see the Cubs play at Wrigley Field or watched the White Sox at Comiskey Park. The most popular activity of all was dancing. "It don't mean a thing if it ain't got that swing," went the song. Everybody danced. We all loved it and it was a great way for guys and gals to mix. Chicago was a hub for great music and big bands and we saw and heard them all: Glenn Miller, Tommy Dorsey, Benny Goodman, Les Brown and his Band of Renown, and countless others.

A peacetime draft for America was a historic first, but hardly the type of thing to lead to serious protests. There was a real debate as to whether the country should get involved in the war, but there was never any question as to whether we should be able to defend it. Under the new conscription law, the government required all males between the ages of 21 and 35, residents and aliens alike, to register for the draft. This process allowed 900,000 "selectees" to be inducted into the army to serve a twelve-month hitch. We knew that this would help make the country better prepared militarily and more likely to deter any attack from a foreign dictator.

The draft certainly seemed reasonable under the circumstances. Nazi Germany and Soviet Russia were still allies in 1940. Hitler also had alliances with Italy and Japan and the only belligerents of any significance were the British and Chinese. It only made sense that American military might be strong enough to give aggressors reason to think before attacking us.

I met the legal criteria for draft eligibility so I walked the two blocks over to Hendricks Public (Grammar) School at the corner of 43rd and Princeton and registered on October 16, 1940. I had attended Hendricks for kindergarten and first grade, but completed the rest of my grammar school education at St. George Catholic grade school. The registrar's report listed me as 6 feet 1 inch, 195 pounds, with brown hair and eyes and a "ruddy complexion." I was order number 765 and my registration serial number was 2,639. I was now a number among the 16,000,000 men who registered for the draft.

I had been employed for two years as a shipping clerk at the Sears and Roebuck warehouse at 1400 W. 35th Street in Chicago. My main qualification for the job had been my Catholic faith. In the days when people and companies were free to practice discrimination of all types, we were asked to list our religion on our employment applications. A clerk at Sears explained to me later that they liked to hire Catholics because, in their words, they felt that Catholics were less likely to steal.

A few years earlier, before the draft and even before the war itself, some of the guys in the neighborhood were farsighted enough to see another world war as inevitable and joined the National Guard with the hope of having some rank and a good assignment by the time war came. They tried to talk me into doing the same, promising me I'd get a good deal, but I wanted no part of it. I was happy to enjoy civilian life and its creature comforts and it literally took an act of congress to get me to give them up.

Despite my love of the creature comforts, I had gone to the Canadians in 1939 to inquire about enlisting in the RAF. I had loved flight ever since I first read about the brave knights of the air who did battle amongst the clouds in World War I. I saw movies like *Hell's Angels, Dawn Patrol* and *The Eagle and the Hawk* over and over again, and dreamed of one day flying in combat.

I had two problems. First, I had no college, and fighter pilots were expected to have at least two years of undergraduate work upon induction. Second, and more importantly, I had problems with depth perception. These became obvious when I took private flying lessons at Lewis College near Joliet. Whenever I lined up my approach to land, I always angled my plane with the wing on my right dipping down. It seemed level to me, but the instructor always had to take the controls. Needless to say, the Canadians rejected me.

I felt no real apprehension or resentment at being drafted into the army. After all, the war was in Europe and the Pacific, and the United States wasn't involved. Roosevelt won his third term as president in large part by pledging at the Boston Gardens a few days before the election, "I have said this before, but I shall say it again and again. Your boys are not going to be sent into any foreign wars." My family and I accepted that presidential campaign promise at face value. The feeling amongst most Americans, as many as 80 percent according to the polls of the day, was that while America should be prepared and the defeat of the Axis Powers was important, foreign wars didn't really concern us and we should make every effort to stay out of them. We had oceans to separate and protect us from aggressors.

We regarded ourselves as wiser in 1940 than we had been in 1917. America would not be "tricked" into war again: we would "walk softly and carry a big stick," making every attempt to stay out of conflict. Still, there was a nagging suspicion, even a fear, that things were getting out of hand overseas. We all knew that something would have to be done, but hoped that England and China would be the ones to do it. Even in 1940 and 1941, however, it was obvious that they were hanging on by their fingernails.

Maybe if we could show foreign dictators that we were no one to tread on, that would be enough. At least that was what many of us hoped. Like almost every other young man of the time, I didn't mind going into the army for a year. It was only the fighting that concerned me.

My selective service records show that on March 13, 1941, the government mailed me an eight-page questionnaire, which I completed and returned within six days. I soon received the famous (I would prefer "infamous") greetings letter from Uncle Sam telling me to report to my local draft board. I would need to answer some questions from the men who would ultimately pass judgment on my availability for national service.

At the time, I was living with my widowed grandmother. I briefly flirted with the idea of seeking a deferment based on the claim that I was her sole means of support, but I knew this was bogus and even if the government bought it, I wouldn't have been able to live with it. Besides, the order to report to the draft board created in me a certain feeling of importance and opened the door to adventure. There was real trouble in the world and the nation needed men capable of putting America's best defensive foot forward. This wasn't a job for just anybody. America needed the best! You have to be 21 to think that way. You aren't experienced enough yet to know any better or wise enough to know that you're not immortal. Every nation of every era has always known that war is for the young.

Local Selective Service Board 101 was located at 5437 South Halsted Street in Chicago, about a mile and a half from where I lived. When the big day came, I hopped the streetcar filled with a sense of adventure. The army "offices" were nothing but a vacant storefront furnished with card tables and folding chairs.

I seated at a table across from three old men, who looked quite ancient to me as a 21-year-old. They proceeded to ask me questions, verifying what was already on my forms. They checked my name, date of birth, and home address, along with a few things regarding my family and health. After about 10 minutes, they concluded the interview and told me to return to my normal routine. I could expect to hear from them in a few weeks.

The draft board wasted no time: I received an order on April 2 to report for a physical exam two days later. Passing the exam was the final step for induction. The army was initially very picky about the mental, moral, family, and physical status of their potential recruits, but their lofty standards dropped dramatically as the war progressed and the need for manpower grew more and more intense. I knew I was in great shape and could count on passing the physical.

As I said, none of this really bothered me all that much. My life at the time was far from perfect. I lived in a cold-water flat on Chicago's south side at 4315 S. Wells with my grandmother in a poor working class neighborhood known as "Canaryville." It was very near the Chicago Stock Yards and local legend holds that the neighborhood got its name because many households put canaries out on their front porches so their singing would drown out the screams of the animals being slaughtered. We did not actually hear the animals dying, but when the wind was right (or wrong) we sure could smell them.

My father, who died before my birth, was an ethnic German who immigrated to the United States when he was 21 years old, just before the outbreak of World War I. He left his home and family in the Austrian-Hungarian Empire to avoid the draft and set out to find a better life in America. A skilled tradesman, he settled in the German community on Chicago's south side and went to work as a cooper (barrel maker), at a local brewery. My uncle became acquainted with him through social events at Saint George Parish and brought him home to meet his mother, my grandmother, who took an instant liking to him. She saw him as a hard-working man with a skilled trade, good looks, German blood, and the Catholic faith. This was everything a woman in this neighborhood could hope for in a man, and so my grandmother decided that her sixteen-year-old daughter would marry him.

My folks were married in July of 1917 and moved into a flat in my grandparents' building. My mother always told me that my father loved life, had a great sense of humor, and treated her very well. She also told me that she quickly grew to love him.

Their circumstances, however, very hard. My mother's dad died just a few weeks after her marriage, and then in June 1918, she gave birth to a stillborn son during her sixth month of pregnancy. I was conceived some three or four months later, but my father died in December 1918 of the flu pandemic, at the youthful age of 26. He and my mother had been married for only 18 months, and now she was a widow and four months pregnant with me. My mother and grandmother reasoned that life was hard and that responsible adults accepted its circumstances. They instilled this same belief in me. They were repulsed by those few who suggested that an abortion was the answer. I was born the following May.

My mother needed a husband to support her and her infant son, which played no small role in her decision to marry my stepfather in January 1920. My stepfather had been a loose acquaintance of my father's and had even been a member of my parents' wedding party. Despite this, he and I never saw eye to eye on anything. My stepfather had us in a typical city bungalow at 4403 S. Princeton. He always took in boarders to help make ends meet, so I slept in the family room on a day bed that was too short for me. Our differences continued to mount over the years, and at 19 I moved in with my grandmother on the next block.

In my grandmother's eyes I could do no wrong and my stepfather could do little right. He was tight with a buck and did little more than tolerate me, and my grandmother paid the dollar-a-month tuition for me to attend St. George's Catholic grade school. My grandmother was old country, typical of her time and background, and believed it was best for people to marry within their own ethnic group and religion. If forced to choose between the two, then choose religion, but in her mind it was best not to have to choose at all.

It was rather understandable that my stepfather resented his mother-in-law. When I was only six years old, my grandmother told me about my biological father's death, instilling in me a feeling of loss. The sense of deprivation I felt over the loss of my natural father's love and affection resonated ever more strongly with me as I grew up. It was obvious to me that my stepfather was in many ways my (and my late father's) complete opposite.

My stepfather considered me and my friends to be nothing more than a bunch of ne'er-do-wells. My friends always thought him bizarre with his rude mannerisms and frequent cursing, and avoided him whenever possible. With his dour attitude, he was always quick to assure me of two dreadful fates that were certain to befall me. First, that I was destined to grow up to be a bum. In this I can say thankfully that he was very wrong. Second, that I would one day "eat wild pears." Here, he was more correct than he ever could have imagined.

The only thing that was really right in my life at the time was Mary. We had met on a blind date in July 1940. She was intelligent and gorgeous both, and she knew it. Far from lacking in self-confidence, she was even a little on the stuck-up side, but she had a good heart and was really a kind person. Mary was about 5 feet 8 inches tall and had brown hair worn in a pageboy, with beautifully matching brown eyes. Her legs were long and slender and her figure was near perfect. She dressed well, but her true sexiness was contained in a cool air of self-confidence and sophistication that made her a real lady.

I was no slouch myself in those days. I was tall with a very full head of brown hair, clear brown eyes, nicely chiseled facial features, and a solid athletic build. My grandmother refused to charge me rent, so I blew most of my money on good clothes. The guys I hung around with respectfully referred to me as the "Esquire Kid." The fact that I frequently dated a number of pretty girls earned me the nickname "lover boy Bilder" among the local ladies.

Mary and I were well suited to each other, and although we didn't have an engagement ring or a wedding date, I proposed to her and she accepted. What possible difference could a year in the army make?

By the end of March 1941, the draft had succeeded in putting some 306,000 American men in uniform, about a third of its stated goal. I knew that within days I would increase that number by one. I reported, as per my orders, on April 4 to the Armory on Madison Avenue in Chicago. My letter stated that I was to keep my draft notice with me at all times during the physical. I did so, even during the part of the exam when I was naked.

When I arrived at the armory it was a near mob scene. The army was quick, though, to make order out of the mess. A serviceman asked me my name, noted it, and instructed me to a room where I was told to undress and carry our clothes around with us. It was a Friday and people must have been anxious to start their weekend, because the exams were quick even by army standards. About eight of us stood naked in front of four doctors seated on folding chairs. The doctors needed to check us for piles (hemorrhoids). They told us to turn around, bend over, and spread our cheeks. There were some poor slobs who didn't know any better and spread the cheeks on their face.

I was in good health and quite active with heavy involvement in various athletic pursuits. Anyone could tell just by looking at me that I was in good shape. I did well until the final medical check, which was blood pressure. "It's a little high," the doctor said with a hint of surprise in his voice. "I don't know whether or not to pass you."

We both hesitated for a second. I was torn. I had a feeling of adventure and importance intrinsic to the thought of being drafted at a time of high international tension, but I also had a half-hearted feeling of common sense. I wanted to be free from all this induction business and what it might entail for my life. Yet despite my reservations, down deep, I wanted to pass and be drafted. The doctor must have sensed this as he looked me over. He reflected for an instant then said, "I'll take a chance on you," and stamped my form as approved.

Once our physicals were completed, we assembled in the main hall, which looked a good deal like a gymnasium, where I encountered a former classmate from Tilden High School. He came over from a separate group of men who had failed their physicals. My buddy had been rated 4-F for a mastoid (ear) operation.

"Hey Mike, why don't we switch places?" he asked. "I'll go into the army in your spot." I thought about it for a second, but quickly realized there was absolutely no hope of pulling it off. "I can't," I said. "Besides, we'd never get away with it," I told him. I watched as he walked back to his group looking dejected. I couldn't help but feel sorry for him. For me, as for most young men at the time, feelings of patriotism made military service a rite of passage of which we were all keenly aware.

A sergeant came in and told us to listen up. He said that since we had passed our physicals we could now consider ourselves in the army. We had less than one week to tie up any loose ends in our civilian lives and to report back to the armory by 7:30 hours the following Thursday, April 10. Any man who failed to report would be considered a deserter.

Mary and my mother cried at the news. My stepfather didn't seem to know how to react. Sears wished me luck and told me that my job would be waiting for me when I came back. I said good-bye to my buddies and prepared myself for a year in the army.

We were instructed to bring nothing but a few toilet articles when we reported for induction; there were to be no suitcases or large bags. At the armory, all the men with any previous training from military schools or the ROTC were told to step forward and given armbands and sticks with colored circles on the end to help direct us. They absolutely loved it.

IQ (proficiency) exams took the better part of the morning; after we finished, we went into the auditorium and sat in folding chairs until our name was called. When my turn came, I was directed to sit at a table with a soldier who had a typewriter. He noticed on my forms that I had dual training in both a Piper Cub and a Stinson, and also saw that my problem with depth perception had kept me from being a pilot. He asked if I wanted to be an airplane mechanic and work at Chanute Airfield in southern Illinois. I declined, saying that I didn't want to be a grease monkey. I guess I figured such work was beneath me.

He noted my answer with a look of surprise. Since I was over six feet tall, 195 pounds, and in good shape, he then asked me if I was interested in being an MP. "I don't like the idea of being a chicken shit telling men to button their collars and straighten their shoulders," I replied. This sealed my fate and I was immediately assigned to the infantry. I soon learned that it wasn't wise to let those in authority know you were carrying a chip on your shoulder.

After about 50 of us were gathered, a sergeant came in and told us to get ready to be sworn in. We raised our right hands and took the oath. We were now in the army. I had just become one of the 923,842 lucky schmucks drafted in 1941. We were directed into yet another room where we joined about 150 other men and a sergeant. It was about noon. We formed up in columns of two and marched across the street to a beanery called Thompson's, where we helped ourselves to whatever we wanted in the cafeteria line. After about 45 minutes, they formed us up again in columns and marched us over to the train station. Out on Madison Avenue, girls passing by made comments like, "Hi ya, soldier" and "Good luck, soldier." We were still in civilian clothes, but there was obviously no mistaking our new employer.

Like everyone else, I was very preoccupied with where we were headed and what was next in store. We boarded a train north out of Chicago and into neighboring Lake County, arriving in about an hour at our destination, Fort Sheridan. We still had to march some three to four miles to the barracks area. This was most definitely a fort. Everything was made of brick and stone; there was nothing resembling the temporary nature of a camp. It reminded me a great deal of a college campus. In a building some four stories high they broke us down from our original number of about 200 into groups of 20 or 25 men, assigned each group a dorm and told us to pick out any bunk we wanted. Around 17:00 hours we were ordered to fall out for chow. We stood at attention as best as untrained recruits can on their first day while sergeants walked up and down our ranks telling us to suck in our guts, stick out our chests, and pull our shoulders back.

After chow, we thought we were through for the day and could relax. We were wrong. They called all 200 of us out and ordered us to form up in a square. A few officers stood in the middle and a major read us the Articles of War. This was eight months before Pearl Harbor, but they did remind us that we were conscripts, not volunteers, who had been drafted to allow the country to be ready for war, should that eventuality occur. The major added that our commanders would read us the Articles of War from time to time at their discretion as a reminder of our responsibilities. Sergeants then moved among us again, informing us who would need to get a hair cut the following day. Tom Spain, a buddy from my old neighborhood, and I were among the men singled out.

Tom and I were individualists. He came from Saint Cecilia's, an Irish parish just west of where I lived. It was more upscale than my neighborhood, and definitely on the right side of the tracks. I had chosen Tilden (public) High because of my aversion to discipline. I met Tom and his Irish buddies at Fuller Park while playing ball. They were a lot more boisterous and fun loving than the Germans in my own parish of Saint George, although I floated with ease from one group to the other. I was one of the few "krautheads" in with the Irish, and some of the older folk in Saint George didn't like it. This was alright with me. I never worried about who approved or did not approve of my actions or my friends.

Tom and I had a good deal in common. We were both athletic, popular with the girls, well thought of by the guys, and accustomed to making the world see things our own way. While the army could force us to conform to its methods, it could never make us like it. We both detested army life.

After the sergeants finished with us, we were dismissed and headed for our bunks. It was Thursday, April 10, 1941. I had gotten up from my own bed in Chicago as a civilian and I was going to sleep in a bunk at Fort Sheridan as a conscript in the army. I was no longer an individual but the property of Uncle Sam. I was now "GI" (Government Issued).

The next day, Tom and I felt we didn't need haircuts, so we ignored our first army order. We were denied weekend passes and spent that Saturday shoveling horse manure. We took advantage of an opportunity to have our hair cut on Sunday. The chip on my shoulder had already grown larger. I had been in the army for just four days and I already hated it.

2

BASIC TRAINING AND SOUTHERN MANEUVERS
Learning How to Soldier

"I Didn't Raise My Boy to Be a Soldier"
—Title of an anti-war song from World War I

On Monday, they marched us back to the railroad tracks and we boarded a regular troop transport bound for Fort Custer in Battle Creek, Michigan, the home of the 5th Infantry Division and the site of our basic training. From the train, I was able to see St. George's Church and my old neighborhood. The symbolic nature of all this was not lost on me. I had a hunch that things would never be quite the same. I tried to see Dorchester, where Mary lived, but we didn't pass close enough for me to do so.

We gave our name as we stepped off the train and were told our unit assignments. I was assigned to Company F (Fox) in the 10th Regiment. They formed us up into our respective companies in columns of two and took us to areas where platoon sergeants were waiting. We were assigned to a platoon, taken to barracks, and assigned a bed. We were now all numbered and pegged.

The barracks were wooden frame and two stories high. I was on the first floor between two windows. We were marched over to the supply depot where we were issued clothes and two pairs of shoes. Some of our equipment was leftover from World War I, including the "saucepan" helmets that the American Doughboys had used. We spent the following few days learning how to salute, stand at attention, march in formation and the like. After about a week, we were issued a rifle, ammunition belt and a pack. I qualified as an "expert" on

17

almost every weapon: rifle, machine gun, and hand grenade. The sole exception was the .45-caliber sidearm, which has a powerful recoil. I thought it kicked like a mule, and I had great difficulty hitting anything at all with it. Somehow, I did manage to qualify on it, though just barely.

Reveille was at 6:00 hours sharp. We had five minutes to get our dress uniform on and fall out into our platoon for roll call. We stood in four neat rows and counted off, man-by-man. The platoon sergeant had to hear four counts of eleven or else it meant that someone was missing. After we were dismissed, we scrambled in a mad dash for toilets and washbasins. We then had to sweep up and mop under our beds and make the beds with military corners tucked so tightly that a quarter dropped flatly onto the bed's surface would literally bounce! Next came mess hall, where we proceeded in line along serving areas where they dumped something resembling food into our mess kits. The tables looked like those at a public picnic area.

There were often extra servings of food at our tables like milk, bread, and potatoes. The standing rule was that anyone who took the last serving of any such item was duty bound to get up and replenish the supply. Outside were 50-gallon drums filled with soapy water for us to clean our mess kits, cups and utensils.

Back at the barracks we received orders on how to dress for the day. It was usually fatigues and leggings. We carefully hung up our dress uniforms, put on our assigned clothes, and head down to the parade grounds for 30 minutes of calisthenics, after which they broke us down into squads to perform close order drill.

To help us keep time when we drilled they had us sing songs. Sometimes we intentionally messed up our marching songs both for fun and to irritate our sergeants. If the sergeant was at the back of our line, the men at the front would start singing something like, "gooey, gooey, gum drops," or some other such nonsense. When the sergeant ran up to the front to see who the culprits were, the men went silent and others in the rear picked it up. Finally, in frustration, the sergeants would just order everyone to be quiet and we marched without any singing.

Our forced marches started out slow with distances of about five miles, then graduated to ten miles, fifteen, and finally twenty miles per day. We were soon fit and trim and able to cover these distances without much difficulty.

The outfit I was assigned to, the 10th Infantry Regiment, was regular army. This meant that it existed in peacetime and was not a new unit created primarily for conscripts. Most of the men in this outfit had enlisted, so I was among the few draftees in its ranks. The 10th Regiment had been activated at Fort Hayes in Ohio in 1933 but in my experience, with the exception of a few Midwesterners who were draftees, most of the ranks were southerners who had come from its previous location at Fort Thomas in Kentucky. This was certainly the case in my barracks, and the southerners obviously had no real use for those of us from the north.

Southern ways and southern men were new to me. I listened to "The Yellow Rose of Texas" and songs with lyrics like "I've got tears in my ears from cryin' in my pillow over you," until I was ready to be sick. I enjoyed Glenn Miller, the big band sound, jitterbug and swing. Country music was as far from my tastes as I could imagine, and seemed as backward to me as the hillbilly lifestyle in general. I had the feeling that many of the southerners got their first pair of shoes when they joined the army, maybe also their first toothbrush. Theirs was a new and different culture, and being in the army didn't make my introduction to it any easier.

I knew we had to put up with some southern hazing, but one guy in particular, a 19-year-old kid from one of the Carolinas, was always pushing the limit. He was a huge guy so he figured he could get away it. "You gotta watch these Yankees," he'd say. "They'll cheat ya at cards, steal yer gal, and lie all the time." I put up with this haranguing for about a week before I finally blew up. "Why don't you shut up, you hillbilly," I said. "We licked ya in the Civil War and we could lick ya again."

He didn't jump, he flew over three bunks and had me on the floor in the tightest bear hug humanly possible. My arms were completely pinned and he was literally squeezing the life out of me. The other southerners were chanting, "Stomp him! Stomp him!" I managed to look over at the few northerners in the barracks, but they just returned a look that said, "What the hell are we supposed to do?" The platoon sergeant came in and broke it up but it didn't end there. "You guys want to fight?" the sergeant asked. "Okay, we'll settle this tonight behind the coal pile after chow."

I was shaken up but the northerners in my barracks reminded me that while my opponent was big and could wrestle, he probably didn't know the first thing about boxing. This was a break for me because I excelled at amateur boxing. I was a very capable all-around amateur athlete: I was in good shape, was a very strong swimmer, and played football and baseball well. I not only had experience in the amateur ring, but in a poor Chicago neighborhood like Canaryville, our main idea of contact sports was bare-knuckle fights in vacant lots.

I knew the trick would be to stay mobile. I had to jab him in the nose to stun him and still stay loose so he couldn't get hold of me with those huge, powerful arms. Once the fight started, he came at me with his arms curved and outstretched. I hit him in the nose with two quick left jabs and jumped away. He still didn't raise his arms to protect himself. He was stunned, but he just kept coming at me as he had before.

I jabbed and backed away, jabbed and backed away. If he got close, I hopped out of his reach or pushed him aside. The jabs had the desired effect, and his reactions became slower and slower. I was only using my left hand (I'm righthanded), but even that drew a fair amount of blood from the kid's nose and lips. He had bruises and knuckle marks on his face, but still he kept coming. It was painfully obvious that this was now a very one-sided fight. The sergeant, who had wanted the other guy to win, finally stepped in and called a halt.

After the fight, there were no more comments from anyone about Yankees or their evil ways. Oddly enough, this southern kid and I ended up becoming very good friends. He was still with the 10th Regiment when it shipped out for Iceland. We both remained in the 5th Division when we got to France, but we were in different regiments. I was truly very sorry when I got the news he had been killed in action.

Despite this incident, I wasn't on the wrong side of many sergeants. One by the name of Kroeger had taken a strong liking to me from the beginning. He had immigrated to the United States from Germany some 18 years before and had spent the last 17 of them in the army. We spoke to each other in German and he even recommended me for promotion to corporal after only six weeks! Nothing came of it since conscripts were not promoted to corporal after only six weeks in the army.

A soldier named Al Carslake, one of the guys who supported me the evening I had to refight the Civil War, came up to me one night pretty much out of the blue and asked me if I wanted to go see the movie they were running that evening. I really wasn't in the mood to go, but I felt kind of obligated to him. Besides, a movie with fresh hot popcorn was one of the few childhood pleasures I carried into adulthood and the base theatre always served up fresh popcorn. "I guess my letters can wait," I told him. "My family's coming up Sunday anyway, so why not?"

After the movie another soldier named Steiner joined us. He and Carslake were both from Soule Saint Marie and had been friends before the service. I guess they must have been homesick for the farmlands back in Michigan, because Al suggested we walk over to the parade grounds. As we were walking, he started to sing and Steiner joined in. They sang a few tunes before they looked at me to take a verse, but they were singing farm songs that I had never heard before. "I'm sorry fellas," I said. "But I don't know these songs."

Fortunately, we all knew classics like "Down by the Ole Millstream" and contemporary stuff like "I'll Be with You in Apple Blossom Time." The three of us harmonized quite well and we got into the habit of meeting at night whenever we could by a particular tree near the parade grounds where we would sing songs and talk of home. The three of us became good friends.

I also became good friends with a couple of other guys. A solider from Michigan named Vern Kelner and I struck up a conversation in the chow line one day. We decided to go to the movies that night and as we talked, we discovered we had many similar tastes. Later, a third soldier named Roger Whitney ended up rounding out our trio.

There was another southern kid that I, all of us, befriended right from the start. His name was McCoy and this poor kid had no business being in the army. He must have been inducted because some southern draft board had a quota to fill. McCoy was only a little over five feet tall and he had great difficulty keeping up with us. Everyone in the outfit did what they could to help him out but he just couldn't make the grade. He was unable to qualify with a weapon, he couldn't perform close order drill, he couldn't dig a proper foxhole: he simply couldn't cut it as a soldier.

Once when we were marching and McCoy was out of step, which was customary for him, some s.o.b. of a buck sergeant stuck a walking stick or a broom handle between his McCoy's legs and sent him tumbling. This idiot had the idea that this would force McCoy to stay in step. After we were dismissed, I walked up to the sergeant and told him privately, "You ever use that stick on that kid again, and I'll make you eat it when I catch you in Battle Creek." He didn't respond, but he never used that stick again either.

We took photographs of McCoy standing next to us and it looked like we were posing with a grade school kid in uniform. We submitted the photos and our comments to the company commander. Sergeant Kroeger took up the cause and the army finally came through with a discharge for McCoy. It may have been a small victory but it made all of us feel good. We had cheated the stupidity inherent in the huge army bureaucracy and given the poor kid an opportunity we couldn't have—a guaranteed chance to grow old and die of natural causes. There were also other guys who didn't belong in the army or at least in the infantry, although none of them was as obvious a case as McCoy. By the time we got into combat, the army, to its credit, had done a reasonable job of ensuring that everyone there could cut it.

I missed Mary desperately. On occasion the army didn't issue me a weekend pass, but that didn't stop me from going home to see her. This was still the peacetime army, and the restrictions on us were nothing like they would be once war was declared. A main road ran right through the middle of Fort Custer and I could get on a bus or hitch a ride right past the front gate. There was no checking for passes on the weekend. They wouldn't even know I was gone until Sunday morning roll call. I never let Mary know if I was AWOL, since she clearly would not have approved. During one of these unauthorized leaves, however, Mary and I ran into someone from Fort Custer in my old neighborhood. "They know," he said to me right in front of Mary. "They'll be waiting for you on Monday morning." I had to let Mary in on my secret and assure her it was no big deal.

In peacetime the punishment for a weekend AWOL was minimal. At first, I was simply given KP duty. I had previously worked as a short order cook, so after I finished my KP work, I'd whip myself up a nice little meal. This the army did not appreciate, so my punishment for unauthorized weekend leaves became to guard the meanest prisoners in the stockade.

Most guys had committed some relatively minor infraction and had sentences of only two or three weeks. I was assigned to guard prisoners who had committed real crimes, like striking an officer, and received sentences of six months or longer. This was too long to be served in the fort stockade, so these men were dishonorably discharged and sent to Leavenworth Military Prison. Leavenworth was not to be taken lightly. Every soldier knew its reputation and regarded it as a fate worse than death. In fact, the thought of Leavenworth later provided me with added incentive to go back and face combat time and again.

On guard duty, I was given a double-barreled shotgun and told not to let any of these guys get within 25 feet of me. The word was that any guard who let a buddy or fellow soldier with a hard luck story escape had to finish out the prisoner's sentence. I don't know if it was true or not, but I wasn't about to take any chances.

I remember one time when a southern prisoner decided to get a little defiant. I pulled back both hammers so he could hear them cock. He was quick to obey any directives I gave him after that. Coming off this detail, I was hopping mad about having had to perform it in the first place. I slammed my shotgun back into the gun rack without checking to be sure that the hammers were no longer cocked. The gun discharged and the buckshot from both barrels went through the ceiling. I was almost court-martialed, but the matter was dropped before the paperwork could be completed.

This type of incredible good luck followed me throughout my entire time in the army. A junior officer once said to me in Europe, "Bilder, you have more shittin' luck in one finger than most men have in their entire body." It was true, and looking back I can say that it was a miracle I made it through alive and free of court-martial.

When Mary came up to visit, she took the train from Chicago and stayed in a room arranged by the Red Cross Club. On occasion, she came up with Tom Spain's girl, Irma. She and Tom had grown up next door to each other and probably had crushes on one another since childhood. Mary hated to make the trip up to Battle Creek alone, and I imagine that Irma felt the same way. The four of us got along well together. Mary and I spent Saturdays walking in the park or window-shopping in Battle Creek. In the evening, we went out dancing at local places like the Post Tavern. I returned to the barracks at night and stood for reveille and roll call the next morning. After Sunday mass, we'd repeat the same routine all over again.

Mary was quite an operator. If I couldn't swing a weekend pass, she would pick up the phone and call the base. Claiming to be my mother, she would ask to speak to my commanding officer. She would explain that she had come up all the way from Chicago to visit her boy and would be terribly disappointed if she had to return home without seeing him. Besides, at her age she couldn't be sure how many visits she had left. Couldn't her son please be granted a weekend pass? My CO was either very kind or very easily fooled because this farce worked every time she pulled it. This was especially funny because my mother was only 40 years old at the time and had another 40 years to live!

Joe Louis came to Fort Custer on a goodwill tour. I saw Louis and his sparring partner and many other members of his crew mix it up in the ring. They put on quite a show and everyone was truly impressed. Afterward, I went over to their truck to tell them how impressed I was by their bouts and to pick up a few pointers. I asked how they were able to keep up such an incredible pace in the ring while sustaining such hard blows. As it turned out, they were more actors than boxers. They handed me a pair of their boxing gloves so I could see for myself that they were made of pure foam rubber. You could get hit by a blow and barely feel it, much less get hurt. I left them much wiser but a little disillusioned.

Another valuable lesson I learned quickly in the army was not to volunteer for anything. Once when we were in formation they asked anyone who could type to raise his hand. A few hands shot up from eager beavers who anticipated cushy office jobs. They were immediately informed that they had just volunteered for garbage detail!

Even in peacetime, the army was not to be taken too lightly, so I tried to do my duty with as little push back as possible. I was not out to be a hero, a career military man, or a leader of men, but at the same time, I would not shirk my duties and responsibilities. I was independently minded, but even when I didn't like it (which was most of the time), I did what was expected of me. In the military, as in civilian life, I got along well with just about everyone.

On one occasion, we were rounded up out of a sound sleep, blindfolded, and driven outside the fort to a wooded area. We were given a compass, the coordinates back to the fort, and an order to return as quickly as possible. It was a crystal clear night and I thought I could see the moon reflecting off of the fort's water tower. Some of the guys weren't sure that I was correct and wanted to trust the compass but I persuaded them to follow my lead. My hunch was right and when we got checked in to our rendezvous point in the mess hall, they said to us, "You made pretty good time." My tone of voice had a definite air of ease as I replied, "It's easy when you know what you're doing."

On May 20, 1941, they got us up at the usual 6:00 hours and we received a better hot breakfast than usual. We were then informed that we were about to begin a 600-mile march from Fort Custer into central Tennessee. We had to gear up and be certain not to carry more than 60 pounds of equipment. This is an infantry standard that goes back to the Romans.

The entire 5th Infantry Division (2d, 10th and 11th Regiments) participated in these maneuvers, covering approximately 80 miles a day. We marched for 50-minute intervals and then received a 10-minute rest period. After marching for 20 to 30 miles, we boarded trucks by company to ride the remaining 50 or so miles. A single canteen of water had to last the whole day, but I usually cheated and carried a couple of smaller beer bottles filled with water. I kept these tucked in near my waist, fastened to my belt with twine.

We lived on C-rations, canned stuff that we swore was left over from the First World War. We had not yet been introduced to K-rations, the boxed breakfast, lunch and dinners, so we were issued peanut butter and jelly sandwiches with some form of sausage that might have been minced ham but had no taste whatsoever. We called it "horse cock." In the evening, weather permitting, they usually set up a field kitchen and served some hot grub.

We pitched our pup tents in open fields by company in perfect straight rows. Each soldier carried half a pup tent so we had to pal up with a guy to construct a place to sleep at night. We dug little ditches around our tents to carry off the rainwater, put our raincoats on the ground, and placed a blanket over them. That left us with a single blanket to cover ourselves. We could place our rifles in an arms holder outside of our tents, but most of us slept with it. We were not allowed to get the weapons wet, and any rainstorm would oblige us to go outside to get our rifles.

One very different thing about the South in those days was the dearth of Catholic churches and even Catholics in general. One Sunday, I jumped in a jeep to go to mass, but ended up in a futile search for a Catholic church. Finally, I pulled up to a Baptist church and stood in the back during services. The preacher singled me out for recognition, saying that the church was honored to have a member of the armed forces in attendance. I just smiled and nodded.

During the maneuvers in Tennessee, our 5th Division was part of the Second Army, which was made up of units from midwestern states. We were up against the Third Army, which was composed of states from the old Confederacy and the southwest, and contained George Patton's 2d Armored Division.

This was the beginning of the 5th Infantry Division's long experience with George Patton. Patton maneuvered his 2d Armored Division around us in the dark of night, came in through the rear lines, and captured the command post. It was a brilliant move. This was the first time, but by no means the last, that Patton won his glory at no small expense to the 5th Infantry Division.

My opinion of General Patton has evolved over the years. I think that most of us who served under Patton during Third Army's campaign in Europe hated him intensely at the time. We would just as soon have shot Patton as the Germans. He was a Prima Dona who loved war and made no bones about it. We on the other hand had to fight it. We were scared, lonely, homesick, depressed, dirty, and underfed. We lost friends frequently and were required to kill people. When they called Patton "Old Blood and Guts," we felt it was always our blood and his guts. The enjoyment and glory of war always seemed to escape us.

Patton's very public disregard of the high number of American casualties we incurred as he won his personal glory and met his personal timetables soured me on him. I was on the frontline on two different occasions when Patton came up screaming because we had not taken some objective or another by a certain time. Imagine! A commanding general of an army knew about some holdup with something as relatively small as a battalion of men! He said in front of everyone present, including the infantry grunts, that he didn't care how many men were lost as long as we took the objective. He would obtain all the replacements necessary to replenish our ranks. For obvious reasons, this failed to motivate us. Maybe it was necessary for him to think that way but for God's sake, he should not have expressed his thoughts out loud to the men on the frontlines!

Then there was the fact that Patton was a tank man. It was a rare day when Patton felt good about the infantry. Many of us felt he tolerated the infantry because he had to, but his heart and soul were always with his tanks. During his great forward thrusts in Europe, the Germans often opened up their lines and let our tanks pass through unopposed. They then closed ranks and waited for the infantry to approach. We were the ones who had to slug it out with them. We weren't really interested in all the praise that Patton was receiving while we were fighting just to stay alive.

With the passage of time, however, I started to say, first as a matter of clarification and then with some pride, "I was in Patton's Third Army," when asked about my military service. Patton was a very capable commander, maybe even a military genius. He moved quickly and hit the enemy hard. He was aggressive to the point of recklessness, although he probably did not end the war sooner than it would have ended otherwise. Patton was a patriot and put his country first, last and always. In sum, these are good characteristics for a general. I wish our government had been as insistent as Patton on the need to take Berlin and keep Eastern Europe free from Soviet influence after the war.

The maneuvers in Tennessee lasted from June 2 to 28, and we were glad when they were over. They worked us hard, but provided us with valuable training that served us well when we got into combat. On the journey back to Fort Custer, a number of us were stricken with severe diarrhea. I think in my case it came from a pin-size hole in a small tin of jelly. Other soldiers drank water from ponds, streams and wells. I was put in an army ambulance and was supposed to be taken to the base hospital at Fort Benjamin Harrison in Indiana, but my drivers didn't want to miss out on their weekend pass so they drove me all the way back to Fort Custer.

I was in a ward with about 20 other soldiers, half of whom had yellow jaundice in conjunction with diarrhea. We spent most of our time soiling our pajamas and showering. Men who still had enough energy tried to move as quickly as possible from bed to toilet, but few made it. Soldiers would get about halfway to the toilets, mutter, "aw shit," and shuffle off to the showers holding their back ends.

Our toilets were out in the open and closely spaced. We could literally reach out and touch the man next to or across from us. I was so drained from diarrhea that when a soldier seated on the toilet across from me started to faint, I put out my arms to stop him, but I was too weak to hold him up. The poor slob continued to slump forward until he slowly dropped unconscious onto the floor.

All they could do in those days was control our diet and give us whatever they had to slow down our bowels. You either got better or you died. Some men did disappear from our ward, but we never found out whether they actually died or had simply been transferred. Mary came up to see me after I had been discharged from the hospital, and she was shocked at my appearance. My collar was open, I was not wearing any socks, and my skin was a ghostly white. I was glad my mother didn't see me this way.

I got back up to speed and returned to my normal duties well in time for our second set of maneuvers, which took place in Louisiana in September 1941. While I was once again in prime physical shape, my morale was low. On August 18, 1941, Roosevelt extended our army hitches by an additional six months, which meant we conscripts now had to serve 18 instead of 12 months in the military.

The Louisiana maneuvers were the largest peacetime maneuvers in U.S. history up to that time. It was very hot and the Mississippi was so low at some points it looked as if we could wade across it. I'm glad I never had to try it. One time I was charging across a stream with my bayonet fixed to my rifle when I simply seemed to disappear. "Where's Bilder?" asked a sergeant who witnessed the charge. "What happened to him?" I had fallen into an underwater hole and damned near drowned. Fortunately, I was a very strong swimmer and pulled myself, equipment and all, to the surface.

Most of our movements and actions took place at night. Maybe our commanders had learned a thing or two from Patton in Tennessee. We moved quietly and slept for 10-minute periods along the side of the road. We had all been cautioned not to sleep in the middle of the road, but so many guys were so tired that when we stopped to snooze they simply dropped wherever they were standing. When word came to get up and move out, sometimes the guys in the road didn't hear the order and nobody noticed them there in the dark. They remained asleep only to be run over by a tank or truck.

These maneuvers proved fatal in other ways too. During one simulated attack, we were charging across an open field when a soldier in our ranks fell through some rotting old planking over a dry well. The well was now a rattlesnake nest infested with deadly reptiles. When this poor GI's body was removed from the well, it was so swollen and bloated that it was almost beyond recognition. Another time, a GI awoke one morning to find a rattler wrapped around his leg. He panicked and tried to kick it off only to be bitten. He was fortunate in that he survived the incident.

I had a close call myself with a poisonous snake. I was resting near a truck when I saw what I thought was a harmless variation of a garden snake. "I'm gonna catch that good lookin' snake," I said to the soldier next to me. "You don't wanna go anywhere near that," he responded. "That's a coral snake and you'll be dead in a couple of minutes if it bites you."

The southern troops never ceased to amaze me. Many could handle poisonous snakes with the ease of handling a kitten. They also could, and did, make moonshine out of everything: corn, potatoes, and anything else that grew in the ground. They even carried their stills around with them!

In those days, the U.S. Army was racially segregated and so was the South. I remember marching at a quick pace down a road and seeing the body of a black man hanging by his neck from a rope wrapped around a tree branch. His body had been riddled with buckshot. "Keep your eyes forward and your mouths shut about this," the sergeant ordered as we all passed by, gaping in shock. "That boy tried to molest a white woman and that's the way they deal with those things down here," he said.

Our divisional front in the Louisiana maneuvers occasionally stretched some 60 to 70 miles in length, but we succeeded in capturing the opposing Blue Army by outflanking them and bagging 2,000 officers and men on their own side of the Red River. This time I was on the winning side. With the maneuvers successfully concluded, I could relax from my duty of guarding an anti-tank gun. I was very disappointed that the gun I had been assigned to protect had not been fired during the maneuvers, so I took it upon myself to discharge its load. It was a dummy, but very noisy. The blast caused all the baking cakes in a nearby civilian farm house to fall, and the woman came out to give our officers holy hell over it. To say that I was dressed down would be putting it politely. I got more KP duty than I thought was possible.

We returned to Fort Custer in early October. On November 11, we participated in Armistice Day parades in Battle Creek and Grand Rapids. It was an impressive show of military might. We gave dictators overseas a reason to think twice before going to war with the United States. Maybe, just maybe, we could somehow stay out of this war.

As early as September 5, elements of the 10th Infantry Regiment began to ship out for Iceland, but the United States was still officially neutral in the war. The 10th Regiment was composed mostly of enlisted men, and draftees were not to be sent overseas in peacetime. As a conscript, I was transferred into Company G (George) of the 5th Division's 11th Regiment. A career officer from West Point told me at the time, "Bilder, you're one of the best field soldiers I've ever seen, but you are by far the worst garrison soldier." I couldn't argue with that assessment.

Many of the southern kids and I had become good friends, including by this time the kid I had fought, and they urged me to stay with the 10th and go with them to Iceland. This would mean signing up for a full three-year tour in the army. "No," I told them. "I've had enough of this man's army. I'm gonna serve my hitch and go home." Little did I realize just how wrong I was and how soon we would all be together, freezing in Iceland.

One thing did remain unchanged. I was no volunteer. I hadn't asked for any of this. I was a conscript, and a conscript I remained right through to my discharge.

3

GOODBYE MARY, HELLO ICELAND
Pawns in the Politics of War

"Sweet love of youth, forgive if I forget thee,
While the world's tide is bearing along:
Other desires and darker hopes beset me,
Hopes which obscure, but cannot do thee wrong!"
—Emily Bronte, "Remembrance"

I was transferred into Company G of the 11th Infantry Regiment in late summer or early fall 1941, around the time of the Louisiana maneuvers. The 11th Regiment remained garrisoned at Fort Custer while the 10th Regiment occupied Iceland. Stationing American troops in Iceland clearly aided the British war effort. It left a rather large credibility gap in Roosevelt's claim that the United States was a neutral nation, since Iceland was designated at the time as a combat zone.

Mary was still coming up to see me at Fort Custer. Sometimes she came alone, sometimes she came up with Tom's girl Irma, and once she came up with my mother and my half-siblings, Evelyn and George. I was now about halfway through my army hitch and desired more than ever to simply complete my service and put army life behind me. My superiors may not have highly regarded me as a garrison soldier, but I always prided myself on fulfilling my duties and obligations, even if I had no tolerance (or desire) for being spit and polish.

On Sunday, December 7, I was back in Chicago on a weekend pass. I had spent the previous day with Mary, and was spending part of Sunday visiting my mother at home. We were talking and the radio was playing in the background when the regular programming was suddenly interrupted with news flashes. They told of the attack on Pearl Harbor.

My stepfather came into the room and asked what all this meant. I explained that America was now at war with Japan and my mother began to cry. Shortly thereafter, a telegram came to the door instructing me to return immediately to Fort Custer. Telegrams were going out to everyone. It was a foretaste of things to come. I was soon on the train back to Battle Creek, where I was issued a loaded rifle and assigned to guard an area of the motor pool. I was given a password and told to be damn sure that only those using it got in. Things were suddenly buttoned down and very military.

A day or so after our return they assembled us in several different groups and gave us each a very general briefing on the attack and the current situation. The United States was now at war with the Japanese Empire, and we were all to remain in the military *for the duration*. War against Japan was bad enough, but on December 11, Germany and Italy also declared war on the United States.

Soon thereafter, we were told to get our gear down to sixty pounds and get ready to move out. We were certain that we would be sent to California and then shipped to the Pacific. Imagine our surprise when we learned that our destination was not the west coast but in fact Fort Dix in Pointsville, New Jersey! How could this be? Why send us around the long way through the Panama Canal, when it was so much easier to send us to the west coast before shipping us out to the Pacific?

I called Mary from Fort Dix and told her that I would love to see her one more time. Mary, always proud but broke, bought the cheapest train ticket available and came up to see me right after New Year's. We both figured that this would be our last time together before I shipped out. Mary's father had been against her coming. He had never been fond of me and felt that Mary could do better. He had even offered her a car at one point if she would stop seeing me. Where he would have gotten the money remains an unsolved mystery to this day.

As an ethnic German who was raised in a largely ethnic German neighborhood, went to the German grade school, and to German Catholic Church at St. George, I spoke German without an accent. I learned "house German" from conversing with my mother and grand-mother, and the rules of proper German grammar from the nuns at Saint George. From fourth grade on, we devoted an hour a day to German language instruction. The strong gravitational pull of the ethnic enclaves thus gave me language skills that served me well in Europe during the war. Unfortunately, that same ethnic pull also resulted in stupid prejudices.

Mary had an English surname (Fairfield) but her heritage was mostly Irish. Her father, an educated man who was born and raised in the United States, still clung to certain old country ideas about marrying your own kind just as strongly as my poorly educated German grandmother did. He told Mary that if she married a German she would always be forced to walk a few steps behind me. On my side, relatives ensured me that if I married an Irish girl I would spend the rest of my life eating out of cans.

I didn't get along with Mary's dad any better than I did my step-father. Mary's dad was no physical match for me, but I still had to show respect for him as the father of my fiancée, so I waited for Mary on her front porch when I came to pick her up. I did this mostly for Mary and her mother. I refused to be intimidated into meeting Mary on the corner, but I wouldn't enter a home where the head of the family did not welcome me.

The saving graces in all this nonsense were our respective mothers. They believed that since both of us were practicing Catholics, the only other thing that mattered was whether we loved each other. If this were true, the rest would work itself out. Finally Mary's mother made her husband come to terms with me. She brought me into the house one evening and forced a truce between the two of us.

Mary paid a last visit to Fort Dix in the hope that we could get married before I was sent overseas. If her father had known, it would have destroyed our fragile truce, and Mary would have had to directly defy his wishes. Mary's mother probably figured out what her daughter was planning since she herself had faced similar circumstances. Back in 1917 she and Mary's dad had wedded secretly in church on the very day of his induction into the army, with nothing more than a maid of honor and a best man. Mary's mother had been in my corner from day she met me. She reminded her husband that

Mary was 21 and old enough to make her own decisions.

This was now wartime and everyone was restricted to base. But in order to meet Mary I needed a pass. I also needed to duck out of the hospital. I was ill with a bad flu bordering on pneumonia. I managed to slip out of the hospital and made it over to the CO's office. I told him that I had gotten my girl pregnant and had to find a priest so I could do the right thing. Don't ask me how but it worked, and he gave me a 72-hour pass.

Mary was a great looker but hardly a likely candidate to become pregnant before marriage. She was a devout Catholic, a kisser and a hugger, but not a believer in free love. Of course, social mores were also different then. She would have died, or killed me, or both, if she had known what I had told my CO to get that pass.

The women that Mary had been talking to on the train had all been bragging about their husbands and boyfriends. They talked of how important they were in their men's lives, how close their relationships were and how eagerly they would be greeted as the train pulled into the station. When the train came to a stop, the women peered out the windows with great expectations. To their surprise, there was one solitary soldier on that platform—me. It meant the world to Mary. She let all the women know that was *her* soldier boy out there, and she got off the train with the strut of royalty.

A friend drove us to Saint Mary's Parish in Trenton in an attempt to enable us to get married. We had nothing in the way of church, military or secular authorization to marry: no official written authorization from the army (required at that time), no proof of baptism (required by the church), no verification that either of us had not been married before (also a church requirement), no marriage license, no blood test, and no attendance record at the church's prenuptial instruction classes. The priest was kind, but explained there was nothing he could do. There was simply no way he could marry us. I knew the odds of any priest agreeing to marry us under these circumstances were slim to none, but I also knew that Mary would never really accept this until she heard it for herself. I was also privately happy to some extent about this outcome. Like a lot of guys at the time, I didn't want to marry a nice (and beautiful) girl only to leave her a widow or forced to spend the rest of her life caring for a wounded invalid.

There was nowhere else to go and nothing else to do, so we simply went back to Fort Dix. Mary was dejected and feeling pretty low. At the main gate we encountered a great deal of commotion. "You missed it, Bilder," the guard said. "Missed what?" I asked. Apparently, white and black troops had arrived simultaneously at the wooden partitions that contained the base showers.

An argument broke out between the two groups about which group would be the first to shower. The argument quickly escalated into a scuffle where the black soldiers, greater in number, prevailed. The white troops had been forced to leave with their tails between their legs and they were none too happy about it. Things didn't end there. One or more of these rebuffed soldiers returned to the showers with fully automatic weapons and riddled the wooden shower stalls with bullets, killing some eight or ten black troops. I saw vehicles and crowds but I saw nothing else, and nothing more was ever said of the incident, official or otherwise.

That night, I walked Mary over to the bus stop just outside the base to see her off. A good buddy by the name of Roland Coderre was with us, perhaps as moral support or to keep me from doing something stupid like running off. Roland was a Native American of the Tejan Tribe from Florida. We affectionately referred to him as "Chief Coderre" or just "Chief," a nickname he loved. I enjoyed listening to him talk about Florida as much as he enjoyed hearing about Chicago.

Even with a torrent of emotions flowing, Mary and I didn't know quite what to say to each other. We had no idea when or even if we would ever see each other again. The Chief walked off a short distance to give us a few moments alone. We stood face to face and looked directly into one another's eyes. It was like something out of a Bogart movie. It was odd, but instead of saying all the things that we wanted to say; we just started to cry. After we composed ourselves, Mary asked how much time we had left. I looked at my watch. "About fifteen minutes," I said.

The Chief must have figured that this was his cue to move things along. "Mike, we better get goin'," he said. "If we get locked off the base before evening roll call, they'll make us use a canoe to get to wherever it is the outfit's shipped." Mary knew our time was up. "You better go," she said. "I don't want you getting into trouble."

"I love you," she said. "I love you too," I said. We kissed and that was it. The Chief and I walked away back toward the base. Mary was a brick. She mustered all her courage and stood there as proudly as she could as she watched us go. The rickety old bus that would take her the two miles to the train station rattled and chugged its way along to the bus stop. It blocked Mary from my view when it came to a halt, and when it pulled away a moment later the bus stop was vacant. I turned and went through the gate to the base with Roland.

The Chief was not only a good friend, but a prince of a guy. Later we were both transferred into different regiments, and it was tough for us to stay in close contact. We inquired about each often in Europe, and when I hadn't heard from him in a while I asked where he was keeping himself. I was shocked and deeply hurt when I found out that he had been killed in action. He was a sergeant by that time and probably yet another victim of command. I can't begin to count all the good men who got themselves killed as a result of accepting stripes or bars. By the time I got the word about the Chief, I thought I had already learned never to be truly surprised by that kind of rotten news. In addition to losing many buddies from my own regiment, I had a lot of good friends in the 10th who never made it home.

I got a chance to see New York City, but I was not all that impressed. It was probably a combination of things. I was partial to Chicago and missed my home there along with Mary. The weather was mild but wet, and a certain glumness permeated everything. Then in mid-January our barracks were quarantined due to a case of small pox. It wasn't the poor slob's fault for getting sick, but we were none too happy with him. Things were bad enough without being confined to quarters.

One day in February 1942 they sealed off Fort Dix. No one could get in or out, telephone calls were no longer allowed, and even our outgoing mail was discontinued! Our overseas gear arrived late. It had been sent by mistake to some southern port, and this delayed our departure. The thing that stunned everyone was that instead of jungle fatigues we had been issued long coats and winter clothes. The army had goofed again!

Then the rumors and scuttlebutt started. We were headed to Greenland. Greenland? Greenland! What was going on? Those guys in

the Pacific needed help and we were one of the best-trained divisions in the U.S. Army. Why in the world would anyone want to send us to Greenland?

Just before we shipped out for overseas I was transferred into the 2d Infantry Regiment. I had now served in all three regiments of the 5th Infantry Division. I remained in George (G) Company, 2d Regiment until a month after the war ended.

On February 19 we boarded troop trucks and headed for the docks. We felt like sellouts. American soldiers, sailors, and marines were hanging on by their fingernails in the Pacific, and here we were on our way to Greenland. They drove us to the port of New York, where we boarded the *U.S.S. Munargo*, a dumpy-looking troop ship built in 1921 that the navy had acquired from the army the previous year. They used it to transport troops in the Atlantic until 1943, when it was re-commissioned as the *USAHS Thistle*, a hospital ship that served in the Mediterranean before being ordered to the Pacific in September 1945.

We were ascending the gangplank when I spotted three sailors leaning against the ship railing. I knew these guys from the old neighborhood and they called out to me. I had my duffle bag in hand, so all I could do was smile and nod my head in return. When we reached the top, a soldier with a clipboard verified our identities before we boarded. "Bilder!" he called out. "Michael C," I responded on cue, and he waved me up the gangplank.

The day was cold and overcast, with a constant drizzle and mist. We watched in a relative, but somewhat profound silence as we passed the Statue of Liberty. I specifically remember wondering whether not I would ever see it again.

Our ship was 432 feet long but still cramped. Our sleeping quarters consisted of bunks made of canvas, rope and GI blankets. The bunks were stacked four or five tiers high with about two feet between each tier. Our dining area was no less elegant. The tables were about four feet high and bolted to the floor. We ate out of mess kits and were usually fed C-rations. We had to eat standing up, but after a day or two at sea few of us had any desire for food.

The rough North Atlantic tossed the ship all about and had us a constant state of seasickness. Vomit was everywhere. It sloshed

about the floors and ran along the tables. Men were so sick that they lay face down on the floor, too weak to move and too ill to care. I was so sick that I hoped that a German sub would sink the ship.

Soldiers were not permitted on deck or in the sailors' quarters, but my three sailor buddies managed to sneak me into their quarters. We spent a bit of time talking about the old neighborhood and the deprivations of military life. I told them how rotten our food was especially on this voyage. I added that my sea legs were none too good. They told me that they ate well and that what I really needed to get over my nausea was a real honest-to-goodness meal instead of military rations. They started to fry up some bacon and the instant the first bit of aroma hit my nostrils, I was sick. Those dirty dogs knew exactly what they were doing and roared with laughter as I ran from their quarters. This was the type of joke I usually played on someone else. I wasn't used to being on the receiving end of such humor.

Now that we were well out into the Atlantic and safely cut off from any personal connections in the outside world we learned that our actual destination was not Greenland but Iceland. As we approached the Icelandic coast, we were allowed up on deck. It was then I saw just how many warships were escorting us. I never was a navy man, and to this day I can't tell the difference between a large cruiser and a battleship, but these were good-size ships the navy had escorting us. We were glad to have them: these waters were prime hunting grounds for German U-boats. The defensive firepower of our troop ship was limited in direction. It had a single 5-inch gun, four 3-inch guns, and eight .50-caliber machine guns. This was reasonable to fend off enemy aircraft or surface vessels, but hardly a match for a submerged German sub. We noticed that one of our escorts had its bow pushed in. They told us it had rammed a German sub one night during our trip.

The coast of Iceland looked bleak and foreboding, and there were no signs of welcome by the local populace. We formed up by companies on deck as the ship prepared to dock in the harbor, and were told to keep our contact with Icelandic civilians to a minimum. The people regarded us as occupiers, or even invaders. Their sympathies were with Germany, but because of its close proximity to the United States and Canada, Iceland became a protectorate of the Allies whether it

wanted to be or not. I was soon to discover that Icelandic was close enough to German to allow me to get by with civilians who did not speak English.

We arrived at Reykjavic on March 3 with the assignment of protecting the West Sector. The British 49th Infantry Division was not far away. The army had established a western defense area on the island extending some 60 miles inland and 40 miles along the coast on the western part of the island. Our 5th Infantry Division was to protect an area east and northeast of Reykjavik along with Hvalfordur, which was an important naval anchorage.

Americans were dying by inches in the Pacific, and here we were in Iceland, guarding the West Sector. In this cold and unwelcoming environment we seemed to be unnoticed, unneeded and unappreciated. Such was our duty for the next 18 months, which earned us the title "FBI": the Forgotten Bastards of Iceland.

4

THE "FBI" OCCUPIES THE ROCK

The Fighting Bastards of Iceland Battle the Arctic Wasteland

"Abandon hope, all ye who enter here!"
—Inscription on the entranceway to hell in Dante's *Inferno*

As we disembarked from the troop ship, it was hard for to imagine that any place inhabited by human beings could be as desolate as Iceland. It was not scenic; most of the population did not want us there, much less welcome us; we were on a war footing; and the culture, surroundings and climate were just about as foreign to Americans as anything we could ever hope (or in this case, hope not) to see.

Iceland is an island nation made from volcanic rock and ash with little vegetation. Rocks were everywhere, but I can't recall ever seeing a tree, at least not in the area we occupied. There were snow-covered mountains and low parts with inactive volcanoes. We regarded it as a hellish reversed image of Hawaii. We referred to it as "the rock," like the prison at Alcatraz Island, and for the next 18 months, we poor Forgotten Bastards of Iceland were stuck there occupying it. We often asked ourselves why.

We all felt we should be on our way to the Pacific. None of us were really happy about the idea of going into combat, but we were well trained and wanted to get a crack at the Japanese. While the enemy was rolling over our boys in the Pacific, we felt our presence in Iceland was serving Churchill's needs rather than America's most pressing interests.

British and American leaders both regarded Iceland as far more sympathetic to the Germans than to the Allies. Iceland's language and culture were practically German, although few of its citizens cared for Hitler. Britain began its occupation of the island in April 1940, and Churchill knew that stationing American forces there would enable him to use geography to bring the States closer to conflict with Germany in both political and military terms. It also freed up British troops for combat who otherwise would be used for occupation duty. Once America came into the war, it was only common sense that our forces in Iceland would be used against the Germans rather than sent to the Pacific.

I was angered (then as now) by the politicians' scheming and lying. I supported the idea of preparedness, but Roosevelt promised Churchill that he would send American troops to Iceland, Northern Ireland, and various British war zones well before the United States was a belligerent. He conducted an undeclared naval war against Germany in late 1941 that got an American destroyer, the *U.S.S. Reuben James*, sunk. German submarines were not arousing the American public's desire for war, as they had in 1917. This was alright with those of us who were soldiers, since we'd be the ones who'd have to do the fighting.

While the attack on Pearl Harbor necessitated war, it still remains hard to imagine that such a huge operation really caught the United States by complete surprise. We had enlisted men in clerical positions at Divisional Headquarters who were often the source of first-hand information and just plain scuttlebutt. It was from them that I first heard the 5th Division referred to as "Churchill's Division." We used this term anytime we felt we were doing England's dirty work.

The American forces stationed in Iceland were free from British military authority. American ground units initially consisted primarily of the First Marine Brigade, which numbered around 4,000, and was led by Brigadier General John Marston. The army in Iceland was commanded by Major General Charles Bonesteel, who had commanded the 5th Division from July to August 1941. Less than two months after the 5th Division arrived, American forces composed two-thirds of the military personnel in Iceland. From December 1941 through January 1942, the British pulled 4,400 men out of Iceland and took them back to Britain. Arriving in March 1942, we effectively served as their replacements. By the end of 1942, almost all of the Brits were out of Iceland.

General Bonesteel officially took over full command of all military personnel in Iceland on April 22, 1942. We stood outside for four hours waiting for and watching the ceremony. Bonesteel presented the British commander, Major General Harry Curtis, with the Distinguished Service Medal. It demonstrated how close and friendly we all were as allies, but it didn't change that fact that it was pretty miserable standing outside in the elements for that long. There were so many of us in formation that only the men in the very front ranks could see the ceremony. Some men even asked who the hell we were waiting to honor. "Churchill" was the common response. I don't know if it was sarcasm or genuine ignorance, but before long most of the ranks actually believed it.

The close proximity of German subs and the occasional activity of German planes made Iceland a combat zone. The Germans usually only gave us a problem when we were in large groups, such as coming out of church on Sunday morning. A fighter might drop down to strafe us, or on occasion the Germans dropped a bomb, but I never knew of anyone who was actually injured as a result of these attacks. How did the enemy know when and where to strike? Was it common sense, or were native inhabitants supplying information about our movements?

German pilots flying over Iceland for recon or attack purposes usually ended up on a one-way mission. Our 19- and 20-year-old hotshot pilots had their P-38 Lightning Fighters in the air so fast the Germans never knew what hit them. Once I was on guard duty at an outside post with a radio when I saw am enemy reconnaissance plane fly over. It was obviously photographing our position. One of our fighters zoomed down and put a burst of machine gun fire into the plane, doing considerable damage.

The German pilot lowered his landing gear, the aerial version of putting up your arms to surrender. He was about 100 feet over the water trying to line up his approach, and pilots over the radio were saying things like, "Don't let that son of a bitch get away," and "Blow that bastard out of the sky." One of our fighters came up behind the crippled plane and fired into it, and it exploded in a ball of flames. I don't ever recall seeing or hearing of a single instance of a captive German plane brought in. This doesn't mean that it didn't happen, but I personally only saw them come down in pieces.

At sea, German U-boats attacked the convoys of supply ships that stopped in Iceland on their way to England or Russia. The subs often struck in large groups known as "wolf packs" in order to coordinate their attacks for maximum effect and to support one another against the destroyers and cruisers that tried to provide protection around the merchant vessels. These subs couldn't return to the Fatherland every time they needed fuel. On guard duty, I once witnessed an Icelandic fishing boat caught in the act of refueling a German sub. One of our ships fired on the boat and blew it into a million pieces. The sub was luckier. Our destroyers pursued it, but it somehow managed to escape.

Our home in Iceland was Camp Arnaholt, in an area known as the Brauterholt Sector. The camp was surrounded by layers upon layers of every type of barbed wire imaginable. The main gate provided the only entrance or exit. In reality, the camp was nothing but a bunch of Nissen huts that the British left us. We replaced them with Quanset huts, simple structures designed to accommodate about a dozen men, which protected us from the elements but nothing more. The winds appeared out of nowhere and reached speeds of 125 miles an hour, so we had to pack three or four feet of sod around all four walls to help keep the huts in place, but this sometimes still proved ineffective.

When our American-made Quanset huts arrived, we hastily started to put them all together. This proved to be a serious mistake. In our effort to get the huts up, we were ordered to concentrate on quantity as opposed to quality construction. We got them up alright, but neglected to cut and pack the necessary three to four feet of sod around the four walls. The next morning, all the newly assembled Quanset huts were floating out in the icy Atlantic.

Even worse, men were sometimes blown in as well. High winds, icy cold water, and heavy military gear proved fatal for anyone unlucky enough to suffer such a fate. Needless to say, this often made guard duty a risky venture. The 5th Division had 40 miles of coastline to protect, and our posts were usually within 100 yards of the shoreline. The concern was that the Germans would use submarines to land commandos: we had to be close enough to the shoreline to make certain that didn't happen.

Once when the captain of the guard came out to inspect the guard posts near the beach, a high wind came out of nowhere and blew him right into the thick layers of our coastal barbed wire. He was completely entangled and had no possible hope of getting out on his own. It was around midnight, and I had just come off a six-hour shift of guard duty, dog-tired. I didn't have a chance to get out of my gear before I was ordered back outside to help. We had to tie half-inch ropes around our waists and crawl on our stomachs against the high winds to reach the Captain. The other end of our rope was tied to an iron pole to keep us from blowing into the sea ourselves.

The cold night air made it difficult to breathe and the high winds threw icy particles of snow into our faces, stinging bitterly and limiting our vision. When we finally reached him, we had to use wire cutters to get him out, which was no easy task. We worked wearing thick gloves, and the high winds kept blowing the barbed wire back into our faces. The Captain was more shaken up than hurt. He was wearing thick winter clothing and goggles, which protected him from the barbed wire. We tied a rope around his waist and he crawled back with us. After that experience, he was careful to conduct his inspections in calmer weather.

A less hazardous and more humorous lesson about Iceland's strong winds took place late one night when one of the men in our hut got up to relieve himself. He didn't feel like making the long cold trek to the latrine, so he simply opened up the door and proceeded to urinate outside. The wind blew every drop back on him, soaking him from head to waist. He simply turned around and got back into bed as if everything had gone normally.

Our quarters featured an army cot, a footlocker, and an orange crate for a table. Light was provided by kerosene lamp, and a potbellied stove provided warmth. I spent a great deal of my off duty time writing letters to Mary. It was a gloomy and depressing place and that's putting it kindly. The routine was monotonous, the weather was intolerable, and the loneliness and homesickness had a real effect on morale.

Guard duty consisted of six hours on and had twelve hours off. I came off duty one night and entered my hut to find one soldier on the floor in his sleeping bag reading a letter and another in his cot reading a book. I sat down on the edge of my cot and used my orange crate to write Mary a letter before going to sleep. The soldier on the floor zipped himself into his sleeping bag from head to foot so that it was completely closed. I went back to my letter with my thoughts, completely fixed on what I was writing.

Suddenly, the blast of a gunshot ripped through the dead silence of our hut and I jumped from my cot. The shot came from inside the sleeping bag. I unzipped it and saw to my horror that the poor guy had put a .45 to his head and pulled the trigger. He had been reading a "Dear John" letter. I saw a lot of guys get these over the years, including married men, and I never saw a man that didn't take it hard.

Needless to say, we didn't get much sleep that night. It was usually tough anyway to get to sleep in Iceland. During the winter, the daylight lasted for 23 hours. It was just one more thing that made our stay there so difficult. Another thing we dreaded in Iceland was mountain duty. This assignment required two soldiers to sit at an observation point on the mountain with an artillery telescope, and look down on the ocean to identify any and all ships headed toward the island.

The merchant marine convoys carrying supplies from the United States to England and Russia left the States together, then split into separate groups after they reached Iceland. Most of these convoys went to Russia. We referred to the waters just in front of our area of observation as "Torpedo Junction." At night, the wolf packs attacked these convoys in force. They started out by hitting the fuel tankers, which exploded in huge balls of fire that burned for hours. This eerie light provided excellent visibility for the enemy subs to finish off their prey. Any poor unfortunates not killed instantly in the attack either drowned or froze to death in the icy waters. The next morning we would have launch duty. This involved sending out several launches, each manned by three or four soldiers, to go up and down a 10-mile area of coastline to collect the bodies from the previous night's attack. I never once heard of or saw the rescue of a single survivor.

Our periods of rest and relaxation consisted of an occasional movie shown in the mess hall or a game of pool in the Red Cross Club, where coffee and donuts were served. Dances were difficult: the animosity of the locals towards their "occupiers" kept the girls away, and the island had such a small population that there was only one girl for every fifty GIs. On top of this, the girls came escorted by their parents! We often clowned around and simply danced with each other.

There was a civilian road, called Sauerbier I believe, just a short distance from the entrance to our camp, where we could catch a civilian bus into Reykjavik. Since we were unwelcome guests, GIs were required to travel in groups of a dozen or so when we took the bus. It was a long ride and there were no formal rest stops, so the driver just pulled over to the side of the road so people could relieve themselves. There was no modesty: the women simply hoisted their skirts and urinated in plain view of everyone.

In our Quanset huts, we often passed the time talking of home, playing cards, and writing letters. Mary and I usually wrote each other every day. I was writing her a letter on one such occasion when a smart guy said to me, "You writing that girl of yours again? She's probably out whoring around with every guy back home." I told him to stand up and say that again. He did, and I landed my right fist square onto his jaw. He went backwards and bounced off a cot. The two of us never exchanged another word again. Like my fight with the southerner back at Fort Custer, this incident caused people to put out the word that I was not a person to take any unnecessary crap.

Those Icelanders who drove often had Ford trucks dating back to the 1920s. Whenever they were involved in an accident with an American military vehicle, which happened with convenient regularity, they received a brand new Ford truck, model 1941, as a replacement, courtesy of the United States. It didn't seem to win over any hearts and minds.

Booze was hard to come by in Iceland, but conditions were so depressing that drinking was somewhat necessary. Our official liquor rations were meager, about three cans of beer a month, and a bottle of whiskey on the black market cost an outrageous $30. Even worse, we had to go down to the docks and buy it from the sailors. Extortion prices were bad enough, but for a soldier to have to go to a swabby for help was just too much to bear.

Guys drank Aqua Velva aftershave, bay rum, and even anti-freeze mixed with lemon extract. Needless to say, we had some cases of blinding. It was safer to drink the white lightening the southerners made. Sometimes we lucked out and an officer who didn't drink gave us his ration.

One day, a civilian approached another soldier named Tom McElligott and me with the offer to sell us a bottle of whiskey for $25. The price was right so we told him he had a sale. When he tried to make a fast getaway with our money, we nabbed him, and after he refused to return our money, we slapped him around. As fate would have it, right in the middle of all this, a jeep with a couple of MPs pulled up and wanted to know what was going on. We told them and they were willing to let it go until our Icelandic friend insisted on filing charges against us and made a such a stink that they had no choice but to comply. We then were told that General Bonesteel had given orders that any Americans who got into trouble with the Icelandic people were on their own. We could probably expect a six-month jail sentence, after which we would have to make the time up to the army with an extension in our hitch.

At trial, I was preparing myself for the inevitable, when the doors to the court suddenly burst open and two British MPs entered the room. They interrupted the proceedings, spoke in hushed tones to the judge, and led our accuser away in handcuffs. Our "Icelandic" friend was in fact a deserter from the British Army. With only minutes to go before a guilty verdict, the charges were dropped and we were free to go. This was another example of my incredible luck. I soon was blessed with another, when I discovered a less hazardous way to obtain liquor.

It was of course illegal to send servicemen liquor through the mail. Back in Chicago, my friend Bobby Glasner was working in a war-related industry because he had a heart problem that kept him out of the military. He was so skilled at soldering that he could weld a can so it appeared never to have been opened. Bobby began his mission of mercy by sending me a carton of large fruit juice, mostly orange and grapefruit, which appeared at first glance to be a ridiculous thought. I was almost resentful. Why bother? Why not send something more useful?

When I finally got around to opening one, I took a big drink and nearly fell over. It was straight bourbon! Bobby, God bless him, had switched the contents. This was one item from home I did not make universally available. I could not afford for loose lips to sink the ship.

Many a time a fellow soldier commented, "Boy, Bilder, you sure are milking that fruit juice," or "Bilder, it sure takes you a long time to finish one of those things." I replied with something like, "Yeah, well, I like to take my time" or "Why rush? What else have I got to do?" The night that poor soul shot himself inside his sleeping bag, I opened up one of those large cans and polished it off with the other guy who was there when it happened. We drank until we passed out. It was the only way to get any sleep after such an experience. I felt that Bobby did a great service to his country, and deserved a decoration.

Another rumor in 1942 was that the 5th Division was going to be part of an invasion force to land in Norway. I was selected for what was to be a ski assault regiment, and sent high into the peaks of Mount Eyjafjallajokull for a six-week training course in mountain warfare. Our rations were meager and I lost weight, but I did learn to ski fairly well. The moves we learned made us proficient skiers, but hardly elite warriors.

This "elite outfit" never materialized, and I have often wondered if the entire operation was part of an intentionally leaked, high profile decoy intended to persuade the Germans to keep vital numbers of their troops and material resources sitting in Norway waiting for an invasion that never occurred. Maybe it was just another duty we performed as "Churchill's Division." At least the artic survival techniques I learned served me well during the Battle of the Bulge.

My most noteworthy, or infamous, adventure in Iceland was an unintentional incident that came very close to blackening my name in the unit histories and getting me a sentence at Leavenworth. Also involved was a buddy of mine named Eugene Brinkman. He had been a reporter with the *Chicago Tribune*, but his military duties were strictly that of an infantryman. Brinkman was also a political lefty. I liked him: he was very smart, loved a good laugh, and was relatively easy-going. While he seemed to have nothing but good things to say about Russia, I never considered him as disloyal or a threat to American security. Besides, infantrymen had no military secrets to give to anybody, and some of his commentary was probably meant just to get a rise out of people.

Because I tended to pal around with Brinkman, I was called in to talk to Lieutenant Siegert, an S-2 officer at Headquarters Battalion. Siegert hemmed and hawed until I finally said, "Look, Lieutenant, I'd like to know why I've been called in." He said he had heard a great deal about Brinkman's leftwing politics and asked if I had ever heard him speak against the U.S. government. I answered honestly when I said that I hadn't.

He then asked me if I would keep an eye on Brinkman and report on a regular basis about what he said and did. I had never been a stool pigeon and was not about to become one now. Besides, Brinkman was a good friend, and I resented even being asked to perform such a duty. I was deferential, but declined the offer. "Lieutenant, I don't think I'd be very good at that sort of thing," I said. "In fact, I'd probably foul it up." Siegert accepted this and as far as I know that was the end of it.

The day that Brinkman and I got in hot water, we were on guard duty. Our sole supply of fresh water was pumped into camp from a single well atop a large hill we called Mount Asia. It was kept under 24-hour guard by two soldiers to protect it from saboteurs. I knew just how boring and tedious a 24-hour stint of guard duty at this well could be, so I went over to the supply depot and got the sergeant's permission to check out an extra 100 rounds of rifle ammunition for Brinkman and myself each to use for target practice. We didn't attend guard formation, but left on foot an hour ahead of our assigned time to guard the well.

At the post, I set up several bottles and tin cans at various distances. We started firing at our makeshift targets and a few minutes later a flare went off in the distance. Brinkman and I saw it, looked at each other, shrugged our shoulders, and continued with our target practice. A few minutes later, a second flare went off. This one was a different color. We continued with our shooting only to see a third flare go off. This one was red. "I wonder who the hell is shooting off all the flares," I said. "Yeah," Brinkman replied. "I wonder what's going on?"

We didn't have to wait too long to find out. Army commandos in blackface with Tommy guns at the ready soon appeared with an armored column as backup. Brinkman and I went out to meet them.

"Where are all the Germans?" the lead trooper asked us. "Germans? What Germans?" I replied.

"We heard all the shooting," he said, "and figured you guys were holding off the first wave of an airborne assault." I couldn't believe it. "We were just getting in some target practice," I said. "We were shooting at bottles and tin cans." The officer in charge immediately relieved us of duty, pulling two men from the ranks to take our place. We were not put under arrest, but we were driven back in a command car to Company Headquarters. By the time we arrived, our company commander had already been informed of the situation, and we were restricted to quarters.

The next morning after reveille, we were instructed to report in full dress uniform to Battalion Headquarters at 8:00 hours. When we got there a full colonel no less was waiting for us. He was regular army and was to serve as our defense counsel. Defense counsel? We didn't know why we would need any defense counsel. We anticipated being reprimanded, but not being charged with any offense.

The colonel told us that General Bonesteel's staff had prepared to be evacuated from the island because they believed an invasion was taking place. The flares we had seen were coded signals to serve as alerts and warnings of imminent enemy attack. A commanding general obviously doesn't have a sense of humor when it comes to such things. When he found out the real cause for all the commotion, he insisted that the soldiers responsible not only be charged, but sent to Leavenworth. This was to be a general court-martial.

The Colonel said he wanted to get our version of the events one at a time. There was no military formality involved. While Brinkman and I were still together in the room, he said, "I suppose you two already know you're in big trouble. From what I gather, they want you both shot." After Brinkman left the room, the Colonel simply said, "Sit down, Mike, and tell me what happened."

"Well, Colonel," I replied, "we just figured that we'd get our target scores up. There's a lot of ammunition left over from the last war in the supply depot and we thought we had a good way of using it up."

"Do you understand your general orders as a soldier here in Iceland, a combat zone?" he asked. "I do," I responded. "Did you understand your special orders when they were read to you?" he continued. "What special orders, sir?" I asked. "No one read or said anything to us before we assumed our post." "Well," he replied, "didn't they read the special orders when you posted guard?" "Sir," I told him, "we simply left on our own, on foot, for the well. We never posted guard."

"Are you sure?" the Colonel asked. "You were not read the orders of the day before taking your posts?" "Positive sir," I said. "This should have been done," he said emphatically. "It's mandatory. In all my years of military service, I have never seen such a breach of duty, such neglect, such stupidity! I want you to go and dictate everything you just told me to the sergeant at the desk." I went out to do so, while Brinkman went in and gave the same story. When our statements were typed up, we reviewed and signed them.

The Colonel then said to us, "Report back to your company and consider yourselves lucky. The chances were very good that you would both have gone to Leavenworth for ten years!" We were then dismissed.

These seemingly pointless military procedures turned out to be our salvation. Neither an officer nor an NCO had read us the orders of the day, which would have stipulated not to discharge our weapons unless absolutely necessary. Nor did any superior officially direct us to march out of the base in formation, or officially post us at our assigned area. We were off the hook. Forget the fact that we were expected to know all this like the back of our hand: the highly centralized management of the army had saved our bacon.

Our superiors had not followed proper protocol. This meant for Brinkman and I got off on a technicality: for me, it was another case of dumb luck. The person who had to answer for it was the officer immediately over us. He was a young and a reserve officer to boot. We heard he was cashiered out of the army. Brinkman and I screwed up big time, but I can honestly say that we never intended to do anything wrong or cause anyone any trouble.

The next time that I fired a weapon it was officially regarded as necessary. Another soldier and I were at our posts watching the harbor, when we saw a mid-sized fishing boat approach flying a foreign flag. Everyone on Iceland, civilian and military alike, knew that all boats had to identify themselves well before entering the harbor. The worry was that German troops, spies, or saboteurs could come ashore in the safety of a civilian vessel.

We watched through our artillery telescope as the boat drew closer to the dock without slowing down or giving the customary signals. Finally, we had no choice. We picked up our rifles and fired warning shots across the bow of the boat. The bullets were tracers and clearly visible to everyone on board. Our action was obviously meant to frighten the crew into stopping the boat or turning it around and heading back to sea.

Despite the tracers, the boat kept coming. We then followed procedure and orders, and fired directly at and into the boat itself. The boat veered away from the dock and beached itself on the shore. We radioed in the incident, and army launches went out and pulled the boat back into coastal waters. The problem was that one of the sailors had been killed by gunfire.

The other soldier and I told our version of the events to an official board of inquiry. We had followed procedure and orders to the letter, which must have been sufficient because neither of us ever heard anything more about it. Which of us fired the fatal shot? What was the boat doing? Why didn't they identify themselves? Why didn't they stop when they heard and saw the shots? If the army got to the bottom of this mystery, they never shared any of the answers with us. It was just as well, because in such a situation, no one wants to know that they fired the fatal shot.

Guard duty could have its lighter sides as well. One evening, I was guarding the airport we maintained for our fighter pilots. They were all hotshot kids whose importance gave them more liberties than we infantry grunts enjoyed. I was walking my post when gunfire came from a Quanset hut where some of the pilots were quartered. I went inside to find them all drunk out of their minds, shooting their .45s at an army helmet in a potbellied stove to see if the bullets would go through it.

I explained as best I could to this happy bunch that they were not allowed to do this and it was time for lights out. They agreed to obey without any fuss and got into their cots. I walked out and closed the door behind me, thinking that the incident was over. No sooner did I start to walk away than I again heard gunshots. This time they were shooting at their overhead light, trying to put it out because no one was sober or energetic enough to get up and turn it off. I decided it was better to turn the matter over to a nearby first sergeant before they put a stray shot into each other, or worse, into me.

Since I had to obey orders, especially during war and in a combat zone, I found I could also enjoy it on occasion as well. This type of thinking might have protected me from another potentially serious incident, or might have just allowed me to blow off some steam. I had sentry duty one night at the post gate when a staff car with a full colonel approached to exit. According to procedure, I motioned for the car to stop and asked for the password. "I can't remember it, soldier," the Colonel said. "It's alright, you know me. I'm Colonel so and so, now open the gate." For all I knew, this could be a test, and I would be immediately placed under arrest if I disobeyed direct orders and allowed anyone, whatever their rank, to proceed in or out of that gate without the proper password.

"I'm sorry sir, but I have strict orders and can't allow you to pass without the proper sign," I said. The Colonel's driver then interjected himself in a way I felt was clearly designed to win the Colonel's favor. "Open this gate or I'll drive through it," he declared. I was angry at such an obvious challenge to my authority and replied quickly. "You do, and I'll put all eight slugs in this clip into the ass end of your vehicle." That was enough for the Colonel. "Turn around," he said in a huff. He returned with the officer of the day, and as soon as he gave me the password and exited, I was informed that I was relieved of my duty. I didn't score many points. I was only following orders, but for once I enjoyed it.

Staying healthy in a climate so cold and unforgiving was not easy. I contracted bronchial pneumonia and spent a week in the hospital. There was a beautiful nurse who thought I was pretty cute and I enjoyed the extra attention. On another occasion, I had to have my tonsils removed. It was nothing like the surgery performed today. I was seated in a dentist's chair and given an injection on the right and left sides of the back of my throat. The doctor immediately proceeded to insert a long wire-like device with a circular end down around the first tonsil. He yanked and it came out before I knew what happened.

The only problem was that I felt every bit of it. The anesthetic didn't have time to work and the pain was unbelievable! Before I could tell him that I could feel everything, he had the second tonsil out. That was it. There was no hospital stay and no slow recovery.

Iceland did have a few bright spots. I remember seeing the northern lights and thinking how beautiful they were. I can still see them in my mind's eye after more than 60 years. Once in the dayroom, where we had a pool table used more for card playing than for pool, I won the deal in a blackjack game. By the time the game ended, I had won $1,100. A little unexpected humor also came my way one night when I was coming off a stint of guard duty. A nurse, drunker than a skunk, wondered off from an officers' party and was sitting on a toilet in our latrine, happy as could be. I got the guys and we all laughed about it for days.

Sports provided me a potential diversion and a lot of real pain. The company commander approached me to represent our outfit in boxing matches as a light heavyweight. The gym was nothing but a Quanset hut with a ring and some boxing equipment. I showed up and had started knocking the bags around when the company barber, a soldier by the name of Carl Sajec, who probably weighed only 145 pounds and was several inches shorter than me, asked if I wanted to go a few rounds. I felt guilty, but thought it might be fun to bounce the guy around a little, so I accepted. We got into the ring and I immediately started to pepper this guy up and down with punches. The only problem was that they seemingly had no effect.

After a round or two, I was tiring out. I asked my corner man as he rubbed me off between rounds if I was actually hitting this guy. "Yeah," he said. "You're all over him." I couldn't understand why this little guy wouldn't go down. By the third round, he started swinging and I swear he hit me everywhere, including my ankles. If I covered my stomach, he hit me in the face. If I covered my face, he hit me in the stomach. He leathered every inch of me and I staggered out of the ring.

I soon found out why my experience as an amateur boxer had done me no real good. Sajec had been in 18 professional boxing matches! He knew how to roll with punches. This allowed him to take with out absorbing the powerful punches I threw. I went to the company commander and told him I wanted out. There was no way I was going to fight with professionals. If a man that much smaller than I could do that well, I hated to think what a bigger guy could do.

Football was my next opportunity. A flier on the bulletin board said that the outfit wanted men to form a team. I told them I wanted to play, but my real motivation was that this was would be a great way to get out of my normal duties. I showed up at the field, where we got a helmet, shoulder pads, and a jersey. The rest of our uniform consisted of fatigues. They asked me what position I had played in high school and I told them right end.

The quarterback called a play wherein I would run downfield straight along the sidelines, cut left, and receive a pass thrown midfield. The ball was snapped and I started to run. I cut left at the appropriate point and caught a pass thrown with picture-perfect precision. The next thing I remember is regaining consciousness on the sidelines. Two of the opposing team had hit me simultaneously. One hit high from one direction and the other low from the opposite direction. I didn't know it, but I had been well covered and set up by the opposition during the play.

Once again, I was playing with professionals. These guys had actually played pro ball back in the States. Yet again, it was back to the company commander. I had to tell him I didn't want to play anymore. Hell, a guy could get killed having all this fun. Regular military duty was a lot less hazardous.

Getting things from home, especially food, meant a great deal. We always shared with one another in our huts, but this became a matter of necessity when the army started serving homegrown Icelandic food, which largely consisted of mutton and pink-colored cheese. We were all outraged that even the army could serve food this bad. When we reached the end of the serving line, we simply dumped the entire meal into the garbage. We were in good with the cooks, who sympathized with us and snuck us sandwiches. The officers saw the garbage cans full of food, and virtually every one of us was very vocal with his complaint. The army soon shifted back to standard issue American food.

I was serving as a temporary squad leader when we stood formation for inspection by a captain who was known to be particularly chicken shit. He looked at the first man in line and said, "This man needs a haircut." He then proceeded to the next man, looked him and his weapon over and said, "This man's rifle is dirty." When he got to me he asked, "Who tied your dog tags?" "That's the way I was instructed to tie them in training, sir," I said. He got angry. "Don't lie to me," he warned in a raised voice. "No one would teach you to tie dog tags like that!"

I didn't appreciate being called a liar. "Captain," I said, "if you didn't have those bars on, I'd get you behind one of these Quanset huts and make you take your words back." His reply was quick. "If you weren't an enlisted man, I'd show you that you couldn't." I felt this comment required a further response. "Well Captain, I'd show you why you couldn't be an enlisted man." At this, the first sergeant jumped in and put a stop to things by telling me to shut up

The inspection proceeded without further incident, but afterwards a notice was posted on the bulletin board that I had been demoted in rank. I was no longer a squad leader. This was hardly a blow: I had only accepted the squad because it was garrison duty.

Rank was something I neither sought nor wanted. It meant the legal and moral commitment to do everything possible for your men's safety while completing your mission. This required sergeants and junior officers to be at the forefront of the action and danger. More importantly, it meant ordering men to do things that would get them killed. My combat experience later confirmed just how many good men this heavy responsibility consumed in terms of lives and mental health. I never felt any calling or desire to take on such a heavy burden.

Later in Europe, when I took out patrols or supervised young replacements in the effort to keep them alive, officers sometimes offered or even urged me to take stripes. I not only declined, but went so far as to say, "You give me those stripes, and I'll say or do something so you'll have to take them away by morning."

"But you're already doing sergeant's work now," they would counter. "It's not the same thing," I'd respond. I simply didn't want the official responsibility for deciding other men's lives. The strangest part of it all was that I broke this promise, at least in spirit, while I was still in Iceland. My friend Tom broke it in practice in France, and paid for it dearly.

I often thought about Mary, and on a couple of different occasions, I even thought I might have a legal way to get back to see her. The bulletin boards stated the air corps needed gunners for heavy bombers flying missions from England over Germany. I thought that if I passed the qualifying test, I would be sent Stateside for three months of special training, which would give me an opportunity to see Mary. The qualifying test consisted of fieldstripping a .50-caliber machine gun and putting a specified number of rounds into a target towed by a plane. I must have initially given my target too much lead, because the pilot radioed down that the fire was coming too close to his tail. I was told to be more careful, but qualified with relative ease. That was the good news.

The bad news came from the major in charge, who informed me that the gunnery training would not be 12 weeks in the States as originally planned, but a mere six weeks in England, not America. We didn't know then, but the high rate of air casualties (50 percent) required the army to speed up training to get more crews in the air.

The Major told me he would submit the paperwork to authorize my transfer to the air corps with a promotion to staff sergeant, effective upon approval of my application. I was shortly informed that my request was denied. The army felt it had invested a good deal of their time and effort in my training, that I had already spent considerable time in the infantry, and I was of more value there than in the air corps. That was that. Decades after the war, when I learned the casualty rates among air crews, I couldn't help but feel that I had been lucky to remain in the infantry.

It was common to rotate jobs during garrison duty. I even had my week of emptying the honey buckets in the latrine. My week on the switchboard, though, created for me a real enemy in high places. I heard one of the Battalion Commanders bum-rapping Lieutenant Block, a friend of mine, to superior officers as inefficient. I clued Block in about it, and he personally confronted the officer. His comments were so specific that the officer to figured out that Block was clued in by someone who heard his conversation over the phone. From there, the officer pieced together who had been on the switchboard that night and put Block in the know.

"I'll fix your wagon one of these days," he said the next time he saw me. When we got to combat in Europe, word came down through the grapevine that he wanted me on every patrol possible. I attended 5th Division reunions for a few years after the war with the primary desire that he would attend so that I could show my appreciation by bouncing him off a wall. I was sorely disappointed that I never saw him again.

Another potential opportunity to get back to see Mary appeared on the bulletin board as a call for applicants for Officer's Candidate School (OCS). I must have really been in love with that woman, because I set out to go against every instinct I had as well as my mutual promise to Tom Spain. Some officers like Smith, Block, and Livingston, not only encouraged me to apply, but offered to act as sponsors. Despite my exchange with the Captain and the fact that more than one officer had told me I was an exceptional field soldier but a terrible garrison soldier, I put in my application along with a fellow soldier, Bob Speidel. Speidel was a good soldier from the family of the famous wristwatch company of the same name. We got along well together.

If accepted, we would be sent to Fort Benning, Georgia, for officer's training. Applications had to be approved at battalion, regimental, and division level. Each review board consisted of about a half dozen officers who reviewed applications as candidates stood at attention before them. They then asked whatever questions they felt were relevant concerning military procedure, tactics in hypothetical situations, weapons, regulations, and the like. I passed all my reviews, as did Speidel, but things did not end there.

I had a good friend in the regimental sergeant-major, Farrell. He was from New York and highly intelligent: like Brinkman, he had been a newspaper reporter in civilian life. Farrell called me down to regimental headquarters to pull my file together, only to find that my application had been disapproved. He was puzzled, as was I, and wanted to find out the reason for its denial. A grizzled old tech sergeant had used his influence to have my application as well as Speidel's denied. He was a career military man with no use for draftees. "I've had 15 years in this man's army," he said, "and if I can't get a chance to go to OCS, no damn conscript is going to go ahead of me."

Farrell screamed and swore at the sergeant. He would even have busted him, but the officer immediately over the tech sergeant either didn't want to be bothered with the mundane job of reviewing OCS applications, or let his sergeant review them and gave him veto power for final approval. In either case, he had a heck of a lot more authority in these matters than he should have had. The end result was that Speidel and I were cheated out of our chance to go to OCS.

Farrell urged me to reapply and said he would personally oversee things the next time to ensure that the tech sergeant was bypassed. It wasn't worth the effort. Two months had passed. By this time it was summer 1943, we were about to leave Iceland. Things seemed to be quieting down, and we appeared to be headed back to the States. "None of this will be necessary," I thought. "I'll get my chance to see Mary without going to OCS."

Neither I nor any of the rest of us could know then just how far off the mark such thinking was from reality. The 5th Division was about to move even further from the States and closer to the fighting in Europe. Within a year, the only way to get back home would be a million-dollar wound or a flag-draped coffin.

5

UNDERPAID, UNDERSEXED, AND OVER THERE
Training with Our Cousins Across the Pond

"We cannot go to the country
for the country will bring us no peace."
—William Carlos Williams, "Raleigh Was Right"

When our exile in Iceland came to an end, we boarded the *USAT Mariposa* in Hvalfjordur on August 15, 1943. Even our departure could not conclude without incident. We ascended the gangplanks by order of rank with our first sergeant leading the way. One of the men on the dock yelled to the sailors at the top of gangway, "Hey sailors, where we headed?" Fully expecting to hear them reply "the United States," we were stunned when they shouted back "England!"

Our first sergeant's name was Williams, but we called him Aacho. He was halfway up the gangplank and completely taken aback with this news. He was a married man with two children and like the rest of us, he felt we had earned a furlough back to the States. "England?" he said with shock and dismay as he slapped his forehead hard with his right hand. This gesture unintentionally knocked his helmet off into the ocean.

We immediately figured it was an act of protest that we should imitate, so we all proceeded to toss our helmets into the sea. Soon the waters all around the dock were filled with floating helmets; others filled with water and sank. Cheers and laughter from soldiers and sailors alike filled the air. We had a great time laughing at our own misfortune.

The officers on the other hand figured they might have a mutiny

63

on their hands. Our laughter and good cheer quickly turned to real solemnity as MPs pulled up to the docks in jeeps with .50-caliber machine guns mounted in the rear. They cocked the guns so we could all hear them and pointed them directly at us so there was no mistaking they meant business. It was no longer a laughing matter. We boarded without further incident, but the army docked the pay of each and every one of us $9.00 for the cost of those helmets.

Aacho was a career man who had worked his way up the ranks from buck private. He lived in Battle Creek and was still a relatively young man. He was a first rate soldier and a heck of a nice guy. He and I got along very well, although he would eventually give up trying to make me walk the army's straight and narrow.

Navy didn't want the responsibility of loading our gear on board so we had to do it ourselves. I don't know why, but no matter how big the crowd, I was selected for one thing or another, sometimes for better, but more often for worse. This time Aacho asked if I could operate a winch. "How come you're always picking on me, Aacho?" I asked. "Because I like you, Mike," he said with a grin.

I was told to operate the vertical movements of the winch while a second man handled the horizontal movements. Together we loaded our gear and supplies onto the ship. A person on deck at the edge of the cargo hold checked to make certain that the area was clear before I lowered my bundle. Things moved along well enough and we were getting everything aboard ship when a crowd started to form. Before long a couple dozen soldiers were gathered around me. The bundle that was moving my way was the liquor ration for the officers. It now dangled above the opening of the cargo hold, waiting to be lowered down.

"Come on, Mike," one soldier said. "Bilder, you're not chicken shit, are you?" asked another. Every last one of them urged me to drop the bundle. The guy at the edge of the cargo hold knew something was up because of the delay and all of the troopers around me. He must have put two and two together, because he looked down into the hold, then looked around, and finally looked up at me and nodded.

That was the final bit of encouragement I needed. I released the brake and the cable ran down at lighting speed, sending the bundle to the bottom of the hold like a comet rocketing down from the sky. The liquor ration smashed to pieces, pouring out all over the bottom of the hold. The officers would now have to endure the impending hardships with the same degree of sobriety as the rest of us dogfaces.

This was my second ocean voyage. It only lasted two days, but it was enough to get me and most of the other men seasick. We arrived at Gourok, Scotland, on August 17. No bands, fanfare or local citizens turned out to meet us. The next day we arrived by train in Wiltshire in Salisbury Plain, about 20 miles outside of London. We were quartered at Tidworth Barracks, the former home of the British 8th Army. The buildings went back many hundreds of years, but living quarters were quite primitive compared to our quarters back in the States or even in Iceland.

Our first quarters were a castle, where conditions took away any romantic notions I might have held about King Arthur and his court. The windows had no glass and were covered with only a curtain. The floors were hard and it was drafty. We had wooden bunks and each man had to stuff his own mattress with straw and cover it with one of his GI blankets because the mattress was dirty and stank. This left just one blanket for sleeping. After about a week we were moved into barracks, but the quarters were almost as bad as the castle. As if this wasn't bad enough, the food was terrible.

Almost as soon as we arrived, I got a two-week furlough. I spent it in London and stayed at the Red Cross Club. My first night out on the town, I was with a two buddies. One was a huge guy, roughly 6 feet 4 inches tall, who had been busted out of the MPs for being too ready to mix it up. The other was from Chicago and stood at about 6 feet 2 inches. I was the runt of the litter at 6 feet 1 inch.

The 5th Division really felt we had earned the right to celebrate after 18 dreary months in Iceland. We were in a mood to tear up the country and probably thought we were justified in doing so. That night I was drinking single shot Scotches, which quickly graduated to doubles. Before long, I was good and drunk. My two buddies were rooming with me and thought it best to get me back to the Red Cross Club, so we started out on foot in that direction.

England was still very much a target of German air raids in 1943 and sandbags were piled up against the windows of almost every store and shop in the city. It was my good fortune to pass a very large plate glass window that was poorly protected. "Look at this," I said. "They hardly put any sandbags at all in front of it! The Germans are gonna smash it in their next raid. Aw, what the hell? I'll save them the trouble." With those words, I proceeded to put my foot through the window.

The window shattered instantly right in full view of two British bobbies. "Hey, Yank, what are doing there?" they called out. They started to grab me when one of my buddies stepped in. "Get your hands off him," he demanded. I was too drunk to fight, but my friends dispatched the two bobbies with relative ease.

The blackout kept the streets in total darkness, so when I saw blue lights approaching I knew who it was. "Let's get out of here," I yelled. "The MPs are coming! Run!" I started off down the street and seemed to run into every lamp and street sign along the way. Somehow I made it to the next street and waved down a taxi. I had him take me to the Red Cross Club. All this excitement had done a great deal to sober me up and I was now wide-awake. I sat on the edge of my cot and waited, but my roommates never showed up. Finally, I drifted off to sleep.

The next morning I rolled over with the hope that I'd see them in their cots. "Aw, shit," were the first words out of my mouth. I went down to the desk and asked the girl to call the American prison compound. She spoke to the Provost Marshall. "They're there," she said, "and he's looking for the third guy who was with them." This meant they hadn't squealed on me. It may not seem important now, but we needed to know we could trust one another, even when one of us did something stupid. A guy who would spill his guts about something like a busted window was not the type you wanted to share a foxhole with.

The two weren't angry with me. They even admitted that it was not my fault they got caught. They heard my warning and could have gotten away, but they had done so well against the bobbies that they thought they could take on the MPs as well. The MPs might have thought the same thing, because they didn't bother to fight. They simply drew their 45s and that was that.

My buddies spent their two-week furlough in the guardhouse and had two-thirds of their pay docked for three months to pay for the window and the fine for breaking it. I of course reimbursed them the money, which came to well over $200. I wrote home and told my mother that I needed the money to pay a fine. I had to be discreet because the mail was censored and I couldn't provide all the details without letting everyone know who the third soldier was.

I managed to get into London about twice a month on weekends. There was ballroom dancing at Hammerschmidt's and Covent Gardens, and I spent most of my time in London at one place or the other. I also spent part of an evening or two in the tube (subway) during air raids. The Brits seemed to regard the entire thing as more of a nuisance than a danger. Talk about a stiff upper lip!

As for the dancing, the Brits had an equivalent to Glenn Miller, but I was disappointed that there was little jitterbugging. The British soldiers and sailors were far superior to the Americans in ballroom dancing, but the tables were turned completely when it came to jitterbugging. I didn't do anything as elaborate as flipping a girl over my shoulders, but I could twirl her with ease and do a walk-about with her as she completed the steps in a circle around me. No one could deny that I was a very good dancer.

I missed having a steady dance partner, and female company in general, so I started to date a girl I met at Covent Gardens called Vicky. She was an excellent dancer. She was also blonde and very cute. We had a brief affair, which was typical under the circumstances, but there was no real chemistry between us. Vicky was much like an American girl and fun to be with, but I was careful not to let either of us get too emotionally involved. From the beginning I let her know that I had a girl back home I intended to marry. Vicky and I went to the movies, saw a few plays, and went dancing. She was very patriotic and we even went to hear Gracie Fields, who was the British version of Kate Smith. It was odd that "I'll Be Seeing You" was the favorite song of Vicky and Mary both.

We were both good looking, at ease in the spotlight, and full of energy in pursuit of a good time. I'm sure if I had proposed marriage that Vicky would have accepted, and we could have even fallen in love, but it would have been more for superficial reasons than for anything we felt in our hearts. It was better to have the moment together and leave it at that. I wanted Mary, and I knew Vicky wouldn't have any problems finding another American boyfriend. After the 5th

Division was sent to Northern Ireland, I got a "Dear John" letter from Vicky. She was throwing me over for an American naval officer. I can't say that I was surprised or even minded. If there was any hurt, it was to my pride and not my heart.

There were a lot of nice British girls and because Americans had money to spend, liked a good time, and might even offer the possibility of American citizenship through marriage, nice girls were easy to find. Soldiers a little more determined for female intimacy resorted to the infamous "Piccadilly Commandos." Their favorite come-on line was, "Hey Yank, got a match?" We joked that the reply should be, "Yeah, a buffalo fart and your breath." The prostitutes were a mess in every way. Most were dirty and downright unattractive.

Aside from morality and the thought that a true man never had to pay for sex, there were health issues involved. The army made a point of repeatedly showing us films on venereal disease that featured real cases of advanced cases of syphilis and gonorrhea. It scared the hell out of me and provided all the motivation I needed to be careful and selective when it came to women.

There was a real feeling of competition between us and our British allies. This was true in the battle for girls, on the training fields, and even on the dance floor. It was so obvious it was almost tangible, yet we still managed to work together. British officers and NCOs supervised our training and tactics, and offered suggestions and methods to improve both. They were tough on us, but on the whole we got along well.

My old buddy First Sergeant Williams selected me to complete a ten-day course in British commando tactics. Soldiers who completed the course returned to their units as instructors to pass on their knowledge to the rest of the outfit. Aacho called me into his office in early October, explained the situation, and told me that I was to represent George Company. I was to report to Saint George Baths in London and follow orders.

The training was given by British sergeant majors. Among us, there were both enlisted personnel and officers, Brits and Americans alike. We were all treated equally, regardless of differences in nationality and rank. The training was rigorous to say the least. On one exercise, we had to crawl on our backs and cut barbed wire as we moved along, while machine guns fired live ammunition over our heads. We had been warned that the guns were fixed in their firing positions so there was no way for their operators to compensate for our errors. Anyone who raised his hands too high to cut the wire or was foolish enough to raise his body would become a casualty.

I didn't appreciate it at the time, but all this extra training played a big role in keeping me alive once we got into combat. Those of us from regular units, as opposed to the commandos and special forces like the Rangers, not only completed the water obstacles portion of the course, but actually became instructors in combat swimming techniques. Everyone knew that Allied troops would one day invade France, which meant crossing the English Channel. Enemy fire was bound to hit troop ships and assault boats, sending their human cargo into the water with full packs and equipment loads. Instructors in combat swimming were needed to teach men how to drop their packs and equipment in the water then swim for their lives wearing uniforms and boots

My instruction in combat swimming began on October 11 and lasted four days. I then assisted both British and Americans in the swim portion of their commando training. Training conditions simulated actual combat as closely as possible. Since the sinking ships would be leaking oil and the oil would catch fire, our trainers were good enough to cover the top of the pool water with oil and then ignite it for us. To graduate, we had to jump into this burning muck from a springboard 20 feet above the water, with helmet, rifle and full equipment, and then swim 75 yards under water! A piece of cake.

I stood at the end of the springboard, and brother was I scared. I knew I was an excellent swimmer, and this gave me enough confidence to overcome my fears. As instructed, I grabbed my jewels with both hands and jumped in. I sank quickly towards the bottom but maintained the presence of mind to follow my training, and immediately unhitched and dumped my pack. I dropped my rifle, shed my helmet, and started to swim like hell.

I couldn't feel any heat from the burning oil on the surface right above me, but I could clearly see the flames. I was worried that I wouldn't be able to hold my breath long enough to make it to the opposite end of the pool, but the fact that there was no pragmatic way to surface provided all the incentive I needed to keep going. Things became blurry and it was difficult to judge distance and stay oriented. I had a brief feeling of intense anxiety bordering on panic, but the instruction had prepared me well and I was able to stay reasonably calm and pace myself. I made it the required length and burst up to the surface. I was dog-tired but I had done it!

Seven other guys from the Chicago area completed the same training, and the newspapers back home all published a small press release from the army about it, complete with our names and home addresses. Mary and my folks both spotted the item and my folks clipped it from the paper. I still have the clippings to this day.

We completed the combat lifeguard course on October 15, got our certification cards, which were valid for one year, and immediately began supervising others in this part of their commando training. Many men on the edge of that springboard, both Americans and Brits, who had started with me at the beginning of this training looked down from that 20-foot height at that burning water and simply refused to jump. They were pulled out of their respective program for reassignment. I couldn't think less of a man who decided not to jump in. The instinct of self-preservation is a strong one, and it was better to learn limitations in training rather than in actual combat.

You won't find this in any official histories of the 5th Division or its component regiments, but I am convinced a race riot in Andover got our unit thrown out of England and sent to Northern Ireland well ahead of schedule. Weekend passes in England had to specify a destination. They would only allow about 20 percent of us to go to London at any given time; the others who got weekend passes had to go somewhere else. If you were lined up for a pass and the company commander said, "You better give somebody else a turn," it meant you were going to Andover.

This was not a bad thing. Andover was a nice little town with pubs and shops, and the city hall or community center usually had some kind of activities for servicemen. There were bands for dancing and the old ladies taught us how to play whist. The Brits didn't break their necks trying to be friendly. They were generally aloof and reserved, but they were courteous and usually did what they could in their own way to make us feel at home.

Black American troops from the quartermaster corps also went into Andover. They knew the 5th Division had a large number of hard-core southerners who had little use for them. In fact, the sad truth is that most troops at that time, regardless of their color, were uncomfortable when races intermingled. It was a bad by-product of the times and I was not immune to it. There was no real love lost on either side, and it only took a small incident to get things really heated up. Naturally, as fate would have it, I was there when just such an incident occurred.

I was fortunate enough to miss the beginning, but got the details after the fact. The girls in Andover, and all over the UK, danced and dated black and white soldiers alike. Some of the southerners in our outfit asked the girls why they danced with Negro soldiers. "They told us they were American Indians," was the reply. That must have been the excuse that some of these guys were waiting for, because they came back to Andover the following weekend armed for bear.

I was out on the street with some other guys when we saw a huge commotion. Civilians and military alike were fleeing from this one pub. We didn't know who it was and why they were fighting, but it didn't matter. It was a fight and we wanted in on it. We ran into the pub and saw instantly that it was a racial fight, so we starting swinging at anyone whose skin was different from our own. The black soldiers were out numbered, so I had to wait my turn to take a swing at somebody. Those of us from the north had certain rules when we fought. There was no kicking, no weapons, and no piling on. It had to be bare knuckles in a fair one-on-one fight. I waited for someone to come at me or intercepted someone who tried to run past.

At first it was almost comical, like something out of a Chaplin movie. If things had stayed that way, everyone might have walked away with nothing more than some cuts and bruises. Then we heard shots ring out. We dove for cover. This had now gone way beyond what almost anybody wanted. We worked ourselves outside and under some cars as shots continued to ring out, then hightailed it out of there before the authorities showed up.

I found out later that men on both sides had made it a point to carry guns and even trench knives into Andover. The brass knuckles on trench knives and eventually the blades themselves were used. I was also told that around 20 soldiers, both black and white, but mostly black, had been killed.

The next thing we knew we were shipping out for Northern Ireland, after only nine weeks in England! We were probably headed there anyway, but this incident sure seemed to speed things up. The quartermaster corps was considered essential because they had to ready all the supplies in England for the upcoming invasion of France, but we were just infantry grunts the army could ship someplace else. This was clearly evident when we discovered nothing was ready for us when we got to Northern Ireland.

On October 22 we were heading up the gangplank of a troop transport in Bristol bound for Northern Ireland when I happened to overhear a British candy dancer (rail worker) near the docks. "There go another bunch of them Yanks, and good riddance," he said. "At least now I won't have to worry about any of them getting my daughter pregnant." That was our sendoff from England.

We docked in Belfast on October 24. Even this two-day trip was enough to get me seasick. As usual, there was no greeting or interest from the local populace. The army quartered us in buildings spread out along the coast boarding Southern Ireland. The political situation was ticklish to say the least. The South of Ireland has 26 counties with a mostly Catholic population, and obtained independence from England in 1921. Northern Ireland consists of six counties that are heavily Protestant and is part of the United Kingdom (UK) along with Scotland, England and Wales. This meant that Northern Ireland was at war with Germany, while Southern Ireland, despite strong pressure from Churchill, remained neutral.

The Irish Republic in the south lacked any real military ability and would have been unable to adequately defend itself if attacked. We often joked that the Irish Navy consisted of a rowboat, which was not all that far from the truth. Ireland had no air force, a few very small naval craft, and nothing more than a token army best suited for parades. Still, Irish President Eamon de Valera, an American by birth, swore that Ireland would fight to the last man against any invader, Axis or Allied.

Some members of the Irish Republican Army (IRA) spied for the Germans and helped refuel their subs. They believed a Germany victory would reunite their homeland. Churchill wanted very much to bring Ireland into the war and make use of their strategic land for air and naval bases. There was always the fear that the Germans would invade and quickly conquer Ireland, hence providing an easy back door entry into Britain.

Many of us wondered aloud whether we were in Ireland to perform duty as "Churchill's Division" and to take over the South for Britain. The Catholics among us deeply resented the idea that Protestant England might force itself upon the Free State. Even the southern Protestants in our outfit opposed such a move. It reminded them of the American Civil War or, as they preferred to call it, the War of Northern Aggression.

There was an overriding reason why Roosevelt couldn't go along with Churchill on taking over the Irish Republic. It would have meant that American Catholics, heavily Democratic in their voting patterns, would switch their political allegiances. Both political and military leaders also had a well-founded fear that large numbers of American troops would outright refuse to obey an order to take the South. At the very least, many of us would have fired our weapons in the air, dragged our feet, or done whatever else we could to show our distaste for such a venture. This would hardly have been good for morale or the war effort in general.

That was how things stood when we arrived in late October 1943. Unlike the situation in Iceland, the Irish did not have a language or culture that enabled them to identify with the Germans: in fact, the situation was just the opposite. The Irish were hesitant to admit it, but with the exception of religion they identified in most every way with the Brits.

Northern Ireland, like England, was very rainy and cold. Our hasty arrival had caught our hosts unprepared. They put us in a little resort town called Warrenpoint located in County Down about half a mile north of Carlingford Lough. Carlingford Lough is a sea loch in the far northeast of the island that divides the two Irelands and leads directly into the Atlantic. We were billeted under a roof, but the space was obviously not designed as military quarters. There were three to four men in a room and instead of bunks we slept on army cots. While we were there, I contracted bronchial pneumonia. The damp and cold were very hard on me. I spent about ten days in the hospital and was sicker than I care to think about.

The "training grounds" were nothing of the sort. We were in the middle of farmland and civilian housing. There was no mess hall, so the army brought us down to the Warrenpoint train station one battalion at a time for chow. We literally had to form up in companies and march to the train station. There was no coming and going as we pleased. At night, the train station doubled as our movie theater.

They fed us mostly C-rations, which were usually awful. Army portions were small and low in calories, which was good in one way and bad in another. It was good in that the food tasted so lousy that we didn't want to eat much of it. It was bad in that we were hungry most of the time.

The official neutrality of the Irish Republic meant that the South was strictly off limits to all Allied military personnel. This left Belfast as the only real city to visit on weekend pass. There were few hotels, and in any case, hotels were still a luxury to us even though we were paid much better than our British counterparts. The Red Cross encouraged families in Northern Ireland to accommodate their Allied guests and "put up a Yank." It was much like a bread and breakfast operation, where the soldier paid the family for this service.

I went into Belfast one weekend and stayed with a nice family that had two daughters. The older girl was 21 and her sister was two years younger. I got into the city on a Saturday morning and looked it over. When I arrived at my lodgings, the family served me tea with a light breakfast and we talked. The girls were very curious about America and Americans in general. I was flattered by their attention and they hung on my every word. Their parents were pleasant enough and they gave me a key to the house so I could let myself in after an evening on the town. I had a good time visiting pubs and looking around and finished the evening without incident.

The next morning I was enjoying some toast with marmalade and tea when I asked where the nearest church was located. "It's about four blocks over," the lord of the manor said. "The services are at eleven and two." Being a practicing Catholic, I knew mass schedules began in the early morning, were spaced about an hour apart, and there were usually five masses in the course of a morning, so when he said "eleven and two," I knew we were of different minds.

"I don't think we're talking about the same church," I said. "I want to go to mass." From the look on their faces you would have thought I had just told them that I was Hitler's blood relative. They gave me directions, but when I returned from mass they made it a point to take their key back. This was their official way of rolling in the welcome mat. The girls who had tittered and squeaked during the previous day's conversation were now as cold as ice and no longer interested in me or anything I had to say.

That night as I walked back to the train, I took note of the local graffiti. "Down with the Pope" and "To Hell with the Pope" were scribbled on the walls in abundance. This was very different from anything I had encountered before. Even during our maneuvers in Tennessee, in the heart of Protestant Bible belt country, I had never seen this kind of animosity towards Catholics.

This was not my only experience in Ireland with different religious perspectives, but my next such experience was a good deal more cordial. Our Protestant chaplain was a huge man from Texas, a captain, and a pretty nice guy. He approached me to act as his chauffeur. I was to report to the motor pool the following morning and get his jeep so I could drive him around. This was yet another example of how seemingly everyone selected me for anything and everything.

I picked him up at his quarters and helped him with some missals and a portable organ that fit into a large carrying case. We drove to an assigned location, and while I was unable to accommodate his request to play the organ, I did pass out the missals. I sat quietly and politely as he delivered his Sunday sermon and everyone sang hymns. I then helped him pack everything up.

During the trip back, I asked, "Captain, can you drop me off here? It's almost eleven o'clock and I have to go to church." He looked a little puzzled. "You just went," he said. "I know, Captain, but I have to go to mass." "Are you Catholic?" he asked. I nodded. He dropped me off as I requested, but he never again asked me to help out with his duties. He remained very cordial however, and continued to greet me with a warm "Hello, Bilder," whenever he saw me. This was more typical of the experiences I had with people of different faiths.

I later saw the horrifying results of Nazi atrocities close up. They showed just how far intolerance could go. This was the type of experience that forever changed the way we thought about prejudice and bigotry.

My time in Northern Ireland also brought me into contact with Mary's family. They had begun immigrating to the United States from Southern Ireland as early as the 1840s. Mary's mother had come from County Galway in 1913. The family had some relatives in Belfast by the name of Cunningham. They were part of a theatre group that traveled from town to town performing in the North. The group was actually a front for the IRA whose purpose was to deliver messages and recruit new members.

It is important to note that Mary's relatives were not terrorists. The Cunninghams were very patriotic but extremely timid. Their paltry actions on behalf of the IRA were about as daring as they could ever hope to get. They had no use for the Germans and supported an Allied victory. As an American, I had no interest in their political differences and, even as a fellow Catholic, I felt nothing more than minor sympathy for their plight.

I stayed for a short time with the Cunninghams, who also had a retired priest living with them. Some of Mary's relatives came up from the South for a kind of family reunion. It was very festive and I was treated quite well during my stay. They suggested I obtain a week's furlough and travel south to meet the rest of the family who were unable to make the trip up north. They offered to give me an Irish haircut and civilian clothes to make the journey. I politely declined. For an American soldier to wear civilian clothes during wartime was bad enough: if caught, he could be treated as a deserter. But to go into the Irish Republic in civilian clothes could mean arrest as a spy. In wartime both offenses could be punishable by death.

The Cunninghams were related to a family in Warrenpoint who owned a small pub where I met a very nice couple by the name of Morgan. Mr. Morgan was a ship's captain on a good-sized fishing boat. He often heard me complain that the whiskey in the North was watered down, and told me he would get me into the South where I could buy real Irish whiskey. I mentioned this to my NCO, Sergeant Farrell, and a few guys in the company who could keep their mouths shut. Together, it was decided that I would go into the South, in uniform, to purchase whiskey for our thirsty little group. What our company didn't drink themselves we sold at cost to others in the regiment. We weren't about to make a profit off our own guys. We only needed enough money to cover our operating costs and maybe grease an occasional palm.

This was a tame, albeit somewhat risky, undertaking. We were not out to run a profitable bootlegging operation, just to get some uncut Irish whiskey for our own consumption. I picked up relatively small quantities, 8-10 cases, in the full light of day from sellers who operated licensed pubs in the South. I also made these excursions with Farrell's full knowledge and blessing. He informed me whenever the supply was exhausted, and suggested I make the trip. He even excused me from my assigned duties long enough to allow me to go, and I usually completed the trip a matter of hours.

Mr. Morgan arranged for me to cross the border the easiest way possible, by water. I left County Down in the North from Warrenpoint and crossed over Carlingford Lough to County Louth in the South, where my destination was a small village called Omeath. Omeath is slightly inland, located about midpoint between Dublin and Belfast. The boat I used was about double the size of a regular rowboat and had a small motor on the back. It reminded me of something that whalers would use.

Two or three Irishmen who lived in the North and knew their way around the South always accompanied me. In Omeath, we went directly to the assigned pub to pick up cases of whiskey that were already stacked and waiting for us, and transported our cargo back to the boat in wheelbarrows. We paid in cash and were immediately on our way.

The purchases were legal, but the circumstances were sketchy. My presence as an Allied soldier on Southern soil and the lack of any import fee on the whiskey were potential problems. Even so, we knew that most officers and authorities regarded such activity as small potatoes and were more than willing to turn a blind eye and a deaf ear to soldiers' mischief in wartime.

I made five or six trips into the South during my eight months in Ireland and the Irish bobbies there stopped me almost every time. "What are you doin' over here, Yank?" they'd ask in a heavy brogue.

"I'm buying some of your good whiskey," I'd say. "Well, get your business done and be off with ya," they'd answer. Back in Warrenpoint, Sergeant Farrell always had a three-quarter-ton truck and a couple of GIs waiting to get our precious cargo back to the company. The only compensation I ever received for my efforts was a free bottle of whiskey.

Mr. Morgan would get fresh meat on occasion and his wife would prepare me a steak. She was very kind and an excellent cook, but her beef was occasionally chewy. I was shocked when I discovered that her "steaks" were actually horsemeat.

Frequenting the Morgans, I became friends with a dentist named Hunter Seath who had offices in Newery and Belfast. He was a member of the Warrenpoint Golf Club, which was very exclusive. I didn't golf, but I went to the club as his guest on Sunday afternoons to play cards. There was a bar and social area in the front and a decorative room in the back for card playing. I may have been the only enlisted man ever in attendance, since club rules technically forbid us entrance, but Seath was a former president of the club and still had great influence. I was popular but always very careful, and even evasive if necessary, about discussing anything of a military nature.

I did obtain a two-week furlough that I spent in Scotland around Attenborough. The scenery was fantastic, but I had great difficulty understanding the English language through the heavy accents. I was also bored beyond belief. One day in a pub, I sat down to drink with some troopers from the famed Scottish Black Watch. This was, and still is, an elite outfit with a very long and well-established reputation for incredible courage and toughness on the battlefield.

They welcomed me to sit down at the bar, and I saw they were wearing military kilts. "Man," I said, "if I had legs like that I'd be on Broadway." One of them hit me so fast that I literally never saw the blow. I woke up on the floor a few seconds later and saw that everything was going on as if the incident had never happened. One of them reached down and offered me a hand up. I took it but was none too sure if I was doing the right thing. I was hoping they weren't picking me up just to lay me out.

"We know you Yanks aren't used to seeing soldiers in skirts," one of them said. "You have to understand that we're pretty sensitive about it." They were obviously great sports. They bought me drinks and we laughed and talked for a long while, as if we had been buddies from way back. It truly was a good time.

Patton came to Ireland and inspected the 5th Division toward the end of March 1944. He was said to be impressed with us and our 18-month tour in Iceland. The 5th Division was commanded by S. LeRoy "Red" Irwin, who had been the artillery commander for Patton's Seventh Army the previous year in Sicily. Irwin was far from a protégé of Patton. He was prudent, and even cautious, but a very capable commander who produced results. He cared deeply about the men under his command, yet was still held high in Patton's regard.

I once saw Irwin sitting on the grass conversing with his staff. There was nothing impressive about his appearance, which was maybe the reason we didn't have any problem with him as a commander. He was not pretentious. He was a professional soldier but still keenly aware of the attitudes, capabilities, and limitations of an army that primarily consisted of citizen soldiers.

By spring 1944, everyone, including Americans, Irish civilians, and even the Germans, knew that the invasion of France was imminent. You could feel it in the air and see it everywhere you looked. I was surprised that Ireland didn't sink under the weight of all the military personnel, supplies, and equipment.

I was in Belfast on a three-day pass having a really good time drinking and card playing with some other soldiers when I realized it was time to get back to Warrenpoint. I hurried to the train station but just missed the train. The next train wouldn't be along for four hours, which meant I was going to be late.

Knowing that combat was drawing near contributed to a certain feeling of abandon. "What the hell?" I said to myself. "If I'm going to be AWOL, why not make it two days?" I turned around and went back into Belfast to enjoy another two days of R and R.

When I got back to Warrenpoint, I walked in the orderly room and the first sergeant said, "Bilder, you're in trouble. You're two days late." My response was classic. "At least I got back." It didn't suffice. He told me to report to the company commander immediately. "Bilder, did you have a good time?" the CO asked. I was honest. "Yes sir, I did. I'm sorry I had to leave." He was very matter of fact and showed no sign of anger. "Well, I've got an assignment for you," he said. "I want you to be at battalion headquarters tomorrow morning at 8:00 hours in dress uniform. That's all, no further questions, dismissed."

The next morning I reported as ordered only to find a number of other men also in dress uniform. I quickly discovered that they were all there for reasons very similar to my own. We were ordered into a deuce and a half (a two-and-a-half-ton truck) and were on our way. "Where are we headed?" asked one. "I don't know," said another. "Why are we in dress uniform?" asked someone else. "They're probably gonna have us pull some kind of guard duty," speculated yet another. It went on this way during the entire trip.

We pulled into an airfield and saw just about every type of aircraft you could imagine. There were gliders, C-47 transports, fighter planes and anything else that flew. "You see," one soldier said. "Guard duty!" A tech sergeant greeted us on arrival. "Alright, everybody dismount. Form up in columns of two and follow me."

He led us into a Quanset hut and gave a one-word order: "STRIP!" There were about 50 of us now. We all started to undress and were getting pretty curious as to what exactly was going on. "Hey Sarge, what's this all about?" somebody asked. "Aren't you guys volunteers for the glider troops?" was his response. In an instant all our eyes made contact with one another. A cold shiver went through us, and it wasn't a result of being naked. We were all getting paid back army style for our infractions.

I went through the physical examination line and passed everything until the doctor saw a bone protruding in my right ankle. "What did you do there?" he asked. "I did it playing basketball," I told him. "Alright," he said. "Go stand over there with those other men," and he pointed to the far end of the room. I went over and joined four or five other guys who also failed to make the grade.

A truck took me back to my company. When I went into the orderly room they were surprised to see me. The company commander wanted to talk to me again and asked what had happened. "Alright," he said. "I can't bust you because everything's been frozen for the invasion. Report back to your platoon." I started to salute in preparation for dismissal, but he still had a point to make. "Bilder, you can rest assured that this hasn't been forgotten." I knew he meant it and I also knew better than to say anything other than, "Yes, sir." He returned the salute and dismissed me but the incident indeed was not forgotten.

Nevertheless, once again, I had lucked out. The glider troops, like the airborne, went in the night before the beach invasions and were killed in waves.

I also had additional dealings with the Red Cross in Ireland that led to my voluntarily accepting further duties. We often went to the Red Cross Club and got something to eat and a sympathetic ear. It was much like the USO. One of the "donut dollies" who served us coffee and donuts was a woman named Jane. She was about ten years older than I was. She was very skinny and nothing to look at, but she was very intelligent and good to talk to, so I dropped by on a regular basis to visit. The officers had long since laid claim to any of the good-looking women there.

Jane invited me to her quarters many times but things never went any further than conversation. Whether she liked me or was simply impressed with my gentlemanly conduct, I'll never know, but she asked if I was interested in serving as a driver and assistant for the Red Cross field representative to the 2d Regiment. I kind of liked the idea so she arranged for me to talk to L.W. Neatherland, a field director for the American Red Cross.

Neatherland and I met in his office at 36 Church Street in Warrenpoint, where he conducted what was essentially a job interview. He was a large, somewhat portly man in his mid-60s who wore small glasses and looked English, even though he was an American. He liked that I had high scores in weapons qualifications and was Red Cross certified as a combat lifeguard. He asked me if I could type. "About 30 words a minute," I told him. "Can you take dictation?" he asked. I said no, but I could write very fast. He asked me to find a few points on a map, and map reading was an area I excelled in.

Finally, he asked if I could anticipate situations well and use sound judgment. In other words, was I a survivor? I couldn't tell him about all the antics I had been involved in or the specifics of my many military experiences but I did assure him I fit the bill. "OK," he said. "You've got the job. I'll get hold of your company commander and tell him that you're not to perform any company duties until I tell him it's OK. I will contact him the night before any time I need you."

The arrangement was that I would still be an infantry grunt who had to fight, but when the Red Cross needed to get a message through to a soldier on the frontline, I would either help the Red Cross representative deliver the message or, more often, I would deliver it myself. When I was needed, the Red Cross rep contacted my company commander and I was sent off the next day in a jeep to whichever company in the 2d Regiment had the soldier I needed to contact. I was then assigned to serve with that company for two or three days before returning to my own George (G) Company.

I served with every company in the 2d Regiment and went wherever they did. If the company was going into reserve status, I went into reserve status; if they were jumping off into combat, I jumped off into combat. It was always a crapshoot, but it suited my temperament. The sense of freedom and mobility kept me sane, helped me to hold up my end of things in combat, and quite probably kept me alive.

Meanwhile, those of us who were certified to teach the Red Cross combat swimming course had to train others to be lifeguards and teach regular recruits how to swim in preparation for the invasion. On May 30, 1944, Neatherland sent me a letter by way of Company Headquarters of the 2d Battalion, instructing me to attend a meeting to plan training courses with the field director and the other men who were certificated instructors. I was also to tell them if I knew of any nearby beaches "suitable for instructing 200 men at a time."

The North Atlantic is very cold even in late May and early June. There was very little swimming. Men seldom brought bathing suits and most of the "instruction" was a discussion of people's past experiences in the water and how to perform different swimming strokes. This was the only part of the training that was not too intense.

All of the other aspects of training for the invasion were designed to toughen men up and weed out those who couldn't cut it. Anyone who couldn't keep up, those overweight, too slow, or deemed not to be fully proficient for any reason, were shipped out, and new replacements took their place. We had to train and perform every waking minute and constantly fight off feelings of complete physical and mental exhaustion.

We performed calisthenics so well and so often that our overseers often tired out before we did. We marched so quickly that we covered five miles in one hour, nine miles in two hours, and 25 miles in eight hours, wearing fully loaded, 60-pound packs. When we finally removed our boots, our feet were almost always blistered and bloody.

No one drove us harder than a certain S-3 (Training and Planning) captain from New York. He had been a lawyer in civilian life and was determined to whip us into the meanest, most effective fighting force on earth. His main problem was one of leadership. He forgot one of the first rules of military command: never order your men to do anything that you can't, won't, or haven't previously done yourself.

He stripped us above the waist down to our T-shirts and had us run flat out at full speed for four miles. He, however, did not participate in this exercise. His arrogance and the air of superiority he projected were another mistake. He wore riding boots and carried a swagger stick, and the fact that he exempted himself from many of the rigors he imposed on us caused some very hard feelings in our ranks. This treatment was not forgotten, especially by a particular NCO, when the Captain led us into combat the following September.

We had to learn razor-sharp precision in battle tactics from the battalion and company levels right on down to our squads. We fired captured German weapons and studied German tactics. We were physically and mentally ready to go. We were even told during briefings that we would be part of the initial invasion force, although this was not the case. I can't say any of us objected after the fact, considering the high number of casualties the army suffered on D-Day.

On June 6, 1944, American forces landed at beaches in Normandy code-named Omaha and Utah, while the British landed at Gold and Sword, and the Canadians at Juno Beach. Hitler had expected the invasion to occur at Calais, so the Allies largely achieved the element of surprise. This helped to reduce the number of Allied casualties, which nevertheless were still appallingly high.

These beach landings were all preceded the night before by glider and airborne troops who went into France with great courage and determination. Often they had opportunity to do little more than die in droves. The 1st and 29th Infantry Divisions and the 2d Ranger Battalion landed at Omaha Beach and took the heaviest casualties of any of the Allied invasion forces to hit the French coast that day. The 4th Infantry Division went in at Utah Beach and, while their losses were not as heavy, it was hardly a cakewalk.

Despite all our training and preparation, we were not sent in as part of the initial invasion force. Instead, we were simply restricted to quarters. Rumors started the next day that the army wanted to have well trained units ready to go in fresh against an expected German counter attack. As it turned out, we wouldn't get to France until early July. The army brought back men fresh from combat in France to teach us the latest about German booby traps and how to go about properly hating the enemy.

In the immediate, I knew my mother and Mary would be worried as news of the invasion flashed across the world. We had to put our letters in unsealed envelopes, and were forbidden to reveal any military details. Army censors screened our outgoing mail, using razors to cut out anything that was, or was even imagined, to refer to location, time, military unit, or any other information that could benefit the enemy. They then sealed the envelopes and mailed our letters.

Our letters home often looked like Swiss cheese and were completely unintelligible to family and friends. With time and experience, we learned the art of wartime letter writing, and were able to limit the surgery performed on our correspondence. We then could at least convey our feelings in a relatively unedited and understandable way.

After the invasions, regulations nevertheless allowed us to send a generally worded cable home to let our loved ones know that we were safe. My cable to Mary simply read: "YOU'RE THE ICE CREAM ON MY APPLE PIE. I'M ALRIGHT. LOVE, MIKE"

6

"LAFAYETTE, WE ARE HERE," AGAIN!

Bloody Combat in the Normandy Hedgerows

"Has this been thus before?"
—Dante Gabriel Rossetti, "Sudden Light"

Most every American of my generation and before learned in grade school about the Marquis de Lafayette. An influential French national, he came to America in 1777 to volunteer his services to George Washington during the Revolutionary War. The Continental Congress appointed him to the impressive rank of major general at the tender age of 19. He then went on to serve on George Washington's staff, where he trained American troops and even led them to victory in battle against seemingly hopeless odds.

He also played no small role in persuading France to enter the war on the side of the Revolutionaries. In short, he received a great deal of praise from American historians, and most Americans credited him for making a significant contribution to the colonies' success in their war for independence. Without France, America almost certainly would have been defeated by the British.

It was for this reason that Americans, in general, still felt in 1917 that the United States owed a special debt to France and was repaying that debt when it entered the First World War on the side of the Allies. According to historical legend, quartermaster officer C.E. Lewis stated in July 1917, "Lafayette, we are here!" Newspapers of the day credited this line to the commanding general of the American Expeditionary Forces, John J. Pershing, but this was hardly the first time that rank was accorded such privilege.

Historians generally believe that the peace terms of the Treaty of Versailles, signed in 1919 to officially end World War I, were so harsh on the defeated nations that it did nothing but lay the seeds for another war. In 1944, a quarter of a century after the fact, American troops were back on French soil to settle any disputes having originated from that treaty. There was no avoiding the fact that Hitler's Germany was not going to quit willingly and America, along with other nations from that first alliance, would again have to fight the Germans in France and elsewhere.

Our outfit had completed ten and a half months of domestic service and training, and spent eighteen months in Iceland and eleven months in the UK, but the war still was far from over before we got into the fray. The hope that it would soon be finished had long since died away, and when the initial success of the Allied invasion was met not by German capitulation but with stiffened resistance, we knew that word was soon to come down from the big brass to send us into action.

At 24:00 hours on June 29, 1944, the 2d Infantry Regiment was put on alert for overseas movement. We were officially "sealed in," which meant that we were restricted to our barracks and billet area. Everyone was prohibited from communicating in any way with the outside world. No one, not even our officers, could leave the area without a pass signed personally by the regimental commander.

We paced, played cards, spread rumors, smoked incessantly, and generally remained in a state of high anxiety. Heavy rains contributed to the dank and dreary atmosphere that hovered over us. It was always the delay that made it so hard to tolerate pre-combat situations. The down time allowed us to build up the worst possible scenarios in our minds. We packed up all of our gear, keeping it at the 60-pound limit, and waited for the word to move out.

That word came on July 5, and we rolled out of Warrenpoint that same day. They got us up to Belfast by truck and train, and over the next 24 hours we were transported with all our equipment out to a dozen liberty ships waiting for us in the harbor. We finished boarding and set sail for France at midnight on July 6.

This was my fourth ocean voyage and I kept my record perfect by getting seasick, just as I had previously on the way to Iceland, England and Northern Ireland. We were briefed on the invasion and the current military situation in company-sized groups on July 7 and 8, and arrived off the coast of France on July 9. It was late at night and our officers, seeking to avoid casualties due to accidents in the dark, wisely decided that only the Regimental and Battalion Headquarters Companies would go ashore that night. They reached shore a few minutes after 22:00 hours. The rest of us would follow in the morning.

The following dawn it was misting as we climbed down the thick roped nets hanging along the outer sides of our liberty ships and into the waiting LCVPs (Landing Craft Vehicle, Personnel) provided by the U.S. Navy. These vessels were also known as Higgins Boats and had been used on D-Day to bring the infantry ashore to assault the beaches. They were capable of carrying troops, supplies, and even vehicles like jeeps.

I looked around at the men as we headed towards shore. Most of them just sat on equipment or the inside edges of the landing craft with their rifles straight up between their knees. Their long faces had a look of despair on them, as if they were certain death were imminent. It was very quiet and quite obvious that everyone was deep in thought. I, on the other hand, had the unlikely idea that I was going to come through this war all right and that only the others could possibly become casualties. I have often wondered how many others may have been thinking that same thing.

Our beach in Normandy had been secured a month earlier, but that did little to put our minds at ease. We were just days away from combat and everybody knew it. We landed just after dawn at a place codenamed Sugar Red Beach. This was part of Utah Beach that had been taken five weeks earlier on D-Day, courtesy of the American 4th Infantry ("Ivy") Division. The 4th Division had fared much better on D-Day than their counterparts at Omaha Beach. Utah Beach had cost 197 dead (60 from drowning), compared to the roughly 3,000 Americans killed at Omaha Beach.

The ramp of our landing craft dropped down in front of us in about three feet of water. I was lucky and aboard a jeep as it drove out onto the beach. Most of the men following had to come ashore on foot in water that was almost waist deep, which meant they had to endure the entire day with wet feet. All of our jeeps, trucks, and tanks had been waterproofed so that they would not stall out in the channel and turn our landing area into a military traffic jam.

The Germans had signs everywhere on the beach, each with a skull and crossbones and the warning *Achtung! Minen!* (Attention! Mines!) Engineers working on the beaches had used a highly visible white tape to mark off "dummy areas" where all the mines had been cleared and we could traverse safely. They used yellow tape to denote the areas with live ordinance. Every man and vehicle was careful to remain within the designated safe zones. To set foot beyond the tape could instantly cost you your life. Despite these precautions, men were still worried about stepping on something even in the cleared zones. "What if they missed a spot?" was often heard as we moved onto the beach area, although it was masked as a half-joke. There was a cemetery on one of the elevations off to the side filled with Americans killed during the preceding fighting, but we all tended to avert our eyes from it for obvious reasons.

We were due east of Ste. Mère-Eglise and we could hear artillery fire in the distance. We had to march some three and a half miles to our initial assembly area ("Transit area B") to stack our duffle bags, get ourselves situated and then take a quick break. The march was especially miserable for those with wet feet, which included just about everybody in the outfit. My good fortune was nothing I could brag about.

That night we spoke of fear. We all felt it, but now we were all willing to admit and talk about it. We were frightened by not knowing what to expect in actual combat. Finding out didn't do much to alleviate that fear.

Soon after our arrival, we had to move inland another 12 and a half miles to the division concentration area, which was right between the towns of Montebourg and Valognes, so that the division could properly organize its units. The 2d Regiment's command post was set up near Huberville and by July 12 our division was organized and ready to join the war.

When we arrived in France two days earlier, it was D+34, but American and Allied forces had made relatively little progress moving inland from the beaches. The Germans didn't have much of an air force left after five years of war, but their fighters still showed up and strafed us. Fortunately, their aim and luck hadn't improved any since Iceland.

The primary reason for the limited advance was that just past the Normandy beaches the farm fields were heavily lined with hedgerows. The French referred to this as bocage country. These hedgerows had been used for a thousand years earlier to mark off the boundaries of properties and to keep cows contained in them. They had grown extremely thick and heavy over the centuries and reached heights of as much as 15 feet. The hedgerows provided an almost perfect natural defense for the Germans holding this ground, as even our tanks couldn't plow through them. The Germans added to this natural defense with barbed wire and land mines. They also put machine guns with varying fields of fire near openings and cross sections, which made it almost impossible to find adequate cover when advancing on the enemy.

Allied soldiers were fighting for yards, even inches, of ground at a time, and dying in excessively large numbers. Meanwhile, men and materiel were accumulating on the beaches in preparation for the big breakout into the French interior. The city of St. Lô, a vital crossroads, had to be taken in order to allow for a breakout and bring this stalemated World War I-type fighting to an end. Once a breakout was completed, the full weight of American military might in the form of tanks and planes could be brought to bear, and a rapid drive across France could liberate the country fairly quickly. That job would fall to Patton once the breakout was achieved.

When we arrived, Patton was not yet on the scene in France. Our 5th Infantry Division was assigned to General Omar Bradley's First U.S. Army, V Corps on July 12. Also with us in V Corps were the 2d Infantry ("Indianhead") Division and the 35th Infantry ("Santa Fe") Division. Both of these outfits had already been badly bloodied and were tired from previous engagements with the Germans. We didn't know it at the time, but the brass was somewhat disappointed in the 2d Division's performance. It seemed they were always disappointed with some outfit's performance. Our turn would come in due time.

The 5th Division was ordered southeast of our landing site to

Caumont, where we were to relieve the American 1st Infantry ("Big Red One") Division on July 13. The 1st Division had been fighting in France since June 6 when they stormed the beaches at Omaha, and they had been in the thick of the action ever since. These poor guys needed a break. Our 2d Regiment would relieve their 16th Regiment. Our 11th Regiment relieved their 26th Regiment and our 10th Regiment relieved their 18th Regiment. The relief of the 1st Division, once it was completed, was orderly and so precise that men not only replaced each other man for man, but in many cases did so with the exact same weapons in the exact same positions. We had the 2d Infantry Division to our right and the British on our left. This put the 5th Infantry Division on the extreme left flank of the American portion of the Allied frontlines.

Bringing this many men to a new area always meant confusion. People move at different speeds especially when there is little room to operate in, and we were forced to share what little room there was with jeeps, trucks, and maybe even an occasional tank. To keep stragglers, the distracted, slow movers, and just plain everybody from getting lost, cardboard or wooden signs were placed on the rear ends of jeeps, each with a large hand-painted letter identifying the battalion's companies (A, B, C, and so forth). All a soldier had to do was to follow or look for his assigned company on the back of the jeep. It was idiot-proof.

Caumont was already pretty shot up when we got there, but even the areas outside the city were hot with enemy activity. Our very arrival there was to become our baptism by fire. The sergeants from General Headquarters were standing in the jeeps, each designated for a particular infantry company, directing men to go this way and that, when the Germans decided to greet us with tree bursts before we could finish settling in. These are shells designed to explode at treetop level and rain deadly chunks of hot steel down on the soldiers below. How the Germans ever knew what was going on and just how vulnerable we were at that time remains a mystery.

One of these pieces of shrapnel struck Sergeant Robert Bass of the 2d Regiment in the head and gave him the tragic and rather dubious honor of being the first man in the 5th Division to be killed in action. As a headquarters man, he was not in the type of position that usually put men on the frontlines or got them killed. We didn't know what to expect, but sergeants and corporals (non-commissioned officers or NCOs) often died soon after the stripes went on their sleeves. The officers who led us in combat varied widely in character and ability, but the vast majority were very capable and exceptionally brave. Captains were in charge of companies and had roughly 150 men under their command. Lieutenants oversaw platoons and had about 45 men under their authority.

Those of us who did our duty in combat and survived long enough to be considered "old soldiers" were often addressed by our first names in private company with our officers. What's more, some of them even allowed us to address them in the same way. I was usually impressed by their abilities and sometimes surprised by their routines, especially those of the academy graduates. One officer, for example, was so military that food was nothing but a utilitarian item for survival, much as a weapon in combat. On the rare occasions when we got hot chow in the field, he would pile all his food in his mess kit so that every item was on top of another from his fruit to his meat. He would then eat it with the kind of detachment we had when we cleaned our rifles.

Captains and lieutenants were considered junior officers and thus had to fight. Majors and above rarely participated in combat. The junior officers, if they were lucky, survived a couple of months on the frontline and went on to higher ranks and staff positions. It seemed that more junior officers died than survived.

I saw one officer who wore hand grenades on his hips like six shooters. While we were fighting in the hedgerows, a piece of shrapnel from a German grenade hit one of the grenades he was wearing and detonated it. As he lay dying, all he said over and over again was, "What's gonna happen to my men?" At the other extreme, we saw an officer confiscate a German motorcycle we had just captured so that it could be used to deliver messages. That was reasonable enough, but before turning it over to headquarters, he decided to take a joy ride in a combat zone. We found his body near the German lines. He had been shot and picked clean of valuables, right down to his Notre Dame ring.

Hedgerow fighting was miserable and totally unexpected. No one had any training or preparation for this type of warfare, which made our casualty numbers very high. The enemy could be just around a corner or directly across from you on the other side of a hedgerow. This caused us to become very jumpy and to get pretty trigger-happy (prone to shoot too much, too often, and too quickly). I remember more than once when we heard movement on the other side of some hedgerows and expended enormous amounts of ammunition firing into them, confident that we were cutting the enemy on the other side to pieces. We then charged around the corner only to discover that all we had succeeded in doing was to kill a few cows.

My circumstances as a rifleman required me at this point to kill for the first time. Another soldier and I were dug in just behind a hedgerow armed with M-1 Garand rifles when we heard running feet approaching from the area directly in front of us. We saw Germans moving towards us to take up positions just opposite us on the other side of the hedgerow. We waited until they reached us and then, before they could situate and secure themselves, we jumped out at them. They stopped and started swinging around to fire at us, but we had the drop on them and killed them both instantly.

I took no joy in it, but I also had no hesitation in doing my duty or regrets about it afterward. In fact, I remember thinking at the time something to the effect of, "You sons of bitches won't kill any more Americans."

The Germans were very clever and many had become highly experienced from years of fighting on the Russian Front. They once use a very successful ruse on us when we were approaching a roadway about 100 yards wide, flanked on both sides by high hedgerows. They had one machine gun set to fire mostly tracer rounds (so no one could miss seeing them) at a height well above our heads. The brightly colored trails from the German bullets kept our attention and gave us a false sense of security, allowing us to believe that their gunners simply could not shoot straight.

We moved forward quickly and confidently into what turned out to be an enemy ambush. The Germans had a second machine gun positioned across the open area in the opposite hedgerow that was set to shoot at a height of about three feet (grazing fire) and without tracer bullets. We advanced unknowingly into their kill zone and learned a very important lesson the hard way. Experienced combat soldiers acquire their experience by being lucky enough to see, and yet survive, someone else's mistake.

German machine gunners and snipers were everywhere, but shot just as often to wound and maim as to kill. It takes two or three healthy soldiers to protect, treat, and carry the wounded, and the enemy knew that we would not disregard our wounded. Thus, wounding one man could put three or four men out of action. We had to ignore our own instincts and leave the wounded for our medics, lest we become casualties ourselves. Only the medics and the chaplains stood any chance at all of avoiding harm while helping the wounded.

Once, an ambulance pulled up and two of our medics and a chaplain got out and were walking with impunity along the roadside checking our wounded while the rest of us were crouched down in a ditch alongside that same road hoping to avoid the German machine gun that was doing so much damage. The chaplain knew me and said, "Come on Bilder, get up here and give us hand with this litter." I stupidly got up and took one end of the stretcher and proceeded off down the road with them. The German on the machine gun must have spotted that I had no Red Cross or chaplain markings on my uniform or helmet. He also must have decided to cut me some slack. He fired a burst that came up around my feet but still missed me.

I dropped the litter and dove back into the ditch. I gave a dirty look up at the chaplain and said, "Don't ever ask me to do anything like that again." If that German had not been feeling decent that day, I would have been a casualty myself. I'm certain that he could have hit me if he had wanted to.

I remember the first time I rolled one of our dead over. He had just been killed and I was stunned into disbelief for a second. "Forget it Mike, he's gone," someone said to me. "But I was just talking to him a minute ago," I said. "Well, get used to it," was the response. "You're gonna being seeing a whole lot more of it."

Some of the Germans in Normandy wanted to surrender to us at the first opportunity. This was especially true of Germans aged forty and older. Their reactions were slower and it was obvious even to them how quickly they were prone to die in battle. They would strip themselves down to their uniforms and approach us with white flags and their hands raised high.

I took one German prisoner who wanted to surrender so badly that he had even thrown away his mess kit. I was curious to talk to an enemy soldier and our exchange became conversational. I happened to mention that I was of German heritage and he asked me my name. I told him, and he said with joy, "Bilder! My name is Bilder, too. I'm Karl Bilder. Maybe we could be cousins?" I was six feet tall and this guy was four or five inches shorter than I was. We looked so little alike that our only physical resemblance was probably our armpits. "Cousins my ass," I said, and I hauled off and belted him. "Get moving to the prison camp," I told him briskly. "Maybe you'll find some of your relatives there."

On the frontline, I once shared a foxhole with a soldier named Ivan Lewis on a forward outpost some 300 yards ahead of our unit. Our mission was simply to watch and listen for the enemy. We were to use our sound-powered telephone to warn the men behind us if the Germans suddenly appeared. Sound-powered phones are activated by blowing into them, which prevents any ringing or other sounds of detection. Their very name explains how they work. To survive this type of assignment a soldier has to be well trained, fairly experienced, and more than a little lucky. We were armed with M-1 Garand rifles, which was often the case when we got this kind of duty.

Lewis and I heard movement on the other side of the hedgerow just in front of us. "Mike, you watch the right and I'll watch the left," he said. No sooner had he completed his sentence than a German scout came around the corner of the hedgerow on my side. I fired immediately and took him out. We could hear a number of Germans scurrying on the other side of the hedgerow, and suddenly they started popping out on both sides. We emptied our clips at them, but I'm not sure how many we actually hit. We both fired our eight rounds and our empty clips ejected noisily, advertising our need to reload in the face of a significantly larger force. It was obvious we had to beat it if we wanted to stay alive.

"Let's get the hell outta here," Lewis said, and we ran crouched down back toward our own lines. We got about 50 yards when Lewis looked back and yelled out, "Mike, hit the dirt!" I threw myself face down just in time to literally feel bullets passing right above me. The Germans had slapped down a tripod and put a light machine gun on it. They were sweeping the area with a hail of deadly fire that would have killed me if not for Lewis' warning.

We obviously, though somewhat unintentionally, fulfilled our mission, as all this noise and commotion alerted our lines to the enemy's presence. Our boys hadn't seen us and thought the fire from the German machine gun was intended for them. A firefight quickly ensued and all Lewis and I could do was stay flat on the ground as the bullets from both sides passed roughly three feet above us. The Germans didn't have the firepower or numbers to compete with our outfit and those Germans that weren't killed outright took to their heels.

As we advanced in hedgerow country, we pushed the Germans out of the farm buildings they were occupying, but the danger didn't retreat with them. They left plenty of booby traps. The Germans were gifted at turning even the most benign things into deadly items. To make matters worse they often used Teller mines in their booby traps. Packed with eleven pounds of TNT and originally designed to be buried in traffic areas for use against tanks and armored vehicles, they didn't detonate until at least 200 pounds of pressure was applied to them.

German engineers modified Teller mines to be detonated by very simple actions like opening a door or gate. Sometimes a break in hedgerows along a footpath would be connected with a cattle gate. One of our men would push the gate open to pass through, only to detonate a Teller mine and be blown into a million pieces. The explosive force of such a powerful weapon turned on a mere man reduced him to atoms.

The Germans had booby-trapped everything, roads, footpaths, wells, doorways, windows, gates, and seemingly anything else you could touch, pick up, or move. We quickly learned not to touch anything until after we carefully checked it. For example, we took a barn once that was just loaded with kegs of all types of booze. It was really something to see, and we stood there motionless for a second in awe just looking. There was beer, wine and hard alcohol of almost every type.

It was too tempting a prize for one soldier, who decided to empty out his canteen and refill it from one of the kegs. He poured out his water and placed his canteen under an outlet, then turned the spigot only to be instantly atomized by a Teller mine. There was absolutely nothing left of him. Even his dog tags were gone. Blood splatters on the walls and ground were the only traces he left behind. We were fortunate that we hadn't formed a line behind him or simultaneously followed his lead to another keg.

German mines planted in the ground varied in type, but all of them were treacherous. There were wood box mines and glasmines, which had a casing made entirely of glass. Neither of these could be located by our mine detectors. There were also the infamous "Bouncing Betties" (S mines). These damn things sprung up out of the ground when stepped on and detonated around a man's groin. This weapon was intended to end a soldier's tour of duty by castrating him.

Armies always send out patrols to judge the enemy's strength and plans. It's an essential element in reducing the likelihood of getting hit by a surprise attack. It also allows the command on your side to determine the enemy's weak points and how to best hit them. An American patrol in World War II usually consisted of a squad of about 12 men if you were lucky enough to be at full strength (which was relatively rare). There was a first and second scout. The first scout was all the way out front at the point about 200 yards or so ahead of everyone else. The second scout was usually half way between the first scout and the rest of the squad. There was a BAR (Browing Automatic Rifle) man with two assistants and seven riflemen. The squads were numbered one through four.

There were four squads to a platoon (roughly 44 men) and four platoons in a company (roughly 150 to 175 men). Platoons were also numbered one through four, while letters of the alphabet were used to designate companies. To avoid being misunderstood, especially on the radio, you referred to your company by a word that started with the same letter of the alphabet. You couldn't choose just any word. The American military used set words to designate each letter.

The first twelve letters identified the companies in an infantry regiment: A was Able, B was Baker, C was Charlie, and so forth, on through Dog, Easy, Fox, George, How, Item, Jig (but there was no J

Company), King, Love, and Mike. There were four companies in a battalion, so a battalion had roughly 600 men in it. Battalions were numbered as well. Three battalions comprised an infantry regiment and three regiments along with all their support organizations (medical, communications, artillery, and so forth) comprised an infantry division.

Thus soldiers in our outfit could identify our organization by saying, "5th Infantry Division, 2d Regiment, 2d Battalion, George Company. Circumstances and casualties often caused your platoon and squad assignments to change for practical reasons. Your official organization assignment only went as low as your company.

The first three companies (A through C) in a battalion were rifle companies and the fourth was heavy weapons. The heavy weapons company had the big mortars, .50-caliber machine guns, and anything else necessary for dislodging the enemy from especially tight places. Since Companies A through D were in 1st Battalion, E through H in 2d Battalion, and I through M in 3rd Battalion, a simple mention or one's company allowed anyone to determine their battalion assignment.

Normally, there are four types of patrols. The first type, used most often, is the reconnaissance ("recon") patrol, which is sent out to obtain information about the enemy's size, strength and position. The object is to spy on the enemy and get back to your own lines and report without the enemy ever knowing that you were there. If the patrol is discovered, its mission is a complete failure, as the enemy now knows what you're up to and will change their position and tactics to protect themselves.

Another type of patrol is the silent patrol, which has the all-important mission of capturing enemy soldiers for interrogation. Things in this type of patrol have to be very precise, very quick, and extremely quiet. Dead prisoners cannot answer questions. German POWs always amazed us. In combat, the Germans were some of the toughest and most feared soldiers in the world, real sons of bitches. Once we captured them, they magically transformed. They smoked their pipes and took on facial expressions that made them look as docile as your elderly grandfather.

A third type of patrol is the combat patrol, where troops are not concerned with secrecy, since their objective is to specifically find and engage the enemy. The trick here is to keep the enemy engaged and stay alive yourself until help arrives. This type of patrol is intended to do much the same thing as the recon patrol only with a good deal more certainty, as nothing reveals as much information about the enemy's capability as their performance in actual combat.

There was one other, especially unpleasant patrol we had to perform while we were fighting in the hedgerows, which I have saved for last. This was night patrol, which could not be performed by squads as such. Very different from other types of patrols, this assignment required a few men to slip in and out of the dense foliage in order to find and then neutralize any and all enemy sentries, outposts, or machine gun nests they encountered. This meant killing silently, using bayonets or trench knives. There were to be no shots fired and the strike was so quick and quiet that the enemy was dead before any of them could yell out or squeeze off a shot.

As terrible as war is, there can be no doubt that killing a man at close quarters is one of the most gruesome and difficult duties a soldier may have to perform. Not everyone can do it, and I never thought less of a man for lacking this ability. Our officers and NCOs always picked those of us who had a number of years in the service and were a little older (in our mid-20s) than the newer recruits or incoming replacements, who could be as young as 18 or 19. Even after 60 years, these are the memories that a man wants most, but is least able, to forget.

This duty was absolutely vital because we often moved at night in order to avoid being spotted and becoming a target for German artillery. Despite our habit, the Germans managed to hit us very hard with their famed 88s. Their fire was so accurate that we all knew that they had to have some first-class spotting and observation. At first, we were all stumped as to how they had achieved this. Then one of our regimental pilots noticed four other piper cubs flying around with him while he was spotting for artillery units. This made for a total of five American observation planes in the air. Something was wrong, because our regiment only had four such planes!

Our pilot relayed this information to Regimental Headquarters via a coded message. Regimental Headquarters responded in return with a coded signal of their own to the five planes, which discreetly peeled off one at a time and headed for home. When the fifth plane did not obey the order and continued to circle the area, everyone knew that it was a captured American plane flown by a German pilot spotting our position for his own artillery. Two P-51 fighters were quickly dispatched and the Piper Cub was blown out of the sky. After that, the German artillery was not nearly so accurate.

Our observation planes spotting for our artillery inflicted so much pain on the enemy that some of the Germans we captured told us they feared our Piper Cubs more than our fighter-bombers. These small observation planes saved us in other ways as well. One time when we were moving forward, one of them swooped down and dropped us a handwritten note. It informed us that there was a German machine gun nest directly in front of us and we were on the verge of walking right into it.

This warning was especially important because the Germans were using a BAR captured from Americans. We recognized its sound in the distance and simply thought it was some of our guys up ahead of us. The information from the plane allowed us to flank the Germans and reverse the ambush. When we got a hold of the BAR they had been using we noticed that they had removed the American stock and modified it with one of their own.

The Allies' near-complete domination of the skies played a major role in our victory. Our P-47s and P-51s could strafe and bomb the Germans at will. They protected us from enemy air attacks and allowed our observation planes to more or less come and go as they pleased. We always appreciated their value, but we had to become accustomed to coordinating their attacks with ours.

We were advancing in hedgerow country on one occasion when an air strike was planned for the area just ahead of us. It was difficult to properly gauge distances and positions in the middle of the bocage, and one of the P-47s dropped a 500-pound bomb so close to our first scout that it blew every stitch of clothing off of him with the exception of his boots. He went stark raving mad after the incident.

The Germans were far from inactive as we inched our way forward amongst the hedgerows. We were just getting settled in some newly acquired real estate and our reserve was in the process of moving up to relieve us. I took advantage of this lull to make a quick move from my foxhole to see a buddy in another, when suddenly the Germans burst through the hedgerows in significant numbers and overran our position. We fell back instantly, but in the confusion of our hasty retreat I was forced to abandon my backpack in my original foxhole.

We counter attacked and retook the ground within hours, but some damn German had rummaged through my personal effects and stolen everything of value including my cheesecake picture of Mary. This was really maddening, because I had worked very hard in my letters to coax Mary into posing for, and then mailing, this picture. It was fairly modest by current standards, and fortunately could be replaced since Mary had the negative, but it was something I enjoyed showing off, and losing it made me mad as hell.

Our M-4 Sherman tanks were no match for anything the Germans had. The military planners back in the Pentagon had opted for quantity over quality when it came to producing a standard tank for the army. The 75mm gun on the Sherman was not capable of penetrating most German armor. Conversely, the armor on the Sherman was not thick enough to withstand German shells, and so we referred to our own tanks as "Ronsons" after the famous cigarette lighter the army issued to us. Our tanks, like our Ronsons, were sure to light and burn with the greatest of ease.

Most tankers put sandbags on their vehicles for extra protection, but Patton wouldn't allow any tankers under his command to do this. He claimed it affected maneuverability, but I think he viewed it as some type of editorial comment against his precious tanks. In any event, we still preferred to have armored support.

On one occasion in hedgerow country, we had a Sherman supporting us against German infantry. Its machine guns were sweeping the area clean and we were relieved to have such firepower at our disposal. Suddenly, the Germans started to hit us with mortars and a round landed directly on one of my friends, George Polazzi, killing him instantly.

We had seemingly just finished clearing the area of enemy when a round fired from a German tank or anti-tank gun hit the Sherman and knocked it out. The enemy didn't follow up on this momentary victory but instead fled. A lieutenant pointed at that knocked-out Sherman and said to me, "Bilder, get up there and get their dog tags." I hopped up onto the tank, and when I looked down into the turret, I was horrified to see that the driver's head had been taken clean off. I could literally see his internal organs through the cavity between his shoulders.

I jumped down from the tank and started to heave my guts out. "What's wrong, Bilder?" the lieutenant asked. I turned to him and said, "Lieutenant, if you want those fuckin' dog tags so bad, you can get up there and get 'em yourself." He chuckled and tolerated my insubordination, ordering someone else to do the job.

Later that evening, I was with two other soldiers in a farmyard we had taken that day, tying one on to forget about Polazzi. Polazzi was a heavier-set fellow with the easiest going nature you could imagine. He laughed at everything and I thought he was a great guy. It was hard to come to terms with the fact that he was really gone.

We all had too much to drink. We saw a chicken strutting around and decided that it not only looked tasty, but it might even be fun to see which one of us was sober enough to successfully shoot it. That chicken clucked, screamed, and jumped, but successfully dodged every shot we took at it. We expended a lot of ammunition all without success. Finally, I told the other two guys we had better knock it off. I remembered from my experience in Iceland just how much trouble a soldier could get into by engaging in recreational target practice in a combat zone and forcing fellow troopers to show up armed and ready for a fight.

I saw some incredible acts of courage fighting in the hedgerows. On one occasion we were moving up with elements of the 10th Regiment when the Germans hit us. We scattered and started to move through the hedgerows in an effort to find cover and attempt to flank wherever it was their fire was coming from. The Germans had caught us cold, and now we were scrambling just to try and situate ourselves.

There was a platoon sergeant from the 10th Regiment who had been in the army for some 15 years. There was some chink in his armor that kept him from becoming an officer, but he was one hell of a leader. This particular encounter in the hedgerows with the Germans had him especially angry. He seemed to feel that the Germans had no business ambushing us.

He grabbed his BAR and charged out of the hedgerows and into the open, firing as he ran. The Germans shot and killed him, but as he fell he went forward with his grip locked on that BAR, the gun blazing away the entire time and its barrel going into the soft ground, so that he actually died standing up. He remained in that position holding onto his weapon after the firefight until his body was removed from the field. I never saw anything like it.

On a similar occasion, when we again walked into an ambush amongst the hedgerows, we were ordered to run flat-out full speed towards a stone wall. I was with two buddies: Don Tower (whom we called "Head" because we thought his was football-shaped) and a soldier named Steponovic, whom we simply called "Step." Both of these men were quite brave, and Tower would go on to become a sergeant and win the Silver Star.

After the Germans opened up on us, everyone was running like mad for the safety of that stone wall. Step inexplicably turned and said, "Tower, you son of a bitch, this is a hell of a time to be throwing rocks. Knock it off!" Tower looked at him dumbfounded as they both continued to run. Step later said he felt something warm running down his leg and glanced down to see his own blood staining his pant leg. Tower wasn't throwing rocks. Step had simply felt a bullet go through his leg.

Step, who not only had guts but a lot of luck, was to go on and demonstrate that he was prone to receiving million-dollar wounds. When he realized what had happened to him he dropped his pack, fell to the ground, and called out, "Medic!" We made it to the stone wall and this poor little medic threw Step over his shoulders and carried him in. His legs looked like they were going to buckle under the strain, but he made it. Step was fortunate enough to have the bullet pass through his leg without hitting any bone. He milked the wound for all it was worth and even limped around on it after he no longer needed to. One day an officer caught him walking normally on it, and he was ordered back up to the frontline.

Our mortar teams were usually close by and ready to provide quick support. A mortar team has to act speedily because their enemy counterparts will quickly determine their position and pour accurate fire of their own down on them. There was one mortar team from our heavy weapons company (Company H) that everyone admired. These four men worked together with ease and skill and appeared to be as close as brothers. They could slam down that heavy base plate, set up their mortar, and be firing in seconds flat. One day an enemy mortar round landed directly on their base plate as they were setting up and killed all four of them instantly. Everyone felt very badly about that.

Everyone, right down to the lowest infantry grunt, knew that a breakout from Normandy was necessary and soon to come. We had been fighting in the hedgerows for about two weeks when General Bradley's battle plan for Operation Cobra, the breakout from Normandy, was set to go into effect. The capture of St. Lô on July 18 had given him the jumping off point he needed.

The plan called for an enormous amount of American artillery fire and aerial bombardment to be concentrated along a section of the German line roughly three miles wide. Concentrated bombing such as this is so massive in its coverage that it is referred to as "carpet bombing," because it covers a designated area as thoroughly as a carpet. The opening created in the Germans' position would enable American ground forces to move quickly through enemy lines and out into the open French countryside. This array of concentrated firepower proved to be so intense that it had nearly the same effect as hitting the area with a small tactical nuclear weapon. (This latter was something that was still a year away from any infantryman's wildest conceptions of weaponry.)

Whenever an army is going to make a massive thrust forward through a relatively narrow area of its enemy's frontlines, there is always a danger that the enemy will counter attack both sides of the rear section of the advancing force and cut it off, allowing the enemy to encircle and then destroy the attackers. This is known as a pincer movement, and the Germans had become the world's leader when it came to this particular military maneuver.

As previously mentioned, the 5th Division was placed to the left of the American 2d Infantry Division. Our two divisions were only to assist in the breakout from Normandy. The objective of the 5th was to take the town of Vidouville and then link up with the 2d near Ste. Suzanne-Sur-Vire soon after the breakout got underway. Our two divisions were together designated to protect the left flank; we were not among the initial outfits that rapidly advanced into Northern France through the massive hole that was soon created in the German lines.

Our position on the frontlines preceding the offensive was somewhat tenuous. We were new and untried. The 2d Division was positioned to recover from the damage it previously suffered in hedgerow fighting. Both our divisions were spread fairly thin across the front and unable to absorb any heavy blows from the enemy. We were lucky the Germans didn't hit us when they had the chance.

Operation Cobra mistakenly began ahead of schedule on July 24, when 300 bombers failed to get the word that the mission was temporarily scrubbed due to bad weather. Some of their bombs fell near American lines and killed some two dozen GIs. We went up against Vidouville, a town southeast of St. Lô, two days later on July 26. The weather had delayed our assault as well; we had originally been scheduled to jump off against Vidouville four days earlier. This would be our first in a seemingly endless number of brutal toe-to-toe slugfests with the Germans for control of a city or town.

We saw the massive formations of our bombers going overhead on July 25. The B-17s were high up and tough to observe, but we saw their vapor trails. The Army Air Corps was sending 2,500 planes into action with a coordinated artillery barrage to hit the Germans about an hour and a half before the infantry advance. As hoped and planned, this created a hole roughly three miles wide in the German lines for the breakout.

This aerial armada was sent in to hit a German force of approximately 3,000 men and 100 tanks. After their air strike, there were 1,000 fewer Germans and only about a dozen of their tanks left. Many of the surviving enemy were so traumatized that they were in no condition to fight. Unfortunately, there were also more than 100 American infantrymen killed along with the enemy by bombs that again fell too close to U.S. lines.

The 2d Regiment jumped off to take Vidouville at 06:35 hours on July 26. The first and third battalions led the attack, with our second battalion held in reserve. We didn't know it at the time, but the German 9th Paratrooper Regiment of the 3rd Paratroop Division was defending the town. The Germans regarded these troops as the best they had in Normandy.

Our attack formation was shaped something like a squared letter "U." On the right was the 1st Battalion, which was to enter Vidouville proper. On the left was the 3rd Battalion, which advanced on the enemy-held woods. Our 2d Battalion was held in reserve, and would advance up the center once the flanks were secured.

Both of the 1st and 3rd Battalions suffered at the hands of German machine gun fire, snipers, mortars and an 88 that the Germans had just outside the town limits. The Germans had also placed trip flares all along our route of advance, which went off if a soldier accidentally tripped or stepped on a wire connected to a flare. The flare would then shoot off and alert the enemy that someone was approaching. Every time someone set off one of these damn things, we knew that machine gun and mortar fire would rain down on the position.

Once the 1st and 3rd Battalions took their objectives, it turned the remaining German position into a salient (an area that faces an enemy force on three sides). The 1st Battalion was on the Germans' left flank, the 3rd Battalion was on their right, and we were in the center. This meant we could advance forward with the aid of the other two battalions, who would bring down fire on the Germans as we moved up. Our objective was to advance straight into the German line, sweep it clean, and link up with the other two battalions just outside the south end of town at Highway 3. Our movement resembled an elevator coming up through its shaft.

We took fire from German artillery as well as snipers and machine gunners as we advanced. The Germans typically used machine guns with the intent of pinning us down and then finishing us off with mortars as we clung to the ground for whatever cover we could find, but we had learned from experience to keep moving forward even in the face of machine gun fire and mortar shells. A soldier might well die advancing, but he was all but certain to die staying put. If enemy artillery didn't kill him, then the enemy snipers would. Failing either of those, our own officers could shoot him on the spot for cowardice.

We definitely got hurt during the advance but still reached our objective. Our artillery had helped reduce the activity of the 88. We thought everything was over and had casually started to walk across Highway 3, when machine gun fire from a German tank opened up on us. We were so green we didn't even notice this damn thing sitting right in the middle of the road just off to our left. The burst of fire killed some men and wounded others. We jumped back onto our side of Highway 3 and hunkered down. Vidouville may have been taken, but it was obviously far from secure.

A soldier next to me said that he was going to go out into the roadway and bring back his wounded buddy. I told him to stay put and keep down until the anti-tank guns arrived and knocked out the enemy tank. He wouldn't listen and reached up from our position of relative safety to grab his buddy. The German tank spotted this and opened up with its machine gun, hitting the soldier in the shoulder. "You stupid son of a bitch," I said to him. "I told you to stay down until it was safe."

The anti-tank guns arrived and took out the enemy tank. The problem was that we had used up most of our ammo during our advance, and our officers knew that we couldn't hold out against the German counter attack that was sure to come. German shells were already starting to fall on our position.

Our outfit received the order to fall back to regroup and rearm. To make certain that the guys in our immediate area had enough time to do this without the Germans on their heels, our BAR man, Rolland Dysinger, and I were ordered to remain behind and delay the Germans before pulling out ourselves. Everybody was ordered to drop any magazine they had with .30-caliber ammunition in it. I was to take all these .30-caliber rounds from other magazines and use them to reload the magazines for the BAR.

The BAR was not a weapon that I was particularly fond of. It was large, heavy, had a fierce recoil, and only held 20 rounds in its magazine. Considering that its user drew such heavy fire from the enemy, I felt its disadvantages outweighed its benefits. I much preferred the Thompson sub-machine gun, but in the hands of an experienced and capable user like Dysinger, the BAR was a highly effective weapon.

Dysinger and I were positioned in a foxhole. He readied his weapon as I worked frantically to reload the magazines. We didn't have to worry about waiting for the Germans. They were approaching our position rapidly, albeit casually, since they apparently thought all the Americans had fallen back. There were about 75 Germans, and they were now within 60 or 70 yards of our foxhole.

Dysinger may have had nerves of steel, but I sure didn't. "Shoot, you son of a bitch, shoot!" I told him. With that, he opened up and the Germans fell like dominos. Dysinger used that BAR with complete ease. I don't know how many enemy he killed, but I saw first hand that their casualties were very high. The survivors ran back to their own lines and we likewise headed back to ours.

My buddies at Regimental Headquarters later told me that Dysinger was put in for the Silver Star for his actions at Vidouville, but since he had been listed as AWOL for four hours before the start of the battle he was denied the award. The 2d Regiment's official history book shows his name on the list of those awarded the Bronze Star Medal in 1944 to 1945.

The fighting was brutal and the Germans not only fought for every foot of ground, but continued to counter attack every time we took real estate away from them. We moved forward with tank support to retake and hold our first positions. The primary reason for this hard fight was not that Vidouville was of great strategic value, but rather that the Germans had adopted a highly aggressive strategy for the defense of France that required them to counter attack with as much determination as possible to regain any ground they were forced to give up. This was the only hope they had to push the Allied invasion forces back into the sea. Rommel and the German High Command knew that a breakout into the open country in the French interior would finish any chance Germany had to win the war or even a negotiated peace.

Artillery on both sides was very active at Vidouville, and the dividing line separating Americans from Germans became rather fluid. The Germans were able to slip small patrols and snipers through our lines, sometimes disguised as medics complete with Red Cross armbands, which enabled them to attack us from the rear. This resulted in so much confusion that our own frontlines were strafed and bombed by German and American planes alike, both of which inflicted heavy casualties. Nevertheless, we prevailed and took the town and the surrounding area.

We paid dearly for Vidouville, and the 10th Regiment still had to take the high ground on Hill 183 just outside of town while we moved ahead to tie up any loose ends along the Torigny-Sur-Vire—Caumont

Highway. Our two regiments jumped off simultaneously at 07:45 hours on July 30. The 10th Regiment by far had the harder time of it. Taking high ground away from an enemy is always a costly thing.

Our regiment was able to advance about half a mile before the Germans hit us with mortars and machine guns near Lamberville. My company (George) pushed ahead, and despite heavy resistance we lined up with the 10th Regiment just before 18:00 hours. That night, we patrolled just south of Bieville along Highway 4, where the Germans were thought to have outposts for artillery spotting, but we didn't encounter anything.

The following morning we pushed further south, but our movement was slowed by an excessive amount of German mines and booby traps. The engineers had to accompany us to clear a path for our advance. They disarmed the German explosives and set charges to blow openings in the hedgerows for our tanks. Some of the Shermans were now equipped with a jerry-rigged array of iron teeth made from the tank traps the Germans had scattered all across the Normandy beaches. Welded to the front of the tank, they acted like giant sheers and usually allowed the tanks to force their way through the hedgerows.

Orders came down for us to speed up our advance. With our tanks in the lead clearing all resistance, we reached the village of La Ferrière near the Vire River at about 02:00 hours on August 1. The British were near enough so that we didn't have to advance any further.

As July came to a close, Patton arrived and took command of the newly formed Third Army, using it like a broom to sweep the bulk of the Germans out of Northern France. We had only been in combat for three weeks, but already we felt like grizzled veterans. We encountered a number of things that we had not been prepared for in any way, including how to deal with the loss of friends we had made over the last three and a half years.

Losing friends at the front was nothing like losing them back home. We simply had to keep moving with no time to really contemplate, much less mourn. We did the only thing we could, which was to become callous to it. We became even more callous when it came to German dead. There were a number of German dead in and around Vidouville and their bodies reeked in the July heat. There was apparently no time for burial, and their bodies were stacked like cordwood, four across one way followed by four across the other, until they formed a tall pile. They were then doused with gasoline and set ablaze. It was like something from the Dark Ages.

It was around this time that I dropped by Able Company to visit Tom Spain. We were still each other's closest friend, and I wanted to see how he was doing. He told me that he was going to accept the next opening for sergeant's stripes, and I asked him why. "It's the letters from home, Mike," he said. "All I ever hear about is how this one and that one got promoted and when will I be promoted?" Tom had accepted corporal stripes while we were in the UK, and I had hoped that would be enough for him. It was hard enough to keep ourselves alive without worrying about the responsibility for others, not to mention the guilt officers felt when their orders got their own men killed.

"I know," Tom said. "But I can handle this. It's what I have to do." I could see he had his mind made up. "OK, Tom," I said. "You must know what you're doing." I knew it was a mistake, but it was his right to do it, and it was clear that there was nothing I could say that was going to change his decision. I wished him luck and left with a bad feeling about things.

More bad feelings and tension soon manifested themselves when another soldier I was worried about asked me to help him carry out an action that was clearly against all the rules. He felt that personal matters required him to get back to England so badly that he even asked me to inflict him with a wound serious enough to send him there. He wanted me to shoot him in the soft tissue along the back of his calf, so the bullet would go in and out without hitting bone. This would have given him one variation of the famous million-dollar wound.

This soldier had a girl back in England who was pregnant with his child, and he wanted desperately to be there for her. His thoughts were consumed with her well being, and he had convinced himself that only his presence at her side could ensure this. He was a descent guy and had proven in combat that he was no coward. I seriously considered helping him out, but if anything went wrong and we got caught, it would mean Leavenworth Prison and that was a fate worse than death. I finally turned him down.

We were sleeping in the open one night in our two-man pup tents. He was in the tent next to mine when a rifle shot shattered the silence and brought us all to our feet. He was screaming in pain as men turned on flashlights and began to light lanterns. Our officers and NCOs went nuts, screaming for everyone to get the lights out before the Germans starting shelling our position or hitting us from the air.

Blankets were used as a hastily assembled canopy over his lower leg so we could safely use flashlights to examine his wound. The bullet passed through his foot, just below and to the right of his big toe. He was bleeding like a stuck pig, and a tourniquet was applied to control the hemorrhaging. He claimed it was an accident.

A field inquest was started the next day, and a number of us were questioned in an official capacity for the record. I was asked if the soldier in question had ever talked about inflicting his own wound. I naturally did not volunteer that he had asked me to do it, so I answered truthfully when I said, "No, I never heard him talk about inflicting himself with a wound."

I was then asked if he talked much about his pregnant girl back in England. I answered that he didn't talk about his girl any more than any of the rest of us talked about our own girls or wives. I added that I thought this man was trigger-happy and careless, in that he usually failed to put the safety on his weapon after we returned from action. Both of these things were exaggerations, but I was never one to tolerate squealing. Everyone handled the questioning the same way I did, and they sent the soldier back to England where he got a medical discharge, married the girl, and as far as I know, remained permanently.

It taught us all a valuable lesson. We had already learned just how fragile the human body could be, but now we knew just how fragile the mind and spirit were as well. These three weeks had taught us a great many things about war and about ourselves.

For instance, we had learned that the Germans were booby-trapping everything, and that you didn't touch anything you couldn't be sure of. We had learned how to fight in hedgerows. We had learned that the Germans had snipers everywhere. We had learned that we had to walk, not on the road, or even on the side of the road, but on the very edge of the road, since it was the only area where the Germans couldn't plant a land mine. We learned how to dive into ditches when enemy tanks or planes suddenly appeared.

We had also learned many simple things about combat that war games and training can't teach you, but can only be acquired from experience. We now knew exactly what an artillery shell sounded like when it was falling on our position. We learned that mortar rounds come in silently, and their use against us would only become evident after the first incoming round exploded. We also knew the fearful sound of a bullet whizzing by our ears and the dreaded thwack it makes when it hits a human being. We developed an instinct that enabled us to drop down to the ground at the first inkling of trouble, but then to adapt and move ahead as quickly as possible. And now, in just three short weeks, we had learned just how well, and how dirty, the Germans could fight.

On a personal level, I had learned a great deal about myself. I now knew that I could handle combat. After the first firefight, I knew what it was all about. Staying alive came down to self-preservation and luck. The only reason that most of us ever stuck our necks out was to protect each other. We fought to stay alive and not for any noble ideals.

While there were many emotions involved, once the shooting started they all passed within a fraction of an instant. First came an almost overwhelming rush of adrenaline that caused an all-consuming fight or flight feeling. Second was a spontaneous reaction that had become instinctual as a result of extensive training. This reaction pushed any idea of flight immediately out of mind and allowed me to respond instantly, whether it was to dive for cover in preparation for fighting back, or to fire my weapon in response to the situation and to do it faster than the enemy.

Still, I must admit that despite all my training, I felt plenty of fear. I was hunkered down the first time the Germans hit us with a rolling barrage, and I can remember wetting my pants. A combatant, especially an infantryman, can't separate himself from his feelings and remain sane, so a delicate balance has to be maintained. Let your emotions become consuming, and you either get killed or have a breakdown. Lose your emotions altogether, and you become a cold-blooded murderer who can even grow to enjoy killing. I saw both and wanted to avoid either extreme with as much determination as I avoided enemy bullets or shells. It's odd, but while training may allow you to temporarily suppress your emotions in combat long enough to kill with little feeling, you can't help but take it personally when an enemy soldier is trying to do that very same thing to you.

Timing was something I had learned about as well. Early on in the fighting, we were moving on a German machine gun nest and I was assigned to throw grenades to keep the Germans' heads down while others rushed the position. I must have been overly anxious because one of our guys yelled out, "Bilder, hold onto those grenades longer! The krauts are throwing them back!"

Another thing that everyone learned was that gut wounds were almost always fatal. Men would often bleed to death in about 15 minutes and while the medics would go through the motions, they could do little to help these men. When such wounds were caused by bullets the sight of excessive amounts of blood was bad enough, but when men had their bellies sliced open by shrapnel, they would often have to hold the wounds closed to keep their intestines from falling out or, even worse, they would make the futile gesture of trying to put them back in.

Men who suffered such wounds would usually scream out how they didn't want to die and then pathetically call for their mothers to help them. Like a small, lost child they would whimper out, "mama, mama" and then finally, as their lives slipped away, they often died whispering the Lord's Prayer or a Hail Mary. It was a horrible thing to witness and it always broke our hearts. We usually left the medics to do their job and didn't stick around to watch.

We also learned the proper way to talk about such things. You learned quickly what words to use and which ones not to use. I never heard anyone say that someone had been "killed" or "died." It was always, "He bought it," or "He never knew what hit him." The same applied to wounds. We said things like, "He got hit bad," or "He took it in the leg (or arm, or wherever)." We would use the word "wound" if it was describing the preferred kind as in, "He got a million-dollar wound." Any wound capable of getting a soldier off the line and maybe even sent home, but still allowed him to make a complete recovery was said to be worth a million dollars.

We learned all this and more at a cost of around 400 casualties. It was now getting harder and harder for men to reassure themselves that they were going to come through the war alive and well. Before we went into combat, we were confident that it was always "somebody else" who was going to get it, but now we were forced to accept what we had always known down deep: that anyone of us could be that "somebody else" at any given moment on any given day.

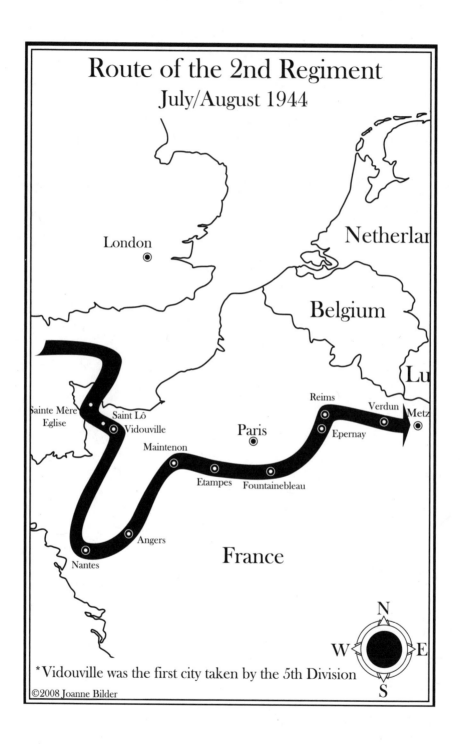

Route of the 2nd Regiment
July/August 1944

London

Netherla

Belgium

Lu

Sainte Mère
Eglise
Saint Lô
Vidouville
Maintenon
Reims
Verdun
Metz
Epernay
Paris

Etampes   Fountainebleau

Angers

Nantes

France

N
W   E
S

*Vidouville was the first city taken by the 5th Division

©2008 Joanne Bilder

7

PATTON AND THE DASH ACROSS FRANCE

Winning the War in Record Time and Making It Look Easy

"Touring France with an Army"
—Chapter title from Patton's memoir

The end of July ushered in complete success for the Allied effort to break out of Normandy. American forces punched a hole some three miles wide in the German lines and immediately began pouring infantry and armor through it, ending the two-month stalemate. The 5th Division's role in all this was relatively small, but we had personally gone up against some of the best troops the Germans had and sent them packing. The 5th even received an official commendation from Major General Leonard Gerow, the commander of V Corps.

The Germans on the other hand were in full retreat. We chased them all across Northern France as they retreated in haste. They were unable throughout all of August to establish a firm or secure frontline. The success of Operation Cobra was the signal to bring Patton into the war. On July 28, Bradley told Patton that Patton would take command of the newly formed Third Army on August 1. Bradley himself would be promoted from command of First Army to command of the newly formed 12th Army Group.

Patton initially had four (instead of the customary three) corps to comprise his Third Army. One of the four was XX Corps, commanded by General Walton "Bulldog" Walker. Walker was a short, stocky man and a Patton protégé to the extreme. Official word came down to the 5th Division just before 17:00 hours on August 3 that it would be assigned to XX Corps. This meant little to us at the time. On August 2 and 3 we enjoyed some down time as the division regrouped, rearmed, resupplied and received replacements for the men fallen from our ranks.

We also got a chance to clean up. Water trucks arrived and set up their strange conglomeration of hole-filled piping, allowing us to shower. We completed this task outdoors with several men at a time standing underneath the spray as they soaped up and rinsed off. It was so refreshing that no one cared about modesty or even left of his own volition. The operators of these mobile showers monitored us, telling us after several minutes, "OK, you look like you've had enough," as they motioned for us to get out.

We then put on clean socks, underwear and fatigues. I was in very good with the laundry sergeant and he kept me well supplied in socks and underwear. Most everyone used laundry markers to write their names in their clothes and the laundry services were very efficient. They had to be, since we couldn't have men trying to squeeze into clothes that were too small or tying up fatigues that were too large. The army, to its credit, did a first-rate job.

Along with the 5th Division, the new XX Corps consisted of the 35th Infantry Division and tank support that frequently shifted between the American 7th and the French 2d Armored Division. Many of us wondered why part of the armored portion of the Corps would be French and not American. Wouldn't it be better to have the French armor held in reserve until the French infantry (eventually five divisions strong) was established and functioning, so that the two could fight as one force?

We were initially concerned because the performance of the French forces in the early years of the war was generally regarded as disgraceful. After all, France had fallen to Germany just six weeks after Hitler invaded the country in May 1940. Considering that the French had held fast for over four years in World War I, their poor performance in the current war made us a little nervous. Our general worry was that international politics might have overridden sound military judgment. Was the agreement to use French tank support just to keep our French allies happy at our possible expense? As it turned out, we had nothing to worry about. Patton would never tolerate second-rate units under his command, especially when they were armored units. It was also understandable that the French wanted to participate in the fight to liberate their country, especially now that it was being fought on their own soil. Since their armor would be one of our lifelines, we just wanted to be sure we could count on them.

In retrospect, the decision of the Allied command was as pragmatic as it was political. They knew that in order to drive the Germans out of France it would be necessary to blow up a great many French homes and buildings to destroy the enemy. It only made sense that this might be easier on the French if they were the ones actually blowing up their own property.

The French 2d Armored had been organized and trained largely by the United States. Their equipment, everything from their tanks to their uniforms, had been supplied by the United States although they bore French insignia. The outfit was commanded by Major General Jacques Philippe Leclerc, who didn't always get along with Patton but shared Patton's views on warfare. Since Patton and the American high command didn't bother to consult their infantrymen on this matter, we had no choice but to put our confidence in our French allies and hope for the best.

They didn't disappoint us. In fact, their tactics against the Germans were surprisingly rough, and that's putting it somewhat mildly. The French wanted payback and their tank crews often asked if they could take our objectives, such as a house, for us. We Americans simply stared at each other, almost dumbfounded by the obviousness of the answer. "Sure," we'd say. "Be our guest." If they wanted to be heroes, we weren't about to stand in their way.

After seeing their country brutally occupied for four years, the French never wasted time trying to coax the Germans into surrendering. If the enemy was occupying a house or building, the French simply rammed a tank right into it, smashing a huge hole in whatever wall it hit. They would then back the tank up and fire a round from the turret cannon right through the cavity. The force from the explosion was strong enough to kill any soldiers inside, and sometimes even brought down the entire house. This was war Patton style. We learned during our first joint encounter with the enemy that we could count on the French tankers, and the Germans learned just as quickly to fear them.

As brutal as the French could be, some of the Scots could be even worse. The Scots could seldom count on getting replacements to replenish their ranks. This meant that they had no men to spare for guarding prisoners in their rear. They dealt with this by telling their German POWs that they were taking them to prison camps, and they should march at the front of the Scots' ranks. When the German prisoners got far enough out in front the Scots rolled hand grenades amongst their feet, killing them all. I knew war was no game, but I never ceased to be amazed by just how brutal men could become. This pertained to everyone, not just Nazis.

XX Corps has been referred to as Patton's "Ghost Corps," as it was known to suddenly appear in front of the Germans out of nowhere. Patton never had much use for infantry, but according to author Nathan Prefer, the 5th Division was suspected to be his favorite. In fact, in a letter Patton wrote after the war to the men and officers of the 5th Division, he said, "Throughout the whole advance across France you spearheaded the attack of your Corps."

The 5th Division's codename was "Dynamite." Patton chose the codename "Lucky" for the Third Army. He planned to proceed further south into France before turning due east to crush anything in his path on the way to Berlin. I'm sure Patton felt that he didn't need any luck. He would simply make his own.

The breakout from Normandy also granted me a little more personal freedom. My special assignment with the American Red Cross meant that I was quickly issued a jeep whenever I they gave me a mission. On these occasions, my orders specified that I was to answer only to the Red Cross field representative and the colonel in command of the 2d Regiment. The 2d Regiment was commanded by Colonel A. Worrel Roffe from the time it arrived in France up until about two weeks before the end of the war.

The Red Cross people were not soldiers, and they were not supposed to be on the frontlines, for their safety as well as ours. The Red Cross representative assigned to the 2d Regiment was a man named Bennet Hove out of North Dakota. He was in his mid-40s and a fairly cool character. I felt he lacked just a bit in the empathy department, but I imagine someone who dealt with so much bad news had to seem detached.

On my first assignment for the Red Cross, Hove was driving a jeep and I was in the front seat navigating. When we got near the frontlines I warned him about shells and snipers, but to his credit he agreed to stay on and drive the jeep up the hill to deliver our messages personally. The problem was that our action gave away an American location to the enemy. After we concluded our highly visible expedition to the summit of the hill, the Germans hit the area from top to bottom with artillery and mortar fire, causing men to hunker down and quite probably producing casualties.

The company commander really balled out Hove for his actions and me for not using my common sense and experience to stop him. After that incident, our orders were clear. Only combat soldiers specifically assigned to assist the Red Cross could deliver their messages to frontline personnel. Hove would give the messages to me and I would personally get them to the appropriate soldier.

In this new responsibility, I would get word to go to one or the other of the companies in our regiment and tell Private Smith that his mother had passed away or Private Jones that his family had not received any letters and that he had to write home. This was an especially difficult thing to ask of soldiers, since they were often covered in mud, living in a hole, and smelled like shit. They usually had more on their minds than finding a clean, dry piece of paper and a pencil to write a letter home to their family.

Once I delivered the message, or messages, I was assigned to that company for three or four days before returning to my own Company G. I did whatever the company I was temporarily assigned to did. If they went into reserve, I went into reserve with them. If they were jumping off for an attack the next day, I had to jump off and fight with them. I served in combat at one point or another with all 12 companies of the 2d Regiment.

The Red Cross duties probably saved my life numerous times. When temporarily assigned to another company, I did indeed have to go with that company whether it was moving to the rear or the front, or simply continuing to hold a position, but I was specifically exempt from any extra duty like night patrol. NCOs looking for "volunteers" would come up to a group of us talking and spot those of us in our mid-20s. They would point two or three guys out and say, "OK, you,

you, and you. Night patrol, let's go." I would pipe up and identify myself and my specialized work for the Red Cross. "Oh yeah," they'd say. "We heard about you." Then they would point to some other poor soul and tell him to come along. On the frontlines it was rare that anybody ever truly volunteered for anything. We took what came and hoped and prayed that everything would work out.

When the guys from another company saw me pull up in a jeep they usually greeted me with something like, "Hi Mike, how ya doin'? Geezz, I hope you're not here to see me." When I told them who I was looking for, they would say something like, "He's up ahead about two hundred yards on the right in a wooden pillbox. Enter from the back. The sign is 'Betty Grable' and the countersign is 'great legs'." I would always report to the commander of the company I was visiting, because they had to keep track of my whereabouts and account for me in their morning reports as well as assign me to some platoon and squad.

On some occasions, I was greeted with silence when I asked about a soldier. Someone would just shake his head from side to side and that was all I needed to know. I would simply write, "Killed in Action," on the outside of the envelope or across the telegram and then have it returned to its place of origin. I still had to stay with that company for a couple of days.

I always had the option of quitting my service for the Red Cross anytime I wanted. In fact, one of my officers seemed to feel that this duty was allowing me to avoid my fair chance of joining the ever-increasing number of casualties in the 5th Division. I don't know why he felt this way because I saw as much action as any of my counterparts, but when he wasn't trying to convince me to end this duty voluntarily, he was trying to convince my superiors to do it for me.

Even this limited freedom to come and go meant a lot to me. It allowed me to keep my sense of independence, but I still had to be careful since I was traveling about in a war zone. Reading a map was no problem so I never had to worry about getting lost, but there were other dangers. The jeeps I drove usually had an antenna-like piece of metal welded to the hood, or wood attached to the bumper that stood about four feet tall. The Germans would attach piano wire to trees on each side of a road, and stretch it out at neck height of anyone sitting in a jeep or riding a motorcycle. The unknowing individual barreling down the road would end up being decapitated.

Hove wore army fatigues but was not actually in the army. He always liked the idea of being near the action. Whenever I captured German cameras, I would use them until the film was gone and then sell them or simply throw them away, as there wasn't any practical access to more film. I gave my completed film rolls to Hove and he had two sets of prints developed, one for me and one for himself.

There was nothing on my service record about the fact I spoke fluent German, but word quickly got out and I was often called in by the local officers of whatever company I was currently with to translate during the interrogation of enemy prisoners. One German officer refused to answer any questions. I was ordered to take my bayonet and press it up against his stomach, which I did. I was then ordered to tell him that I was going to push it clear through to the other side if he didn't start cooperating. That German officer sang like a canary. I'm glad he did, because I honestly don't know what I would have done if he hadn't.

Because of my interrogation experience, Colonel Roffe occasionally requested to see me for a debriefing. He asked me about things like the morale of the enemy and the age and condition of their troops. He asked me about our boys as well and how they were doing. He was a fine soldier and officer. He was very capable and it was obvious that he cared about the men under his command.

My movements amongst the 12 companies of the 2d Regiment meant that I usually was assigned to whatever platoon and squad needed an extra body and I usually got whatever weapon was most appropriate for that job. I quickly learned what weapons I did and did not care for. I have already mentioned my dislike for the BAR, but there were also other weapons that I preferred to avoid.

The M-1 Garand was a reliable, durable, and accurate rifle, but it was heavy and the clip only held eight rounds. Once it emptied, the clip automatically ejected from the rifle with a very recognizable ring. If it struck a hard surface like pavement (or ice during the Battle of the Bulge), it provided an additional clue to the enemy that you had to reload. In close-quarter combat the Germans waited for this sound and then moved in for the kill. We sometimes carried empty clips to throw down and trick them into revealing themselves.

My least favorite weapon of all was the grease gun. This submachine gun was the government's cost-cutting response to the Thompson (Tommy gun) and it looked exactly like its name implied. It never felt or looked reliable. The gun was cocked by a crank-like mechanism on its right side and it was more prone than any of our other weapons to misfire. The safety was nothing more than a flap on the top of the weapon that had to be closed when the operator wanted to put it in safety mode.

I was once sitting in the back of a jeep about to go out on a motorized patrol, holding a grease gun in my right hand. I had the weapon barrel slightly up and its stock resting on my right hip. My finger was on the trigger and I had forgotten that the safety was not on. When the driver hit the gas, the jeep bolted and my right hand clenched around the weapon, firing a burst that clanged along the top of the metal rim of the windshield. You never saw men scatter and dive for cover like the guys in that jeep. Thank God, I didn't hit anybody. "Give this damn thing to a plumber," I said, as I replaced it with a Thompson. I always hated the grease gun.

By contrast, I found the Thompson submachine gun to be a highly effective, reliable, and predictable weapon. It could fire in semi- or fully automatic mode at the switch of a lever. Its very sound sent shivers down the spines of the enemy. The drawbacks were minimal and common to almost every other machine gun. These were the weapon's heavy weight and, of course, the fact that anybody using a machine gun was responsible for laying down a lot of covering fire for his comrades and thus became a prime target of the enemy.

The Germans had a gun somewhat similar to the Thompson. It was the MP-40 Schmeisser or Machinenpistole (machine pistol). It fired a 9mm slug (comparable to our .45-caliber) and had a magazine that held 32 rounds. It fired in a semi- or fully automatic mode, depending upon how far back the trigger was pulled.

Using enemy weapons on a regular basis was not a wise move because the Germans were prone to execute prisoners caught with these items in their possession. I did it on rare occasions as a matter of necessity. We couldn't always find an ammo man around in combat so we would have to grab whatever ammo or weapon we could to keep fighting. I felt the MP-40 was the only weapon the Germans had that compared to our own. (I can't ever recall seeing Germany's famed MP-44 assault rifle during the war.) Since it was carefully machined and not mass-produced, the MP-40 was usually reserved for the Waffen SS. When we came up against these guys we wanted all the firepower we could get and took it any way necessary, including off their dead bodies.

My weapon of choice above all others was the M-1 carbine. It was very light, easy to use, easy to clean, and had little recoil. It had been designed for personnel who, while not specifically trained for frontline combat duty, might become frontline combatants nonetheless, such as truck drivers, clerks, cooks, and so forth. The magazine held 15 rounds of ammunition, but by removing the feed spring from the bottom of a magazine loaded directly into the rifle, an operator could load, and secure with tape, a second magazine and then have 30 rounds of ammunition ready for use. I did this often.

The .30-caliber round the carbine fired was short rifle ammo, but still had excellent stopping power at close range and worked well enough at reasonable distances. In September 1944 the army issued a longer magazine that held 30 rounds. They must have reasoned that if we poor dumb GIs could figure out how to make a 30 round magazine so could they. I was always a big believer in firepower. I sometimes felt as if I alone sprayed enough lead around to double the national debt. I did my best to kill enemy soldiers as far away from me as possible. The carbine fulfilled this function well and saved my life more times than I can count.

Our skirmishes with the Germans were often over in a matter of minutes. Afterward, we had to check their dead for intelligence items. Their NCOs or senior riflemen usually had a sketch or some notes about their alternate or secondary targets. We then used this information to warn our people before they were hit. Searching a fresh enemy corpse, I often had the bad luck to open an envelope or pocket folder that had pictures of the poor guy's girlfriend, or his wife and kids. That always put a stab in my heart, and I always stuffed the personal effects back into their pockets as quickly as possible.

The 5th Division moved out on August 4 to join up with the other outfits that would make up XX Corps. We rode on trucks and tanks over paved roads and in pleasant summer weather covering a distance of some 50 miles to rendezvous at a point near Cherencey-Le-Heron. Our movements south of the assembly area were without incident: the French 2d Armored cleared all resistance in our path. We traveled through many towns and villages, and whenever circumstances allowed, we were greeted by cheering French who showered us with fruits, cheese, eggs, wine, cognac, and kisses from beautiful young women. The portrayal of such scenes in movies is one of the few things about the war that filmmakers have been able to recreate with any real degree of accuracy

Everyone, even the Germans, knew in the early fighting on the newly created Western Front that American tanks were no match for their German counterparts. Despite this, we were always glad to see our armor. I remember once on patrol we had to hide out in a cellar as two German armored cars roamed the town square patrolling in search of Americans. "Nobody even breathe," I told the guys with me as I peered through a window, wishing we had some tank support at that moment.

The city of Nantes was our next objective. It was thought that a single German regiment was garrisoned there, but no one could confirm that as a fact. The 10th Regiment was ordered in virtually blind to take the city in a preparatory movement to the division's objective of an even bigger prize: Angers, just east of Nantes. It was a fairly big gamble of human lives, but that never deterred Patton. The 10th Regiment moved in and took Nantes and its 2,000 German defenders, but it was a pretty dicey venture considering how little was known about German strength there. Patton is said to have commented, "I am sure he (Bradley) would think it too risky. It is slightly risky but so is war." Typical Patton!

It was around Nantes that a new lieutenant took us out on a patrol around 16:00 hours. His name was Capparrelli and he had been in the army for some 15 years, but he was from the quartermaster corps and so was not an experienced infantryman. He had only recently graduated from OCS and we were his first command.

We knew the area was hot, so when he told us to advance through it in a skirmish line formation we balked. Skirmish lines tend to work well when an enemy is known beyond all doubt to be in front of you and half expecting an attack. It allows men to advance into a fight without bunching up. But when dealing with unknown situations, a first and second scout are sent out and everyone moves forward in a single file line to reduce the visibility of potential targets.

"Lieutenant," I said. "I think you're making a mistake. This area is unfamiliar and very dangerous. It would probably be better to move forward in a line column." My suggestion was not well received. "I'm running this patrol," he said. "And I'll say what goes," and with that, he ordered us to move forward. It wasn't long before we encountered a German machine gun nest with supporting infantry, and when their machine gun opened up it hit three of our men. The rest of us dropped flat onto the ground and from here on in everything became surreal.

Our medics showed up and like a time out in a kid's game, everything stopped while they picked up those three men. I couldn't tell whether the men hit were dead or alive. Once the medics had them off the field, everything resumed. The lieutenant yelled, "Bilder, get up and get that machine gun." I pretended not to hear him. I knew from experience that any move against that gun would be suicide. He was the officer, and if he wanted that gun taken out he should lead the charge. Then we'd all be duty bound to follow him. I wasn't about to throw my life away for no reason other than to obey the orders of an officer who didn't know his job.

He yelled out a second time. "Bilder, I said to get up there and take out that gun." I yelled back, "Fuck you, I'm pinned down!" My buddy Steponovic was lying next to me. Step was too brave for his own good, and he jumped up on one knee with the intent of throwing a grenade at that machine gun. He never got as far as pulling the pin, and I thank God that he didn't, because as soon as he got up he took a bullet in the left shoulder while another grazed his left ear. He fell back and dropped the grenade. If he had managed to pull the pin before he was hit, we would have all been killed.

We stayed flat on the ground with our noses in the dirt until dark, when we crawled away from the area and then walked back the rest of the way to our lines. Step was able to walk back with us. This was the second time he had been wounded, and once again he had been fortunate enough to have the bullets miss his bones and pass through soft tissue. I was one of the last back, and my company commander was waiting for me when I got there. The lieutenant who led the patrol wanted me court-martialed for disobeying a direct order under fire, a serious charge to be sure. It was a capital offense.

Our company commander, Captain Churkland, liked me and had confidence in my combat abilities. He decided to hear my side of things in private. "What's your story, Bilder?" he asked me. "You're a good soldier. What happened?" I told him the entire thing in detail. I told him that if the Lieutenant had been any kind of an officer he would have led the charge. We all would have been killed, but we all would have followed him. "I just put in the paperwork to have you promoted to sergeant," Churkland said. "But that's all over now. The Lieutenant has no confidence in you and I have to stick by my officers."

I was actually glad to know that I wasn't going to be made a sergeant. I had not even known until that minute that I had even been considered for promotion. I was, however, disappointed at being on the wrong side of Captain Churkland. He was a first-rate officer and a hell of a good man. It was obvious that I wasn't going to be charged with anything, but since it looked like my captain might now have doubts about me, I said to him, "Captain, I'd like to put in for a transfer."

His response was quick. "I'm the only one who decides who transfers out of my company," he said briskly. "I'll transfer you, but only to another platoon, understood?" I felt his anger was mostly manufactured and that he was not unsympathetic to my circumstances, but this was as close as he could come to letting me know his feelings. "Yes sir," I said. I saluted him and left his quarters.

Angers was now next on the map. A city of 80,000 inhabitants, it was a major German communication and transportation center at the junction of the Maine and Loire Rivers. It had significant strategic value, and we put everything we had into place to take it.

The primary goal now was for the 5th Division to secure the bridges leading into Angers and then take the town. The 2d Regiment had won the division's first significant engagement back at Vidouville. The 10th Regiment had followed suit in taking Hill 183 and Nantes. It was now the 11th Regiment's turn to do the lion's share of the fighting and take Angers.

Unfortunately for us, our company wouldn't just be sitting this one out in reserve. We were assigned to Task Force Thackeray, a makeshift unit commanded by Lt. Colonel D.W. Thackeray from Divisional S-2 (intelligence), whose mission it was to secure the bridges leading into Angers. The task force consisted of the 5th Cavalry Recon Group, Company G (my outfit) from the 2d Regiment, engineers, mortar teams, machine gunners, and even the photo and counter-intelligence units. We pulled out towards Angers in support of the 11th Regiment at a little after 13:00 hours on August 7.

We moved about 25 miles southeast towards Chateau Gontier and had no opposition. The Germans were supposed to be some 200-strong in Coudray, and when we got to within a mile and a half of this objective we skirmished with them. We overran their position and took some prisoners, but the real fight was still to come. When we got to within 800 yards of the town, the Germans hit us again. They took out three of our six tanks and the infantry was rushed forward to take some heat off the armor.

The Germans brought down a hail of machine and small arms fire on us. They were hidden in the hedgerows; the fire seemed to be coming from everywhere, but we couldn't see anybody. It was mass confusion and we fired blindly into the hedgerows. We took the heat off of the armor long enough for the remaining tanks to regroup and coordinate their turret cannons with our mortar crews, who together put down enough fire on the hedgerows to force the Germans to retreat.

The Germans slipped out of Coudray that night and we entered the town without a fight on August 8. We went another seven miles before we encountered gradual resistance in the hedgerows, which got heavier as we advanced. Our divisional history states that we killed about 15 Germans and took an equal number prisoner, whom we left behind with some French and some of our engineers. We also captured some heavy weapons which included four 20mm guns, but it was all for nothing. We got to the bridge at Chateau-Neauf-Sur-Sarthe just in time to watch the Germans blow it up.

On August 9 we moved another six miles and entered the towns of Le Lion and Champigne without a fight. Some 500 SS troops managed to stay one step ahead of us, and they made certain that all the remaining bridges had been blown. This is probably why they hadn't stopped to fight us. In their haste to blow the bridges, they did manage to strand some of their own troops on our side of the river. I remember these men couldn't do anything but walk to our lines and surrender. Our mission, however, was a complete failure, and the division ordered us back that same day.

The SS were a tough bunch of bastards. It was not uncommon for them to fight to the very last man, regardless of how hopeless their circumstances. I remember one incident where it must have taken over a dozen of us to surround and finally kill one who absolutely refused to be taken alive.

Aside from medics, who risked death from the same hazards we did, along with the added danger that some coldhearted bastard could still shoot a man with red crosses all over him, I quickly developed an exceptionally high degree of respect for two other military specialists. First were the combat engineers. These men worked under constant enemy fire to create or repair bridges across rivers for our tanks and infantry. They had no means or opportunity of fighting back. They had to continue working no matter what and depend on others for protection. They were phenomenal.

The combat MPs were also incredible. They directed military traffic under fire and, like the combat engineers, they continued to perform their duty regardless of what was going on around them. They knew from the serial numbers on our vehicles who was supposed to go where, and they directed us accordingly. They thought and acted clearly in the midst of chaos and terror. We were all in awe of them.

As I later read my regimental and divisional histories, I saw how neatly and orderly the regiments of the 5th Division leapfrogged from town to town, with each outfit having its own turn in taking an objective. In reality our movements were not that clear-cut. Our regiments almost always assisted each other, and often ended up overlapping in ways that the official histories couldn't accurately record, so they were largely ignored.

Frequently during attacks, we found ourselves sharing a bombed-out house with another man or men from the 5th Division whom we didn't recognize, and vice-versa. When we inquired what outfit the other guys were with, we were often surprised to discover that we were from different regiments altogether!

Nantes had been one such occasion. Our advance had brought the 2d Regiment to a point just above the city where we could block any attempt by the Germans to move north into our rear area or simply to escape. The 10th Regiment had taken Nantes itself, but directly following Task Force Thackeray on August 10, our 2d Battalion was ordered to outpost the city perimeters and to assist in clearing out snipers. I was very scruffy-looking at the time. I needed a shower and a shave desperately, and I sure didn't look or feel like anyone who had ever held the nickname Esquire Kid.

We came to this three-story structure, a massive complex of apartments with twists and turns. I remember clearly how odd it seemed. There was no separation in the building: it was all connected in a seemingly endless row of linked apartments. I had a Thompson submachine gun as I cautiously moved along, checking apartments. I came to one door and crouched down as I reached for the doorknob with my left hand. We weren't worried about booby traps because the retreating enemy was still too busy running to have time to properly withdraw. I opened the door quickly and jumped inside the room with my machine gun at the ready.

I was confronted by a beautiful French whore lying in bed, only partially covered with a sheet. We were in a house of ill repute! On the wall next to her bed were notches from her previous encounters. "'Ello baybee," she said in a French accent thick enough to cut with a knife. "I don't have time right now. I'll catch you later," I told her, knowing she probably had no idea what I was saying. The Germans were running out the back door into captivity, being caught literally with their pants down.

I can't recall the exact time or place it occurred, but I remember well another mission that I believe was near Nantes. We were dug in with the Germans directly in front us, but all was quiet as the late afternoon approached. To all appearances, it was going to be a calm and uneventful time. We had some bacon and everybody began talking about how great it would be to have fresh eggs to go along with it. Since I was the type that usually volunteered for such missions, I spoke up and offered to go. I took off my helmet. "Alright, give me all your trading material," I said, pointing into my steel pot. Within seconds my helmet was filled with cigarettes, chocolate bars, razor blades, you name it. I was ready to go.

Whenever I set off on such a mission, I moved in a straight line from a point directly to the right or left of our lines. There could be nothing in our rear but the command post, and the enemy was directly in front, so this only left the sides to maneuver in. I got a little less than a mile, when I saw a barn and farmhouse that were probably the biggest I had yet seen in France. These structures were in a very open area and unoccupied by military personnel. The reason was obvious. As a target, it was impossible for either side's artillery to miss, and therefore no one wanted to take possession of it.

I approached the rear entrance and knocked. An older French couple opened the door and greeted me with a smile. None of us knew more than a few words of the other's language but I was able to make my intentions known and the man nodded enthusiastically and said, "Oui, oui." He was insistent on pouring me some calvados (cognac) while his wife took my helmet to exchange its goodies for their eggs. I belted down a few shots and was feeling no pain. They had no extra liquor, but she returned with my helmet filled well above the rim with fresh eggs. I nodded, as these would do nicely.

It was time to head back, when suddenly I heard the sound of clanking armor and approaching engines. The old man looked out the window and said one word: "Boches!" I knew what that meant and carefully peered out the window. My heart sank down to my ankles as I saw a German captain standing in the back of a Volkswagen directing armored cars and light tanks in the immediate vicinity of the house. This sobered me up immediately and I made a beeline for the cellar. I opened the rear door a crack and saw that it was clear, so I decided not to waste any time in getting the hell out of there.

In my haste I left my precious cargo of fresh eggs. When I got back to our lines, I was so flustered that I reported to Easy instead of George Company. I went to the company commander and reported what I had seen, but he told me that he already knew all about it. Our scouts had spotted them before I had and reported it in. It turned out the Germans were preparing to hit us that night and were checking out the area. We would be ready for them.

I was then ordered to get back to my own company, who were

none too happy with me for expending their goodies but leaving their eggs behind. To make matters worse I had been drinking, which only added fuel to the fire. I had to do some fast talking, and even then it took a while for things to blow over.

Meanwhile, the poor guys in the 11th Regiment didn't fare any better in taking the bridge near Angers than Task Force Thackeray had fared with the bridges leading up to it. The 11th Regiment had started attacking the edges of Angers on August 8. The Germans blew the bridge at the Maine River and a forced crossing was necessary. Fortunately, there were other avenues of attack and by August 10, the city was liberated. It was a nasty fight, but the 11th did their job, and even the SS were no match for them. The capture of Angers cut off the Germans' only major avenue of escape from the Breast Peninsula and opened wide our communication and supply lines.

The 5th Division was to keep moving, but this time dame fortune smiled on us. The 2d Regiment was ordered to garrison and defend Angers while the other two regiments continued to advance. The French locals treated us like kings, and we enjoyed a wonderful two days that were the closest thing to a vacation that a frontline soldier could have.

In our drive across France, the Germans couldn't set up an effective defensive line, but they sure as hell did everything they could to hurt and delay us. Their actions consisted of a good deal more than just mines and booby traps. For starters, they used snipers liberally. Our training never included anything at all, not even a mention, about snipers. We learned about them through experience and heavy losses. There was always something especially eerie about these well-hidden, silent killers. They had an aspect of the grotesque, like a spider popping out of its hole to snatch and devour its prey.

In pitched battles snipers slowed our advance, forcing us to be especially careful when moving up. Often during firefights someone who seemed to be very well protected by cover and out of the line of fire would suddenly get hit and collapse from a shot that seemingly came out of nowhere. We knew immediately that the shot had come from a sniper. As we advanced toward an objective that appeared quiet, sometimes a single shot rang out and took down one of our men. Everyone dove for cover, and the inevitable question, "Anybody see where that came from?" resonated throughout our ranks.

As I mentioned previously, snipers often aimed to maim and not to kill. During one incident, an enemy sniper kept hitting our guys in the back of their ankles, blowing out their Achilles' tendons and crippling them for life. The screams of agony these men let out as they were hit made our hair stand on end and our blood boil. What's more, the pain of these wounded men was so excruciating that they couldn't stop screaming. The natural tendency was to run out and help whoever was hit, but this is exactly what the sniper wanted. It was a tactic intended to produce new victims.

We spotted the sniper and sprayed fire in his general direction, which sent him scurrying down out of his tree. He jumped down in front of us, threw up his hands, and yelled, "Kamerad!" The GI closest to him hesitated for a moment then said, "Comrade my ass," and shot him with a burst from his BAR. I wouldn't have done it, but on the other hand I didn't suffer any angst over it.

I can't begin to describe how often replacements came into our ranks only to be killed a day or two later by snipers. We knew what to do and how to survive through our experience, but these green kids served as nothing more than target practice for German snipers. Yet despite their experience, even veterans made fatal errors on occasion. I remember one lieutenant colonel who was always preaching cover and concealment to us when it came to snipers. He forgot his own teaching one day, and stepped from a jeep and walked across an open field rather than hugging the tree line around it. He was struck by a sniper's bullet and dead before he hit the ground.

Officers serving on the frontline normally wore no insignia, diligently scrubbed the white vertical line off the back of their helmets, and threatened any soldier stupid enough to salute them. All of the above were considered open invitations to enemy snipers. Sergeant and corporal stripes also drew the additional interest of snipers, but NCOs did not have the luxury of being able to hide their status from the enemy.

Some of the enemy were very well trained for this duty and volunteered to stay behind when their units retreated. Others were ordered to do it and had no choice. Either way, they meant trouble for us. When we entered a town or village one of the first things we did was send some men to check any steeples, bell towers, or other high points for snipers. We had to take turns for the duty. This included being the first man to go up the winding staircase of local hotels we had to check. Sometimes snipers were perched in an attic entrance or overhang, waiting for the first unlucky man to come around those winding stairs. My heart would beat so strongly that I could swear everyone else could hear it. I was very lucky that I never encountered a sniper when it was my turn to be the first man up those stairs. The men who did seldom lived to tell about it.

Another deadly delaying tactic the Germans employed was the use of pillboxes. These could be made out of logs and timbers or concrete. The wooden ones were not as great a problem, and could be taken out from a safe distance with a bazooka. I was a pretty good bazooka man. Shooting a bazooka took a little more expertise, because it was not a matter of simply looking through a set of crosshairs and pulling a trigger. There were different sights for different distances, so a bazooka user had to have a keen knack for judging distances.

A bazooka man first dropped down on one knee with the bazooka over his shoulder. Then someone immediately behind him loaded the projectile in the rear opening of the bazooka. Once this was completed the soldier loading tapped the user on his helmet or shoulder, and ducked down out of the way. The user lined up the target in the appropriate sight and fired the round. This was a highly effective way to destroy enemy machine gun nests and wooden pillboxes.

I don't ever recall using a bazooka against a tank, though. German armor was known to be too thick for a bazooka round to penetrate. Only the underside of a tank or its treads were vulnerable, and a man with a bazooka had to get far too close for comfort to have any chance of scoring a hit against either one. However, there were heroes who did do it, and they deserve a lot of credit.

Concrete pillboxes were more common and much harder to take out. If we outflanked an enemy pillbox and got behind it, we usually had free reign. One time our combat engineers planted charges at the rear door. They blew it off only to find that there was a second steel door three feet behind the first. We often dropped hand grenades down the airshafts and watched the Germans race out the rear. They came out with their hands raised high above their heads and blood running out of their noses and ears.

We discovered that pillboxes were sometimes manned by Czechs, Poles, or other foreign nationals the SS had forced into German uniform. In these circumstances, the SS had two men at the inside rear of the pillbox with their guns on their foreign conscripts. If they refused to fight, they were shot. We often encountered pillbox occupants who wouldn't (or couldn't) surrender. During one of these instances, we had a tank come up that had an enormous bulldozer-type blade on its front (a Sherman-dozer). It moved forward with impunity, pushing up earth all the way right to the pillbox, and buried the enemy inside alive.

The arrival of Allied troops allowed the French resistance (FFI, or Free French of the Interior) to step up their activities. Supposedly they provided valuable information about enemy strength and carried out a number of successful acts of sabotage that slowed and pained the Germans. I only saw the resistance after we took objectives, never while we were in combat. This was apparently the way our commanders wanted it.

The FFI were partisans and not regular troops. Since partisans almost by definition lack formal military training, their reliance in combat is always subject to question. Because of this, and the fact that they had a number of communists in their ranks (no one ever never knew just how many), we were instructed to be friendly, but to keep our distance.

Whenever we occupied towns or villages in areas where the Germans were active, we forced the residents from their homes and out into the elements to fend for themselves. This was not intended as an act of cruelty. These people could spend a night or two in the fields or with someone they knew. It was a small price to pay for liberation. When there was a fight coming on, we needed the structures as protection from enemy fire. This in turn made the homes targets, and we didn't want to cause unnecessary civilian casualties in the midst of a fight.

We tried to be as accommodating to people as possible when we fought in Allied lands, but once we were in Germany the courtesy ended. The orders that came down regarding civilians were always the same no matter where we were: no murder, no rape, and no looting.

Obeying orders against rape and murder came naturally for almost all American troops, but the orders on looting were largely ignored when we finally reached Germany.

The Third Army never idled in August. We were always on the move. I can't begin to count the number of times we expended great energy and effort digging first-class foxholes, only to hear some officer or NCO bark out, "Alright, gear up, we're moving out," the minute we finished.

We usually had very good support when moving up to take a town. The Germans often had two or three machine guns set up along a defensive perimeter to hit us while we were still out in the open. These machine guns each had their own field of fire and could provide support to one another as well.

I remember one particular time in France when we were moving up on foot over some hilly countryside. Our first scout was a fine young soldier by the name of Roy Downs, out of southern Illinois. The customary enemy practice in such cases was to allow the first and second scouts a free pass, and then open fire on the approaching infantry once they were in clear view. This particular German machine gunner must have been trigger-happy, because he opened up on Downs as soon as he saw him. We saw Roy's helmet fly off and knew that he had been hit in the head. We dove for cover and called for support. After some four hours of heavy skirmishing, we took the ground from the Germans.

Roy's body was nowhere to be found, so we all just figured that he would be listed as Missing In Action (MIA) and presumed dead. I got a very pleasant surprise a couple of years after the war when he showed up unexpectedly at my front door in suburban Chicago. I was so shocked when I first saw him that my first words were actually, "You're dead!" He quickly assured me that he was no ghost. He had been hit in the head and paralyzed on one side, but our medics picked him up and our doctors saved his life. He spent the war recovering and when I met him, he was driving a specially modified car, courtesy of the Veteran's Administration. He had survived the war, and that was what it was all about.

I had plenty of other buddies who didn't fare as well as Roy Downs. My friend Roger Witney had accepted sergeant's stripes and moved to 2d Battalion Headquarters. Like so many others, he died wearing the rank that helped kill him.

During one of our advances, Witney was out front scouting for a new location for the battalion HQ when we fell under attack from German mortars. According to author Michael Doubler, German mortars accounted for about two-thirds of the combat casualties inflicted on Americans during the fighting in France. Witney ended up being hit in the gut by a piece of shrapnel. His wound was fatal, as gut wounds almost always are, and there was nothing any of us could do but watch helplessly as a fine man and brave soldier bled to death. It took almost 15 minutes for him to go, and he spent almost all of it calling out in a pleading tone, "I don't wanna die," over and over again. It still rings in my ears and haunts me more than 60 years later.

Enemy machine gun nests were another hazard and could be very difficult to take out. They almost always had infantry and mines around them for support. Getting close enough to use hand grenades was often impossible. This type of situation called for a bazooka or possibly even heavier firepower. If we didn't have tanks leading the way, then we might have air support, or our artillery and mortar crews might reduce much of the enemy's strength before we got there.

When all else failed, we could always use smoke grenades and advance across open ground to flank the enemy and take the objective. Our company commanders were accountable for the men and weapons they lost, which mandated a certain degree of caution. Command over human lives weighed very heavily on most men.

An officer once directed us very specifically about where to dig our foxholes. On this occasion, like many others, we dug them wide enough so that each foxhole held two men. Soon after we were in position, the Germans opened up on us with mortars. A round landed directly in one of our foxholes, killing both of its occupants instantly. This poor officer had a nervous breakdown right there on the spot. It seemed only General Patton could tolerate and get away with high casualty figures.

Even when we thought a town was unoccupied, we had to approach and enter it cautiously. Soldiers never walked down the middle of a street. We split our outfits in half, and advanced simultaneously up both sides of a street, with the men hugging close to the buildings. The men on the right hand side of the street kept their eyes and guns fixed on the left hand side, while the men on the left did the same for the men on the right. This allowed for a quicker and safer advance since it provided us with a wider view and greater opportunity for a fast response, if the enemy suddenly appeared. This is only one of the many ways a soldier puts his life in the hands of his comrades simply as a matter of routine.

Occupying a town was no guarantee of safety. We had one kid who got into bed with a woman who was previously unknown to be a Nazi sympathizer. During intercourse, she pulled out a knife and stabbed him in the back. He was mortally wounded, but managed to strangle her before he died. When we found them, she was still holding onto the knife in his back and his hands were wrapped around her throat. I asked the company commander how he was going to report this soldier's death. "Killed in Action," he said without missing a beat.

Army policy on homosexuality was "Don't ask, don't tell," even then. We were in the open when a German artillery barrage started to fall on us. Everyone dove for any kind of cover possible, and I ducked into a recently captured concrete pillbox. I discovered another GI crouched down inside, shivering from head to toe. "I'm not even supposed to be here," he said for no apparent reason. "Well, that makes two of us," I said. "What's your excuse?" He looked at me rather squeamishly and said, "I like boys," as if looking for a sympathetic response. I didn't know if he was on the level or simply looking for a witness to get him out of the army. "Well, you better keep it to yourself," I told him. "It's already dangerous enough around here."

Later, an officer I knew fairly well got wind of what this soldier was saying, and mentioned to me that he was considering sending him home. I couldn't resist pulling his leg. "Sir," I said, "if it'll get me off the line, then I have to admit that guys are starting to look pretty good to me too." He shot an angry glare at me and snapped, "Go to hell, Bilder!" as he walked off in a huff. It took every ounce of discipline I had not to laugh out loud.

Aside from Paris and a few major cities, France consisted of small towns separated by large farms and open country. Sometimes as we moved across three or four miles of open space on our way to the next objective, the Germans turned tanks, artillery, or antiaircraft guns

(20mm) on us. On one such encounter, we actually received air support in the form of four P-51 Mustang fighters. Three of them climbed high into the air and then dove down on their targets, but the fourth pilot decided to come straight on at the Germans, flying about 100 feet off the ground and right into their sights. The German anti-aircraft gunners easily hit the plane. It flipped over before crashing into the ground in an upside down position. After we took the ground, we saw how badly the cockpit canopy was cracked and busted. The remains of the poor pilot inside looked like he had been put through a meat grinder.

Booby-trapping souvenir material was another deadly tactic the Germans used to delay our advance. They understood that Americans love to touch things. They also knew that everyone wanted something to send back home. Guns, daggers, or anything we thought was worth picking up, or even just plain useful, was liable to have an explosive charge attached to it.

Some crooks and souvenir hunters would go to any lengths to get what they wanted. There was a sergeant from Graves' Registration whom we all despised. It was bad enough that he was from Graves' Registration, but we understood that everybody had a job to do. This man, however, robbed the dead, German and American alike. His close and constant physical contact with the dead made him smell like a rotting corpse. Whenever he tried to buddy up to us, we'd say, "Get the hell out of here! You smell like a walking cemetery."

The man was heartless. We regarded him as nothing more than a ghoul who would try to pal around with a soldier one day and then loot his corpse the next. Justice came the day he reached into the pocket of a dead German officer and a booby trap went off, taking his hand with it. I wasn't there to see it, but I was told that everyone actually cheered.

We got the hell scared out of us on August 13 and 14 when we were placed on alert to prepare for a heavy German counter attack. Word had come from the French that a well-equipped enemy force of as many as 5,000 men and supporting armor was moving our way. It turned out to be a bogus rumor originated by jittery civilians.

We moved out again on August 15, heading northeast towards Chartres aboard tanks and trucks. While German tanks were superior to ours at this point in the war, the enemy couldn't compensate for our vast superiority in numbers. We had numerous tanks, and American artillery and air power were so powerful that the Germans could not effectively challenge us in the open countryside.

With no sleep, we traveled 113 miles over narrow, bumpy roads to our new assembly area near Authon du Perche. We arrived around 5:00 hours on August 16. German fighter planes strafed us during our journey but did little damage. We were able to move so rapidly because opposition was relatively sparse. Our divisional history accurately describes that when we did encounter problems, a coded radio signal was sent out to our company commanders. If it said to "rally up," we were ordered to dismount and attack along our left flank. If it said to "rally down," we got orders to dismount and move along the right flank. It was very effective and I remember its use, but they didn't share the code universally with the infantry grunts. Some guys had big mouths and there was also the danger of someone getting captured by the enemy.

We were ordered to move again at 8:00 hours to a point just east of Illiers. We then got some rest and conducted motorized patrols. The 7th Armored Division held up just outside of Chartres while the 11th Regiment took the city. We had moved on foot to a point about 11 miles southwest of the city to defend it in the event of an enemy counter attack.

Things were relatively quiet. Action was limited and we took a few prisoners. I remember that Dysinger and I captured some half a dozen Germans in the cellar of a house when we were out on patrol. Most of them were enlisted men, but one was a junior officer who spoke English. Dysinger told them to empty their pockets and remove everything else except their uniforms. The officer quickly spoke up and said, "You can't do this. It's looting and against the rules of the Geneva Convention. I am going to report this to your commanding officer." Dysinger's father was dead and his 18-year-old kid brother, his only sibling, had joined the service to help his older brother out. The kid had been killed in the Pacific and Dysinger was none too happy about it.

"Bilder, go out and check the yard," he said. I should have realized how volatile the situation·was, but the yard had not been checked, so I headed out without hesitation. I heard BAR fire while I was out there and saw Dysinger emerge a minute later without the prisoners. I don't know the details about what happened or why. Maybe they tried to rush him, but he didn't offer any explanations and you just didn't ask a guy about something like that.

I heard Ernest Hemingway and some of his left-wing buddies in the FFI showed up and were escorted to our regimental command post presumably to booze it up. The cathedral in Chartres had been taken intact along with a captured German limo, which years later I learned had been given to Patton. We got a few days rest.

On August 21 we moved towards the city of Etampes. I was riding shotgun in a jeep with a soldier manning a .30-caliber machine gun mounted in the back. We were following another jeep that was equipped the same way as part of a motorized patrol checking the approaches into the city. The men ahead of us slowed to a crawl in order to drive around some debris in the road.

Suddenly German paratroopers, camouflaged so skillfully that they seemed to materialize out of thin air, emerged to surround the jeep. They pointed their guns directly at the three men ahead of us. The driver and the machine gunner immediately threw up their hands to surrender, but the GI riding shotgun resisted. The Germans didn't hesitate, and we were close enough to hear the shot that killed him. We hastily made a sharp U-turn and were able to get safely out of the area, but there was nothing we could do for the men just captured. It seemed like we did the only thing possible under the circumstances, but something like that always makes you wonder if you may have turned chicken shit.

For the attack on Etampes, the 2d Regiment was split into two groups. The 1st and 3rd Battalions were to attack from the north while our 2d Battalion was to attack from the south. The group in the north got hit heavy around 11:00 hours from German mortars and artillery. We were stopped an hour later by enemy fire. The Germans had obviously decided to make a stand, and they had a hell of a lot of automatic weapons to do it with.

We pushed ahead from the south and gained about 400 yards, but the going was slow. By 19:00 hours our reserve company was thrown into the fight from the west and the Germans were being hit from three sides. By the following day, we were well into the city and civilians were ordered to stay inside while we patrolled the streets.

One of our soldiers wore an asbestos glove and carried a .30-caliber machine gun in his hands like it was a Tommy gun. A curious old man must have wanted to see what Americans looked like, because a set of shudders suddenly burst open on the second floor of a building as he popped out to have a look. With the speed of pure instinct, this soldier pulled up that .30-caliber and fired a burst from left to right across the window. The old man slumped forward dead as a doornail. "Nice shooting," someone said. "That's the eye," said another. We continued our patrol.

By the August 22, we had taken the town and sealed off the escape routes to the east. We were then transported to Maisse, where we were held in reserve. The following day we were ordered to secure a bridgehead at Misy in our continued drive east. We did this and took the town of Bray, which was occupied by a small German force.

We were denied the honor of liberating Paris that I know Patton so desperately wanted. Supposedly, Eisenhower and the Allied high command did not regard the French capital as strategic enough to warrant the diversion of any American units for its liberation. They were willing to give it to the FFI, but De Gaulle worried that might result in a communist government, so the French military was ordered to take it. It's hard to imagine that Paris was considered of no strategic importance. Maybe the brain trust in Washington actually wanted the FFI to take the capital, or maybe there was a legitimate political concern on De Gaulle's part about who controlled the French capital, but whether it was politics or pragmatics, it was the French regulars under De Gaulle who took Paris.

Our rapid advance through France had raised our confidence and demonstrated to us that an Allied victory was inevitable. We got so cocky that we even had our own marching song, which drove our officers crazy whenever we sang it.

Oh, we're a lovely bunch of morons,
Morphodites are we,
Scum of the earth,
The men of com-pan-ee gee.

Oh, we're a lovely bunch of morons,
Morphodites are we,
We'd rather fuck than fight
For lib-ib-erty!

We crossed the Seine River on a repaired bridge at Nogent on
August 27 and got word two days later to get ready to take Reims.
Our advance was held up when the retreating Germans destroyed the
bridges. Our engineers had to construct treadway bridges to allow the
tanks of the 7th Armored Division to move forward.

We usually didn't have the luxury of using bridges when crossing
rivers. The Germans did a pretty good job of blowing them up. This
meant the infantry had to go across first, almost always under heavy
fire, in wooden assault boats, and secure a bridgehead on the opposite
side so our engineers could lay down something for the armor and
other support groups to use in their crossing.

As previously mentioned, I was certified by the Red Cross as a
combat lifeguard. There was usually one such man in every boat.
During contested river crossings, we had to dive in and try to bring
back to the surface any soldier who fell or was knocked out of the
boat. Those of us performing this duty were often kept very busy,
because a German shell could explode alongside an assault boat, tip it,
and spill eight or nine men into the water. We would then dive after
them and do everything possible to save them from drowning. The
trick was to get their packs and ammo belts unhooked as quickly as
possible, since few men were strong enough to swim with this extra
weight. After we accomplished this task, we then pushed them back
up towards the surface and to the relative safety of enemy mortar
rounds and machine gun fire. The guys in the nearest boat lent a hand,
pulling them aboard.

I once dove in after a kid and found him frozen with fear. He was
sitting in about eight feet of water with his rifle between his knees as
if he were still in the boat, only he looked like he was deep in a trance.
I unhooked his gear and pulled him back up to the surface with me.

Whenever I completed these actions, I swam to the guys in whatever boat was closest, and after they pulled me in, I put on a helmet,
grabbed whatever weapon was available, and resumed my duties as an

infantryman. I collected my regular gear, assuming both it and I survived, once the fight was over.

The action at Reims started just before midnight on August 29 with sharp skirmishing. The following day (Sunday), we took the city. It was rainy, but any day that ends in victory and allows you to walk away whole is a good day. I read later that there were general services held in the cathedral that day.

I had fought along the edge of the city, and I entered downtown Reims the next day in style riding atop an M-10 Wolverine tank destroyer from the 5th Division's 818th Tank Destroyer Battalion. Reims is not only a beautiful city, but also a major producer of French champagne and it was warehoused up to the rafters with bubbly. Our advance had been so rapid that when we took a champagne factory we caught the Germans inside by surprise. Many of them were falling down drunk and still half dressed from recent visits to brothels.

Eight months later, Germany would surrender unconditionally in Riems, but the end of the war was still a long way away, and a lot more good men would die before then. Meanwhile, we were left behind to garrison the city while almost everyone else continued east towards Verdun. This was not our proudest moment. We all got falling down drunk on champagne. We didn't know that champagne needs to be sipped and we guzzled it like water. I got heartburn so bad that I actually thought I was experiencing a coronary at the age of 25, and believed that I was dying. I had never gotten drunk on carbonated liquor before, and the headache from the hangover was even worse than the heartburn. A captain had placed himself in charge and was still there enjoying himself a week later. The rest of us moved up and covered for him as long as we could, but when the commanding officers found out what the force they had left to garrison the city had done, there was hell to pay.

The party was over in more ways than one. There would be no more mad dashes and sweeping advances. From here on in it was one bloody, costly, and slow-moving trek into the Reich. We were about to go up against the fortress city of Metz in a slaughterhouse of a campaign that would last for four months. Before it was over, 90 percent of the riflemen in the 5th Division would become casualties.

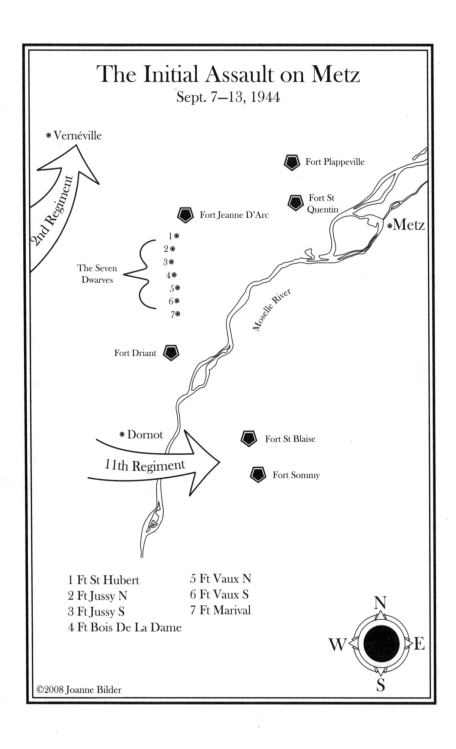

The Initial Assault on Metz
Sept. 7–13, 1944

Vernéville

2nd Regiment

Fort Plappeville

Fort St Quentin

Fort Jeanne D'Arc

Metz

The Seven Dwarves

1
2
3
4
5
6
7

Moselle River

Fort Driant

Dornot

Fort St Blaise

11th Regiment

Fort Sommy

1 Ft St Hubert
2 Ft Jussy N
3 Ft Jussy S
4 Ft Bois De La Dame

5 Ft Vaux N
6 Ft Vaux S
7 Ft Marival

N
W E
S

©2008 Joanne Bilder

8

METZ THE MEAT GRINDER
Paying the Price for Patton's Folly

"What passing bells for these who die like cattle?"
—Wilfred Owens, "Anthem for a Doomed Youth"

We moved up towards the ancient city of Verdun, getting closer and closer to the German border. In the First World War, the Germans threw everything they had at Verdun from February to December 1916, attempting, in their words, "to bleed the French white."

General Henri Philippe Pétain was charged with defending Verdun in 1916. Pétain was later disgraced in World War II when he took charge of France's Vichy Government, which was no more than a puppet state for Hitler. But in 1916, when he was still an honorable representative of French resolve, the order he issued for the defense of Verdun became a rallying battle cry: "On ne passe pas!" (Nobody gets through!) The ten-and-a-half month campaign ended with the city still in French hands, bought and paid for with the blood of countless thousands.

Time and technology alter the methods and outcomes of war, and Patton's Third Army took Verdun from the Germans in a mere day. In fact, the Germans ran while the 7th Armored Division rolled through the city largely unopposed, with the 11th Regiment following right behind. This all took place on August 31. That night, the Germans hit the city with artillery and an air strike that damaged buildings, but caused few casualties. Their action was more harassment than anything else. The German infantry never attempted to follow up with a counter attack. The bombings did shake up our headquarters people

145

considerably when the enemy scored a direct hit on the luxurious and regal hotel where they were staying, but this didn't break any of our hearts.

A friend from my days at Fort Custer was transferred to the field artillery and made an aerial observer after the army discovered that he had earned his pilot's license back in civilian life. He flew a Piper Cub and took me out to their little version of an airfield, which was only some tents and flat grassy fields. He asked me if I wanted to go up, and I jumped at the chance as he figured I would.

We flew over the trenches of World War I. They were overgrown with grass, but still left deep scars in the earth. It was an awesome sight from the air. I remember thinking about the mass slaughter that had occurred down there and how far our methods of warfare had since progressed. Little did I realize how much these same conditions would return with on the killing fields awaiting us at Metz.

With Patton, things were always "go, go, go!" No grass grew under our feet. We started out of Verdun the following day, moving east toward the great fortress city of Metz. Metz is located in the province of Lorraine, a piece of geography that has been exchanged many times between France and Germany as a spoil of war.

We were having a problem with the enemy's self-propelled guns when we left the relative safety of Verdun on September 2. I had delivered some Red Cross messages to Able Company and was with them as they were moving up. We were advancing on both sides of a road in open ranks in route step (a more casual, but practical way of marching in combat areas). Suddenly a German tank, skillfully camouflaged, appeared near the road roughly 500 yards ahead of us. I know that American soldiers are often faulted for calling every German tank a Tiger, and we did often use the terms "tank" and "Tiger" interchangeably. It's also true that there were only about 90 German Tigers actually deployed on the Western Front, but I can say without fear of contradiction that this particular tank was, in fact, a Tiger.

In any event, the tank surprised us as it fired off a round from its cannon and started to rake the area with machine gun fire. We all ran for the fields and ditches along the sides of the road and dove for cover. I saw Tom Spain, who was then a staff sergeant responsible for the men under his command, get down on one knee, yelling out orders and giving hand signals directing his men. The turret cannon of the tank turned in his direction and fired off a round that exploded just a few yards from him. I saw Tom fall, but there was nothing any of us could do. We had no anti-tank weapons, and any attempt to take on that tank without them was mindless suicide.

The Germans in the tank and their supporting infantry must have been die-hards because they simply would not leave. They seemed a good deal more willing to get themselves killed than any of us did. They stayed right there planted alongside the road, spraying machine gun fire everywhere. After about 15 minutes of this, our cannon company came up from our rear with anti-tank guns and took the tank out. The coast now clear, we all scurried from the ditches towards Tom. A crowd had formed around him and the medics were already at work bandaging a very bloody head wound before I could get there. My view of him was obscured, but I could see that he was thrashing about, although he wasn't making any sounds that I could hear. I glanced over and saw his helmet on the road with a huge gash in its side.

Because Tom had a head wound they couldn't give him any morphine. They restrained his arms and legs on a litter and carried him over to a jeep. The litter was secured to the jeep and an eighteen-year-old kid was told to drive Tom immediately to the battalion aid station. The kid took off like a shot. Later, I glanced down the open hatch of the German tank and saw that the crew had consisted of one man and three women. They were all wearing black uniforms and the man, a corporal, had been the commander.

That night, about six hours later, I was sitting in a foxhole when someone came up to me and said, "Bilder, you're a friend of Tom Spain, aren't you?" I looked up quizzically and simply said, "Yeah." The soldier then pointed and said, "Well, he's over there behind that hedgerow." I didn't say anything as I got out of my foxhole but I was thinking, "What the hell are you talking about?"

I came around the hedgerow and saw Tom lying on a litter, and for a fraction of an instant I thought he was sleeping. I knew a second later that I was mistaken. I never saw, before or since, a look of such serenity on a dead man's face. There was a dead German lieutenant on the litter next to Tom's.

"What happened? What's he doing here?" I asked. "He bled to death," someone said. "That kid couldn't find the battalion aid station so he dropped him off at a French hospital." This of course was a death sentence for Tom. The French never had the kind of supplies that Americans did, and they were especially short of things like blood plasma. Then someone told me that because everything had moved up, they had nowhere to send the body, so they sent it back to the front-lines. That was why he was now lying there in front of me.

A sense of rage came over me and I felt myself come close to snapping. "Where's that kid?" I demanded. I saw him before anyone could point him out, and I grabbed him with both hands by the front of his fatigues. "What the hell is wrong with you, you idiot, I'll tear you apart!" I said all this with clenched teeth and in enraged tones. The kid had a look of sheer terror on his face as the other guys started to pull me off of him.

"Take it easy, Mike," one said. "The kid did the best he could. The aid station had moved up and the first thing he came across while try-ing to find it was the French hospital. It wasn't his fault." My grip loosened and the kid squirmed free and took off. Deep down I knew it was nobody's fault. But Tom Spain, my closest friend and one of the finest men I've ever known, was dead, and there was no way to go back and undo it. This was a fortune of war and I had to accept it. I walked back to my foxhole and got into it in a funk.

One of the Catholic chaplains with the 5th Division, Major (later Colonel) Harold O. Prudell, wrote Tom's family a letter and assured them that Tom had made a final confession, been given communion, and received the last rites of the church before he died. All this would have allowed Tom to go in relative peace. He was posthumously awarded the Purple Heart. I still feel after more than 60 years that his death was a terrible waste of human life. I have always tried to con-sole myself with the thought that had he lived, he might have been so reduced mentally and/or physically that his life would have been a per-petual hell. Who knows? Who can say?

Not too long after Tom was killed, either the next day or the day after, we began again moving east. We were crossing open ground and our right flank fell a little behind us. Our outfit was in the center por-tion of the line during this advance and I was about 100 yards behind the point, which consisted of Second Lieutenant John Bennett and an 18-year-old kid who was serving as his runner.

I liked Bennett and he liked me. He was only 21 years old, but he was a first-rate officer and human being. He was a southerner and a graduate of the Virginia Military Institute (VMI). He loved the South and we joked that he probably carried a Confederate flag in his back pocket. Bennett kind of looked up to me like an older brother, and this naturally made me feel somewhat protective of him. He was young, but he knew how to lead men and he didn't flinch.

All of a sudden a German machine gun on our right opened up, and Bennett and his runner went down. The rest of us had enough time to dive for cover. We were pinned down for a moment before the men who formed our right flank, who would have been the target of this ambush if they had not fallen behind, moved up and drew the attention of the Germans, who turned their machine gun fire in that direction.

We got up to Bennett and his runner. It was plain to see that the kid had been killed instantly by the first burst. He was riddled with bullet holes. I rolled Bennett over and saw three bullet wounds in his lower right side, each about the size of quarter. "Are you hit bad, Lieutenant?" I asked. He opened his eyes and just said, "And how!" And with that he died. Bennett was the epitome of an academy graduate. These men lived, and unfortunately all too often died, putting concern for the safety of their men ahead of their own well-being.

Command of our platoon then went to Tech Sergeant Bruno Mankus, a big guy from Chicago standing tall at around 6 feet 4 inches. He was Lithuanian and very proud of it. Twenty minutes later he died, much the same way Bennett had, hit by enemy machine gun fire while leading us across open ground.

No matter how long I'd been in the frontlines, and no matter how much I thought I'd seen, combat experience often provided with me some ugly new twist of fate and another lesson to learn. Such was the case when I glanced over to my side and saw a soldier by the name of Robert Collins suddenly jerk his head back. I knew immediately that he had been hit. I got over to him and was relieved to see that he had received what appeared to be a relatively minor wound. A bullet had grazed the side of his head but penetrated deep enough through his scalp that I could see his skull bone. The bullet had not done any damage to his skull, so it looked like he had received a million-dollar wound. "Don't worry Collins, you're gonna be alright," I told him, as I sprinkled some sulfa powder on the wound and dressed it with a bandage. By this time, there were other guys helping me. Someone then headed off to find a medic.

We helped Collins in every way we could and tried to reassure him. He was shaking terribly and didn't really respond to anything we said. We watched in utter dismay as he died right before our eyes, a mere five minutes or so after being hit. A moment later the medic arrived and took a brief look at him. "It was shock," the medic said. "You have to keep 'em warm. Next time, elevate the guy's feet and put a blanket over him." With this parting advice, he was off to treat the next victim. I was amazed and stunned to see how someone could die from something as seemingly simple as a graze on the side of the head. It was this type of thing that forced a man to think about everything going on around him. It was another sharp reminder of reality and mortality, and it contributed to the tremendous sense of unease that we all carried around with us.

As we approached Metz we were running out of gas, and I don't just mean for our vehicles. We were dead tired and low on men, ammunition, and gasoline. We had dashed across France and we needed to stop and take a break. We needed rest and supplies. This was not true of just the Third Army but of the entire American advance on the Western Front. The 1st Infantry Division was bogged down outside of Aachen, Germany. The 28th Infantry Division was slowed to a crawl in the Hurtgen Forest, and now we were stalled outside of Metz. Metz turned out to be a bigger travesty than anyone could ever have imagined. Initially, the Germans' situation at Metz was the same predicament they had earlier discovered in France during the Allied push in August. They had had little time to properly prepare defenses and garrison the city. The whole place was wide open for the taking, but we couldn't get there because of the shortage in gasoline. This down time allowed the German Gestapo to truck back the units necessary to fortify the city and turn it into a real source of pain for the Third Army.

The gasoline and general supply shortage that affected us and everybody else on the Western Front was largely the result of Allied

This is my official portrait taken in the fall of 1941. The insignia on my garrison cap is the 11th Regiment's. I spent about three months with them because the 10th was being sent to Iceland and they had to get all the conscripts out of it. I was transferred to the 2nd Regiment just before shipping out in February 1942 and remained with them until mid-June of 1945.

Below, left: My cheesecake photo of Mary that ended up in the possession of some German soldier. Fortunately, she had the negative.
Below, right: With my mother (also named Mary) and stepfather, Frank Pavell, in their backyard in the summer of 1941.

Hurry up and wait. In May 1941, getting ready to depart Fort Custer for long marches and maneuvers in Tennessee. The Army was still issuing WWI-era helmets.

Our outfit did everything it could to make "Little McCoy" feel head and shoulders above everyone else, even if he needed a few helping hands. I'm the guy on the right.

A semi-quet moment during the Tennessee Maneuvers of 1941, on the same ground over which Union and Confederate armies once vied.

At first the army was not only issuing WWI-style uniforms but seemed to be planning WWI tactics. This is Army Postcard 101: "Cold Steel for the Enemy." I sent this home from Fort Dix in January 1942 because I needed to bum a few bucks from the folks.

Lt. General George S. Patton, Jr. speaks to men of the 5th Infantry Division after they completed an assault demonstration near Kikeel, Couny Down, Northern Ireland, on 30 March 1944.

Officers studying a terrain model in France during a visit to 5th Infantry Div. HQ by General George C. Marshall (right). Shown from left are Lt. Gen. Patton, Col. Paul Franson, Maj. Gen. H.C. Walker, and Maj. Gen. S. Leroy Irwin, 5th Div. CG.

August 30, 1944, entering Reims in style. That's me in the top center with a wave of my left hand. We're riding on an M-10 "Wolverine" from the 5th Division's 818th Tank Destroyer Battalion.

A 155mm howitzer from a section of the 21st Field Artillery Battalion firing on German positions near Berdorf. Note the camouflage against air attack as well as the muddy, rain-soaked ground, typical of conditions we encountered in 1944–45. (SFD)

My wallet photo of Mary was autographed on the back by Bing Crosby when he came to entertain the troops at Metz on September 27, 1944. "It looks like you've got a fine girl there soldier," he said.

Tom Spain (1919–1944). Tom and I had been friends since our days palling around back in Fuller Park in Chicago. He was killed in action just outside of Verdun on September 2, 1944. Even in death he remains the finest man I've ever known.

In Metz after its capture in late November 1944.

5th Division infantrymen move through the streets of newly taken
Frankfurt, 27 March 1945. (SFD)

In the Ruhr Pocket, the town of Meschede was taken by the 5th Division
in April 1945. (SFD)

Company K of the 2nd Infantry Regiment skirts the town of Grevenstein to attack a nearby hill the Germans are using as an OP. (SFD)

A more grueling kind of advance was endured through the ruins of Bitburg, fearing snipers at any moment. (SFD)

The 5th Infantry Division advances near Luxembourg City to help repel the Germans' Ardennes Offensive on 22 December 1944. (SFD)

The weather, terrain and roads varied—from bad to terrible—after the 5th Division crossed the Sauer River and approached the front. (MNHM)

The impact of the brutal cold during the Battle of the Bulge can be judged by the state of this jeep-mounted machine gun. (MNHM)

Aside from forested terrain, snow reduced visibility even further, putting marching columns at great risk of ambush. (MNHM)

Obviously amused, these 2nd Infantry Regiment soldiers find civilian bed-sheets handy for camouflage in destroyed Diekirch after the town was recaptured on January 20, 1945. (MNHM)

2nd Regiment infantryman take up positions around Diekirch. (MNHM)

This was taken inside the Ruhr Pocket in April 1945. From left, Captain Churkland, commanding George Company, Bennet Hove, Red Cross Representative to the 2nd Regiment, and me. Notice the Red Diamond of the 5th Division on the front of the captain's helmet. I'm wearing one of the famed Eisenhower jackets.

President Harry Truman (center above) along with Major General Albert E. Brown, who commanded the 5th Division in 1945, reviewing the troops' gala "welcome home" parade down Michigan Avenue in Chicago. Unfortunately, many of the 5th's combat veterans were unavailable at the time the parade took place. (Both photos: SFD)

Another parade celebrating our victory in World War II, this time in Washington, DC. (SFD)

This photo was taken in Luxembourg City in January 1945 during the Battle of the Bulge. I was sent there (officially!) on a booze run.

Clowning around with my captured German booty back home in Chicago around the start of December 1945. We spent the entire afternoon giving everyone in the neighborhood a chance to be photographed in this get-up.

Most of the photos in this section are from the authors' collection. For the remainder, originating with the US Signal Corps and U.S. Army, we are grateful for the collections and courtesy of:
SFD: The Society of the Fifth Division; and
MNHM: National Museum of Military History in Diekirch, Luxembourg

bombing. The Germans had been planning long before D-Day to bring up men and equipment by rail to repel the invading allied armies. Our planes had made certain that the rails were in no condition for the Germans to use them, but unfortunately, after we took them, neither could we. Our replacements of men and materiel had to be brought up by way of the famed Red Ball Express, but the trucks could deliver only a fraction of what we needed. As a result, we had to halt our advance until we could be properly resupplied, a process that could take months.

I once saw a supply truck from the Red Ball Express that was zooming up the road run over and detonate a German land mine. It blew the front wheel and fender off the driver's side of the truck. Racial prejudice at the time deemed the black soldiers who drove these trucks to be unreliable for combat duty, and therefore they had not been properly trained for contact with the enemy. A soldier is only as good as his leadership and training, and if his leaders expect less of him, it's all but impossible for him not to disappoint. The driver jumped from the truck cab and started to run back in the direction he came. I yelled out, "Hey, get back here and stay with your truck," but he just kept running down the road.

I'm amazed at how the history books and movies about Patton and World War II always detail with awe his fantastic dash across France in August 1944. In one month, he had all but liberated the country. Related books and movies then skip ahead to December and the relief of Bastogne during the Battle of the Bulge. Rarely do any of them mention the long autumn of that year and the terrible bloody mess that was Metz.

On September 3 we learned for ourselves what Patton had already known for days. We were out of gas. We were just east of Verdun in Eix, France. We were ordered to maintain outposts but got a chance to shower and see a movie. The weapons, including the heavy stuff, were all being test-fired, so we knew this respite wouldn't last long. The plan was to issue what remained of the gasoline to the tanks in the 7th Armored Division, which would in turn provide us support as we moved forward on Metz. We were to cross the Moselle River and assault the fortress city. Zero Hour was set for 08:00 hours on September 7. We had no idea of what was right before us. It would be the worst combat I ever saw during the entire war.

The biggest motivating factor for Patton in this battle was that Metz was a prize he simply could not resist. Here we were, tired, our units under strength, our lines overextended, and short of just about everything we needed. On top of this we were going to make a direct assault on a city ringed with forts, when we had no training whatsoever in attacking fortifications! All military commanders knew, then as now, that attacking fortifications is a highly specialized procedure in the very deadly art of war.

Military strategy and Patton's own superiors encouraged him to sit tight and wait it out. Flank the city and encircle it maybe, but if nothing else, be certain to bypass its strongholds. Unfortunately for us, this was not Patton's way. In Eisenhower's own words, Patton continued to attack so long as he had a battalion standing. Metz had not been conquered by assault since the year 451 A.D, but Patton intended to take this historic stronghold, even if it cost him every man he had. His inability to sit still and his unquenchable thirst for glory cost us dearly.

In *Patton at Bay*, John Nelson Rickard describes Metz as the most heavily fortified city in Europe. Metz had 43 forts that formed two defensive rings around the city, 15 forts in the outer ring, and 28 in the inner. While a number of these forts were not even garrisoned and others had only a few large guns in operation, the Germans had more than enough men and firepower to stop us cold and hurt us badly.

The key to taking Metz by direct assault was thought to lie in the area just southwest of the city. That key was Fort Driant, a name that even 60 years later makes me shudder. Heavily protected by its defenders, Fort Driant sat on high ground surrounded by moats 20 yards wide and 30 feet deep. There were countless mine fields covered with layers upon layers of barbed wire, and well concealed machine nests providing interlocking fire. The elevations up to Fort Driant were "steps" roughly ten feet wide and ten feet high. The Germans had machine guns locked in place so they would always fire directly at the edge of a step, which prevented any attacker from being able to scale over the top of one step up onto the next.

Even if it were possible for an infantryman to make it through all this, the concrete composing Fort Driant's walls was seven feet thick and all the entrances were covered with a 20-foot depth of barbed wire. A number of the forts had either 150mm or 105mm guns, and Fort St. Quentin had two 210mm guns that could rotate and rise in concrete turrets impervious to air and artillery attack. The forts could protect one another by bringing down artillery fire from one fort onto another with the assurance that the fort would be unharmed, but any attacking soldiers outside of its walls would be annihilated.

I saw P-47s drop 500-pound armor-piercing bombs directly on these forts, only to have them bounce off harmlessly. It was like trying to take down the Eiffel Tower with a screwdriver. Anthony Kemp has described Fort Driant as the most heavily fortified position that the United States Army tried to take in all of World War II. Anybody who fought there would not doubt the accuracy of his assertion.

Fort Driant had tunnels and an underground rail system, much like the small trains in amusement parks, which ferried men and ammunition wherever they were needed. It was just south of a string of smaller forts in the outer ring we called "the Seven Dwarfs." To take Fort Driant was to take Metz, to take Metz was to take Lorraine, and to take Lorraine was to secure the liberation of France and provide Patton with his jumping-off point into Germany. The Germans knew this all too well. For this reason they lined up everything possible to hold onto Metz and Fort Driant, and were determined to fight to the last.

I know that hindsight is 20-20, but the logic in avoiding a direct assault on Fort Driant was so obvious that even a blind man could see it. Colonel Charles Yuill, commander of the 11th Regiment, must have been deaf in addition to blind, because he persuaded General Walton Walker, Commander of XX Corps, that a single regiment (his) could successfully take the fortress. This was beyond the reasonable expectations of any single regiment in the U.S. Army at the time. It was simply impossible and everyone down to the lowest grunt knew it. Still, Walker took the plan to Patton, who loved it and in turn took the plan to Eisenhower, who approved it. This all took place despite the strong reservations of General Irwin, our divisional commander.

The plan was given the green light and we got the order to make ourselves ready. The weather was no more sensible or accommodating than any other part of that campaign; right from the first day of the attack, even it was against us. Lorraine had seven inches of rainfall that autumn instead of its customary two and a half inches. This made conditions far more miserable than usual on the battlefield during the entire three months of the campaign. The rain ponchos the army issued us did nothing to keep out the water. We always found ourselves soaked to the skin whenever we removed them. Being wet and cold outdoors is a miserable experience, and we lived in rain, mud and cold at Metz.

At 08:30 hours on September 7, the 11th Regiment headed off to cross the Moselle at Dornot and caught holy hell from the 17th SS Panzergrenadier Division. We were sent out towards the tiny Village of Verneville, a German outpost northwest of Metz, in what was essentially a frontal probe against Driant and its adjacent forts. Military strategy dictates that when attacking a fixed position, the attackers should have a three-to-one numerical superiority. In this case it was the defenders who had not only the advantage of a very secure position, but a three-to-one superiority in numbers.

Fort Driant and the city of Metz were being held by a hodgepodge but very capable mixture of German troops. The German 462 Volksgranedier Division was hastily put together to defend Metz and the areas southwest of the city. It consisted of recruits from the Non-Commissioned Officer's (NCO) School, the Officer's Candidate School (OCS), the 1010 Security Regiment, and other various outfits. These men were well trained and fought as fanatically as any SS outfit we encountered. The goofy bastards even yelled out "Heil Hitler" during their counter attacks.

Unaware of our numeric inferiority, we moved on Verneville. From the response we got, you would have thought we had just invaded hell. The Germans brought down a curtain of fire and steel like nothing I'd ever seen before; a torrent of machine guns, small arms, sniper fire, mortars, and even artillery rained down on us. I saw the bodies of our boys flying into the air from explosions, while others were cut down in a hail of machine gun fire. I saw one poor soul who had his jaw and the entire bottom of his mouth shot clean off. I now had an idea of what the poor bastards who had stormed the beaches on D-Day had gone through.

We advanced slowly at first, and only by small distances, staying very close to the ground. The temptation to just lay low and stay put in a safe spot during an advance this deadly is very strong, but aside from officers and NCOs screaming for you to go forward, you realize that you have to do your duty, especially since the other guys moving up are depending on your support. You simply have to take your chances and keep going.

We probably cursed our commanders for getting us into a mess like this, but no matter how terrified we were, no man wanted to let his buddies down. Everyone knew what was at stake and could see what was happening, and the mere thought of being labeled a coward made every man aware that there was truly a fate worse than death.

The artillery fire our gunners returned was equal to or superior to what the Germans put out. That was a real plus, and we needed it desperately. Trying to displace the Germans from Verneville was extremely difficult. They hung on and fought ferociously, but we fought with even more determination than they did, and by 19:00 hours we amazed even ourselves when we took the village. We secured our position and established a line about 300 yards east of the village itself.

Patrols were going out and everything seemed in good order until around 03:00 hours on September 8, when the Germans succeeding in infiltrating our lines and hitting us from the rear. It was similar to our first full-scale assault back in Vidouville during the Normandy Campaign. Our initial reaction was shock and confusion because the Germans caught us by surprise. They even hit us with shells containing white phosphorus, which continues to burn its way under the skin until dug out with a knife or some other object.

Our artillery opened up on what we knew to be the last German position, but they had to be careful because our lines were no longer distinct, and they didn't want to kill us with friendly fire. We fought through the night and all into the next day to reestablish our position and clear some of the nearby woods of enemy troops. The Germans were so numerous that everywhere we looked one of them popped up and started shooting. We could clearly see that we were outnumbered.

During an assault in the open area before the woods, one of our officers was killed in action with more than a little assistance from one of our own men. This was the arrogant officer with the swagger stick who was so disliked, primarily because of the harsh training tactics he had used in Northern Ireland. Even his fellow officers had warned him when he was given a frontline assignment that he all but had a target on his back.

This officer was hit, presumably by enemy fire, and lying on his back out in the open in no man's land. He had been shot in the arm, but even from a distance it was clear from his blood-drenched uniform that he had been hit in an artery. I saw a German medic race up to the officer and kneel next to him with the intention of treating his wound. The officer made a motion to reach for his sidearm, clearly signaling for the German to leave him alone. The German obliged, but returned a short time later. This time the officer drew his .45 sidearm and waved the German off. The German medic shrugged as if to say, "If you insist on dying, I can't stop you."

At this point one of our medics said, "I'm going out there." An NCO responded with, "You do, and you'll be lying next to him." Our medic stayed put, and when we retook the ground four hours later the officer had bled to death. I don't whether or not that NCO actually shot this officer, or merely capitalized on the situation, but either way he got the result he wanted.

There is an old adage, a warning perhaps, that the wheels of justice grind slowly but they grind exceedingly fine. I know for a fact that this same NCO was killed in action a couple of weeks later by a German grenade. Like the vast majority of soldiers I served with, I restricted my killing to enemy soldiers, and even then it was only in combat and when I had no other alternative. I never knew when and if circumstances might suddenly and quite unexpectedly require me to be standing before God. For all my faults, there were certain lines I just didn't cross. Cold-blooded killing was one of them.

We were only two days into the Battle of Metz and already it was Normandy all over again. Our progress was slow and the dead mounted in ever-increasing numbers. This was nothing like August, when the Germans usually retreated so quickly that we had to race just to catch up to them.

On September 9 we were to advance with armored support after our artillery laid down a 15-minute barrage. Just before 13:00 hours, we finally caught up to the 1st Battalion of our regiment. They jumped off towards the town of Amanville, and ten minutes later the Germans opened up on them with artillery. The enemy came up on their right flank screaming and firing.

The 1st Battalion bravely fought off the attack, but the Germans regrouped and came at them again. The battalion started to fall back, and for a moment looked like it might even be overrun. Our 2d Battalion was ordered into the fight to assist, and together we repelled the second German counter attack. I remember thinking then about the Germans, "What the hell keeps them coming? Why aren't they running away?" That night we had to fall back quietly under the cover of darkness.

The 2d Regiment had racked up 14 officers and 332 enlisted personnel as casualties after just two days fighting. Our regimental commander, Colonel Roffe, argued against further attacks using infantry against forts. He wanted air support, which he got, but only in conjunction with another assault by the infantry.

At 09:00 hours on September 10, we moved out to secure the crossroads a little more than a mile east of Verneville. We were harassed by small arms fire for much of the way and also later while we organized along the crossroads. The Germans held a sunken road that would have been too costly for us to assault without armored support, so we had to hunker down and dig ourselves in for the night.

The German line immediately in front of us was spread thin, but it was very deceptive in its apparent innocence. The Germans had camouflaged their machine gun nests and pillboxes so that they appeared to be harmless haystacks or straw mounds. Intelligence had reported to our command that the Germans had outposts in front of us that were spotting for artillery, and therefore we had to take the area. Our artillery took out a number of the machine gun nests and wooden pillboxes, but some of these positions were concrete and still very much in operation.

By this time, the battle plan for quickly securing Metz was deteriorating. The 11th Regiment had taken horrific casualties along the Moselle River, our 2d Regiment had advanced nowhere near what they had planned, and the 10th Regiment was making some progress, but still in a slugfest trying to advance on Arnaville. The 10th Regiment's bridgehead was screened by an oil-fog smoke that the 84th Smoke Generator Company produced for them. This was the first use of such smoke by the American army in all of northwestern Europe. Unfortunately, it hampered the engineers building the bridge across the Moselle and had to be turned off.

With support from the XIX Tactical Air Command (TAC), the area in front of us, Amanvillers, and the adjacent high ground (Hill 339) were bombed from the air by P-47 Thunderbolt fighter bombers dropping 500-pound armor-piercing bombs. Our objective was also hit with artillery fire to soften up the way for the 1st and 2d Battalions. The 7th Armored moved in to attack the village from the south, and we moved on the high ground near Verneville.

It was an extremely bitter battle of wills, with each side determined to emerge victorious. The fire on both sides was so loud and intense that I can remember turning to men next to me and being completely unable to hear anything they said or even hear my own words. The Germans were close enough that the fighting in some instances was hand-to-hand. The dead on both sides were everywhere, but by 21:00 hours our 2d Battalion was king of the mountain.

I had completed a cozy foxhole, and was settled in and dozing when the Germans counter attacked us around 04:00hours. They had terrific fire support, including 20mm guns. They hit us so hard that their bullets almost seemed to be coming up from the ground below us. They drove us off the high ground all the way back to our starting point of the previous day. We left in such a hurry that our withdrawal could be considered more running than retreating.

We counter attacked some two and a half hours later, and by 08:00 hours we had fought our way back to the bottom of the hill. It was foggy and our officers thought it wise to wait for the fog to burn off before sending us up the hill. Patton now showed up and wanted to know what was causing the delay. "Keep moving and don't worry about casualties," he barked at our officers. "I'll get you all the replacements you need. Just take that hill." The cold-hearted bastard actually said this in front of all of us!

We moved up the hill by inches, losing many good men along the way. I saw one of our officers on one knee holding the lower portion of his right arm. When I got close enough, I saw it was Lieutenant Capparrelli, the same man who had tried to have me court-martialed a month earlier for ignoring his order to take out a machine gun. His right hand was gone and tears were running down his cheeks.

I knew as an infantryman it was my job to keep moving and leave the wounded for the medics, but I could see he was in shock and needed help. I put a tourniquet on his arm and sprinkled sulfa powder on the wound before bandaging it as best I could. I covered him with his blanket to keep him warm and prevent shock. I told him to take his sulfa pills and to head back down the hill. I wished him luck, but he never said a word. He must have been too stunned about losing his hand. I continued to move up and never saw him again. We fought for eight hours and secured the hill at around 17:00 hours. It had been a bloodbath.

If this wasn't enough, the Germans counter attacked yet again. Our flanks below us fell back somewhat, but we continued to hold onto the hill. It was a worthless piece of earth, but holding it suddenly meant everything. We all seemed to feel pretty much the same way: we had paid dearly for it, and were not going to give it up again. We picked our targets carefully as we had been trained to do. We didn't know then whether or not we had been cut off or whether we would be able to get more ammunition.

We held on against the counter attack, but the Germans still refused to quit. They counter attacked again some five hours later in the dark of night, but this time our artillery opened up on them and broke up their assault. This was total war. We had never seen anything like this even in Normandy.

We got a day to catch our breath and reorganize, but on September 12 we were ordered to clear out La Chamoise Woods. I can't swear to it, but I believe it was here that Sergeant Joe Russo was killed. Russo was a good man and knew his business. We were moving up when I saw him sitting against a tree with his eyes closed. I thought he was sleeping and said to him, "Come on you Daigo, this is a hell of a time to take a nap." I nudged him and he slumped forward. He must have caught a machine gun burst, because his back looked like an axe had hit it.

At 17:00 hours the same day we were ordered to take Montigny, but the German artillery and machine gun fire were so intense that our offensive went nowhere. W e didn't fare any better the next day. The Germans had the position well zeroed in and made the most of it. We restricted the movements in our lines to night, but the Germans wouldn't give us any peace. They hit us continually with artillery during the night of September 14 to 15. We stayed hunkered down in our foxholes.

Foxhole living is miserable. Aside from the fact that you are literally balled up in a mud hole, it's sometimes far too dangerous to stick your head, much less your ass, up out of it. I once had a bowel movement that refused to wait, so I removed the liner from my helmet and used it as a toilet. It's none too easy or comfortable to sit on, and I flung the contents up and out of my foxhole as quickly as I could.

In order to bind my bowels up and fill my stomach on our meager rations, I took hard tack and spread melted cheese over it. I then sprinkled bullion powder on the melted cheese and ate the whole mess. It was hardly tasty, but it served the purpose. Many of us carried small German heaters (Esbit stoves) we'd taken from POWs, which operated very effectively. All you had to do was simply drop a small capsule into them.

Another problem with foxholes was water. We took the lining out of our helmets and used them as buckets to bail the water out. I sometimes forgot to put the lining and helmet back together. Once we were moving out and all I had on my head was the damn liner to the helmet. Somebody said to me, "Mike, what happened to your helmet? Did somebody shoot it off, or what?" I felt the top of my head and knew immediately I had left my helmet back in my foxhole. Much to my chagrin, I had to run back and get it accompanied by a chorus of laughter from the guys.

As I mentioned earlier, I was a survivor. As such, I was often assigned to look out as best I could for new recruits. The high casualty rates at Metz meant we were getting younger and younger replacements. These kids were often 18 or 19 years old and had been pulled from places like Air Corps schools, where they had been training for the non-pilot duties on bombers such as radio, navigation, and tail gunner positions. Suddenly, they were told that they were going to become riflemen in infantry companies.

By September 17 we had been on the frontline for ten days. Our 2d Battalion was put into reserve at Buxières, some five miles west of the Moselle River, to train the new recruits coming in as replacements.

I saw trucks of these kids arriving in the woods at assembly areas in our rear. I heard them say in an almost pleading voice things like, "But I've never even fired a rifle before." They were issued the weapon all the same and told, "Don't worry, you'll learn." All most of them learned was how to die.

These kids tended to view me like baby chicks view their mother. When we were moving up or out on patrol, they tended to bunch up around me. "Spread out, don't get so close, you're gonna draw fire," I'd have to say. Despite my best attempts, these young boys seldom lasted long. We saw their dead bodies carried away in mattress covers a day or two after their arrival.

There were so many dead that they were piled into trucks like debris. Two soldiers, each one holding an end of a mattress cover, would swing the body inside back and forth and then fling it up into a truck. I used to think if only the mothers of these poor boys could see how their sons were being treated what hell there would be to pay.

I did what I could for these kids. In fact, what was probably my most unselfish action in the war took place looking after these boys. We were hunkered down in our foxholes during a barrage, undoubtedly praying, as incoming German artillery was falling all around us. I had lived through this type of thing before, so I knew enough to time the intervals of the barrage and count the number of guns. The enemy rounds came in followed by a period of about 20 to 30 seconds of quiet. The German pause only meant they were reloading, but during the lull, some soldiers, especially green kids with no experience, often got up to run to what they thought was a safer area. This was very dangerous. The pause in shelling would cause a false sense of security similar to what a person experiences when they're in the eye of a hurricane. When the enemy resumed their shelling, those men out in the open were the most vulnerable. Thirty seconds was nowhere near enough time to get out from underneath a barrage.

I observed these kids in their foxholes and saw that they were getting panicky. I could tell they intended to make a break for it down the hill, and might not even wait for the shelling to stop. I knew that they would be cut to pieces if they tried it, so I crawled from foxhole to foxhole during and between barrages to tell them to stay put and wait it out.

This action may have contributed to the award of my first of two Bronze Star Medals. The cause for the uncertainty is that my 1945 citation listed the reason for my award as "Distinctive Service," with no mention of any specific action. The cluster (additional award) to my Bronze Star Medal was the result of an executive order signed by President Kennedy in 1962, which authorized awarding the Bronze Star Medal for "Meritorious Achievement" to those who earned either the Combat Infantry Badge or the Combat Medical Badge. The order was retroactive to 1941.

If my action during the barrage was the reason for the medal, it was, oddly enough, observed by the same officer who had it in for me since Iceland. He probably didn't know it was me, and simply told his aide to see to it that that soldier (me) got a medal. I didn't care about any medals, but I did manage to keep those kids in their foxholes and alive for the moment.

During the fighting at Metz I ran into a kid from my old neighborhood. I was going to headquarters when I saw this runt of a GI sitting down on some steps. He had his Garand rifle between his knees and it looked like he was holding a cannon. "You're Johnny Davis," I said. "What are you doing here?" I stupidly asked. He told me how he had been drafted and had even seen action. He had been nicked in the nose by a piece of shrapnel.

I didn't know it, but he was now gun shy. This is when a soldier wounded in combat loses his nerve to return to the front. He will even accept a court martial rather than go back to combat. This is exactly what Johnny did. He refused a direct order to go out on patrol and was placed under arrest and put on trial for his life. He was found guilty and sentenced to death. This little guy had no business being in the army in the first place. I sometimes felt we were almost as bad as the enemy when it came to filling uniforms with bodies.

I knew that one of the priests back at Saint Cecilia's had a lot of political pull, and in a political town like Chicago that means a lot. My commanding officer agreed to personally censor my letter so I could write my mother without fear of the details being cut out. I still had to avoid all mention of where we were, but at least I got all the other details of the incident to her, which would have been impossible going through the normal channels where letters were censored.

My mother got hold of the priest, who in turn got hold of the politicians, who in turn got hold of the appropriate military people. Johnny's sentence was reduced to life, which in actuality turned out to be a couple of years served in a labor battalion in England. I ran into him after the war and he thanked me for what I did. I was just glad he was alive.

Inexperienced youth weren't the only soldiers we had who didn't belong at Metz. We had a 35-year-old florist from Brooklyn who was married with five children. This poor guy had no comprehension whatsoever about diplomacy. He was in serious need of what's now called anger management. Everything with him was an argument.

They tried to give him every rear echelon job there was in an effort to keep him out of the frontlines. He prepared food, cooked food, and served food, but was always required to shift jobs because of his constant arguing, until finally there were no more jobs in the rear to give him. I figured he should have beaten the draft as a married man with five kids, but he probably argued with his draft board as well. A 35-year-old man moves too slowly for serious combat, and when he finally argued himself into the frontlines, he didn't last long. There was a big stink about his death and I'm sure some officer had some real explaining to do.

While we were in reserve, the 1st and 3rd Battalions of the 2d Regiment were engaged in some nasty fighting. Fate had spared me yet again. Even so, I had been getting pretty difficult to be around when they pulled us off the line, and my superiors knew it. My attitude was as sour as my body odor. Aacho called me in to tell me this personally, but also informed me that I was being given a four-day leave to go to Paris and fix myself up.

I grabbed a carton of the best cigarettes I could and got on board a two-and-a-half-ton truck bound for Paris. Before I left, Al Carslake asked me if I'd swap boots with him. His were water logged from the mud. I could probably obtain a replacement pair in Paris a lot easier than he could near Metz, so we swapped boots.

Boots were a funny thing in the army. They came to us on the frontlines via supply trucks. When they arrived we lined up as soon as we could to turn our old boots in for new ones. The main problem was that a single truck would be filled with boots all the same size and there might only be one or possibly two trucks loaded with boots. This meant that the entire company, roughly 150 men, might all be swapping and struggling to fit into boots of a single size. When we marched, you could always tell whose boots didn't fit by the man's step. Some poor guys had their feet swimming inside oversized boots, while other guys were in agony from jamming their feet into boots that were too small.

While in Paris, I did many things, but resting wasn't among them. During the day, I went sightseeing like a civilian tourist and saw things like the Eiffel Tower, Notre Dame Cathedral, and Napoleon's Tomb. At night, I went to cabarets, drank myself silly, and enjoyed the intimate company of beautiful French women.

I remember one cabaret where women, wearing nothing more than high-heeled shoes, walked out on stage to be critiqued by the men. Middle-aged Frenchmen all around me casually made comments like, "Her calves are too muscular," or "Her breasts are too small," and so on. I had never seen anything like it and it was incredible to watch. Nevertheless, it was hard to enjoy myself all that much in Paris. The entire time I knew that I had to go back to the hell that was waiting for me at Metz. When I returned to my outfit, Aacho told me that I looked worse than I had before I left, but at least my attitude was somewhat improved.

We were ordered back to the front on September 24 to a place called Vittonville. Both sides were running low on men. The Germans were cannibalizing their specialized units for men and we were pulling kids out of the Air Corps for our rifle companies. We had just left the road and gone into the woods to be briefed on our new situation, when suddenly the area over our heads ignited from an enemy barrage of tree bursts. Somebody yelled out, "Hit the dirt," and we were diving for cover when I saw Al Carslake grab his stomach and double over.

There was nothing I or anyone else could do but hug the ground or the nearest tree and pray to be spared from the hot steel raining down. Our artillery got the enemy's range fairly quickly, and after they fired a counter barrage things got quiet again. Standard operating procedure in such a situation still required that we stay put until our officers gave us permission to move out from under cover.

The lieutenant called out to me, "Bilder, Carslake's been hit. Get him up to the road!" I was off like a shot headed towards Al. I grabbed him quickly and tossed him over my shoulder in a classic fireman's carry. I ran as fast as I could go, hoping that I wasn't causing him too much pain because his stomach was resting against my shoulder, but there was no alternative. I had to get him to a medic as quickly as possible. He had been hit in the gut and every second counted.

We cleared the woods and I raced up along the roadside towards a medic. "It's all right Al, we made it," I told him. I carefully laid him out along the road so the medic could treat him. My immediate attention faded a moment as I caught my breath, but the medic snapped me back to reality when he said, "You wasted your time fella, he's dead." My head jerked a little. "No," I said. "He can't be." The medic stepped back and said, "See for yourself." I looked down at Al and saw all the familiar signs in his face: that whitish gray color, the frozen expression, and an appearance that looked more mannequin than human.

Al's blood had soaked my backpack and the upper part of my fatigues. My hands were covered with it. I must have experienced some degree of shock because I acted without thought. I wiped my hands on Al's fatigues and then on the grass. I took the clean pack off him and removed the bloodstained pack from my own back. I emptied the contents from both packs out onto the ground. I put all my things into Al's clean pack and in turn put his items into my bloody pack. I then carefully placed my old pack, filled with his belongings, on top of his lifeless body and put his pack, now filled with my own stuff, up on my back.

Al was a sergeant, although command hadn't cost him his life. It just seemed that stripes and bars were cursed. I took one more look at one of my closest friends and started back to rejoin the company.

That September, I lost two of my best buddies within weeks of each other. Whenever I had friends killed, I immediately did everything I could to block them out of my mind. I knew, and immediately resolved to accept the fact, that I would never see them again. It was a protection against insanity. I did, however, make up my mind after Carslake's death that I would not allow anyone new to get close enough to me to become a buddy until after the war was over.

Despite all the madness going on around us, on September 27 we got a visit from none other than Bing Crosby. We were assembled in an abandoned factory a little over two miles from the German lines and ready for a good show. The only problem was that the show we ended up with was courtesy of the Germans, not Crosby. He had finished his first and, as it turned out, only song, when the enemy started to shell and probe our lines.

About 600 of us were bunched together in a factory, which would mean huge casualties if any enemy shells fell on our position. We were immediately ordered out and everybody started exiting in good military order. As fate would have it, Crosby was sitting calmly on the back of a three-quarter-ton truck barely moving along in a sea of green uniforms, as soldiers moved out as best they could on foot in these cramped quarters. I looked over and there was Crosby right next to me. He wasn't wearing his hairpiece, and I was shocked to see that the top of his head was bald. "Hey Bing, could you give me an autograph?" I asked. "Well sure, soldier," he said.

I quickly frisked myself but had no paper, so I handed him a wallet-sized portrait shot of Mary and asked him to autograph the back. He looked at Mary's picture. "It looks like you have a fine girl there, soldier," he said as he signed his name on the back of the photo. He also said something like, "I hope you get back home to her safely." In any event, I thanked him and continued to march out of there with everyone else. That night, many fine men in the 11th Regiment died in another one of the countless and fruitless assaults on Front Driant. It was a bad day for everybody, but at least I finished it alive.

Before the end of September, yet one more of the many fine men I knew was killed. The Germans attacked us when we were holding a position on a small hill. Carl Sajec, our company barber and the little guy who gave me such a peppering in the ring back in Iceland, was manning a .50-caliber machine gun. We knew we couldn't hold our position and would have to retreat under fire.

Sajec was hit in both legs and couldn't move. The Germans were coming up fast and there was no way for us to take him along. In one of the most courageous acts I have ever witnessed, he told us to get going and that he would hold off the enemy for as long as possible. There was nothing else to do, so we scurried off the hill and left Carl

Sajec there to cover our retreat. We could hear his machine gun blazing away. Finally, things up there went quiet and the Germans took the hill.

We all knew what happened to Carl. I can personally attest that he deserves one hell of a high decoration, although it would have to be awarded posthumously. "Bloody September" at Metz claimed 94 KIAs from the 2d Regiment, and we still weren't any closer to taking the city or any or its forts.

A new assault against Fort Driant kicked off on October 3 and lasted for ten days. Fighting went on above the fort and below it in its tunnels. Our engineers even prepared a special type of bangalore torpedo called a "snake," which was supposed to do a phenomenal job of destroying all the barbed wire around the forts. It was a joke. Whenever the Germans saw any bangalores sliding towards their lines they simply fired a shot into them, and the land torpedoes exploded well short of their intended target.

One night I was sent out around 01:00 hours as part of a team escorting combat engineers. Their objective was to plant high explosive charges in the walls of Driant, so they could blow a hole large enough for the infantry to swarm through. I had to go ahead with other members of the team to neutralize the outposts of the sentries guarding the entranceways to one area of the fort. This involved sneaking up on the sentries from their rear. As the attackers, we used our left hand to grab the enemy sentry under the chin to keep him from crying out, and pulled his head back to expose his throat. Simultaneously, we placed our right knee in his back to pull him off balance, then ran the knife blade across his throat. When you perform an action like this you know there has to be a God in heaven, because there is certainly a devil in hell.

We got inside the fort but the tunnels underneath had water in them some six inches deep. No matter how careful we were and how slowly we moved, we couldn't help but make sloshing sounds. The tunnels were only about three feet wide and very dimly lit with blue lights. It was very eerie and claustrophobic. Between our noise and the fact, unknown to us then, that the sentries we had neutralized were supposed to report in every few minutes, the Germans were now on to us. They started to fire without even seeing us.

The cement tunnels had rounded corners. All the Germans had to do was to shoot at the corners and their bullets rode along the curve and came out on the other side, ricocheting in every direction. Water or no water, we threw ourselves down and immediately began to think of getting the hell out of there. We returned some fire at the Germans in the same way they were firing against us, but we knew it was totally ineffective. The engineers scrambled to place their charges while the NCO commanding our group ordered everybody out.

We were moving on all fours almost as quickly as if we were running. Men were crawling over one another like lobsters in a restaurant tank. We reached the outside safely and ran full speed away from the fort and back to our lines. The moon was fairly bright and lit up most of the area. We didn't know it then, but the Germans inside the fort had radioed ahead to a tank (a Panther as I recall) that they had waiting for just such an eventuality.

We got a few hundred yards away from Driant and thought we were in the clear, when all of a sudden that tank opened up on us. The first shots fired hit a friend of mine, Bill Neilson from Idaho, in the head. We heard the clunk as the shots hit his helmet and knocked it off. We knew he was most likely killed. In any event, it was a job for the medics, and our NCOs ordered us to keep moving. There were no explosions from the fort and no hole in the wall, so the Germans had obviously found and disarmed the charges the engineers had placed before they could be detonated. The entire operation was a screw-up from beginning to end and we were lucky to make it out of there alive.

Patton was furious that Driant could not be taken, especially since he had hoped to present it as a prize to the Army Chief of Staff, General George C. Marshall, when he visited on October 7. Indeed, the big brass wanted Patton to account for the high casualties and minimal gains. By 13 October, the casualties had risen so high that all infantry assaults against the fort were ordered halted and our guys were pulled out of there.

Around this time, I had messages to deliver for the Red Cross to some men in Able Company, which meant spending several days assigned to their unit. All of us at Metz were severely hampered by the mud that the horrific rains created. It was so thick and consuming that it would literally pull the boots off a soldier's feet.

I was heading back on foot to a perimeter position when all of a sudden, two German self-propelled guns appeared on a hill directly in front of me and started to fire. I think they were Hummels, which had bigger howitzers than the Wespes. The noise from their cannons was deafening and it seemed as if they were aiming directly at me. I was caught out in the open with no cover of any kind whatsoever. I had no choice but to spread my arms wide and throw myself face down in the mud. I needn't have bothered. The Germans weren't shooting at me: they had observed many jeeps and trucks parked around a single house, and easily deduced it was the company command post. They scored a direct hit on it, causing all four walls and the roof to simply disintegrate. Our artillery opened up and started to zero in on the two German vehicles and they were quickly forced to withdraw.

I got up out of the slop and shook myself off as best I could. I saw that a big group of our boys were already frantically clearing away the rubble from what had been Able Company's CP. I immediately ran to join them. Fortunately, all of the company personnel had been in the basement, and although they were buried in rubble they were still alive. We all threw debris out of the way as quickly as we could. We then began to pull, and in some cases lift, men out the basement who were covered with sawdust, dirt and other assorted rubble.

I was helping some others lift out a soldier, when I noticed it was Joe Malloy. Malloy was the cousin of Frankie Boehm, a friend of mine from the old neighborhood, who was serving with the 28th Infantry Division. Malloy was quivering from head to toe. While he was relatively unhurt and made a quick recovery, the shock of the incident rattled him badly. Before he ended up developing combat fatigue, the army wisely gave him a permanent reassignment to the rear when the Battle of the Bulge broke out in December.

Despite the ferocity of the battle, the army set up areas in the rear for soldiers to cast absentee ballots in the presidential contest between Roosevelt and Dewey. I didn't bother to vote. I knew I wasn't voting for Roosevelt under any circumstances, but I couldn't yet bring myself to vote Republican either. That wouldn't come until I was a civilian again, living a comfortable suburban life.

On October 18 we were relieved by elements of the 95th Infantry Division, and two days later we were in the town of Morfontain, just south of the French border with Luxembourg. The famed Maginot Line, now utterly useless, ran through Morfontain, and it was here that we would spend the next ten days learning how to properly assault and take fortifications. The training was rigorous and conducted by experienced instructors and commandos. We did, however, get opportunities to shower, rest, and see a few movies.

We got back to the frontlines on October 31. Our ranks were filled up again with plenty of green recruits from the States who were all too soon to die in big numbers. We also found that the 95th Division had lost virtually all of the ground we had paid so heavily to take.

Finally, the big brass made the decision to do what they should have done in the beginning: bypass the forts, encircle Metz, and cut it off. XII Corps under Major General Manton S. Eddy would use the city of Nancy to come up around the rear of Metz. Our 5th Division would secure everything to the south, while the 90th and 95th Infantry Divisions would assault from the north to complete the circle.

The 90th Division jumped off out of Thionville, and it was no picnic. I was sent there once just as shells from a German rail gun were falling on the city. It was fortunate that I was nowhere near the points of impact, but I could hear those shells coming in long before they hit. They sounded like railroad boxcars falling from the sky.

In preparation for this big offensive, and to satisfy Patton's longing for revenge, the Air Corps units from the XIX Tactical Air Command were coming in to soften up the area. It was November 5, and once again our shells and bombs bounced off the concrete forts like rubber balls. It was nothing but a complete waste of ordinance. We learned from POWs that the Germans no longer had running water and were now down to bringing in militia and supplying Metz police with military arms. Fortunately, they sent the bulk of the civilian population out of the city, but many people chose to remain in their cellars hiding.

Our jump off started at 06:00 hours on November 9 when we crossed the Seille River in assault boats. The Germans fired rockets at us from their Nebelwerfers that we called "screaming meemies." By itself, the very sound of a screaming meemie was enough to make a soldier soil his pants. The Nebelwerfer (meaning "smoke thrower") consisted of five or six tubular barrels resting on a carriage that could be hauled by a half-track or mounted on its back. Its rockets were three feet long and weighed about 75 pounds each. They carried almost five and a half pounds of TNT, and were accurate for a little over four miles. They were very destructive and greatly feared.

Although the screaming meemies scared the hell out of us, luckily this time they didn't cause any casualties. Our Company G easily took the town of Cheminot, which was defended by a sole German soldier who greeted us with a white flag. Cheminot gave us the high ground over Louvigny, which we used to good advantage to provide cover fire with mortars and machine guns as the 1st Battalion took Louvigny. Once Louvigny fell early that night, our outfit continued to push east. At the end of the day, the 2d Regiment had secured all its objectives. We patrolled that night.

The weather the following day was rotten yet again. It was cold and wet as always. The 5th Division's three regiments were now aligned with our 2d Regiment on the right flank, the 10th in the center, and the 11th on the left. Our jump off time was set for 07:00 hours. The 2d Battalion's objective was the town of Vigny, which was relatively lightly defended. Our Company G was at the tip of the spearhead, and we were fortunate enough to have tank support. We secured the town by 13:00 hours, but our regiment's 1st and 3rd Battalions had a much harder time of it as a result of German artillery. Again, by day's end, all the regiment's objectives had been taken, along with some 700 German prisoners. It was now evident that the enemy was beginning to give up the ghost.

On November 11, Armistice Day, we had early morning services at Saint Mihiel Cemetery at Thiaucourt before pressing on to our next objective, Beux, which we took by noon. We then moved to high ground in preparation for crossing the Nied-Française River. We were ordered to sit tight on the west side of the river.

That night, a patrol from the 6th Armored Division found that the bridge over the river at Sanry-sur-Nied was intact, and our battalion crossed over before dawn on November 12. The Germans skirmished with us at Sanry, but it was clear now that we weren't going to be beaten. Still, the Germans weren't quitting just yet. We pushed further east on to Bazoncourt and then Vaucremont. We had both towns shortly after 15:00 hours. The problem was that the Germans continued to pound Sanry with heavy artillery as well as mortars and 20mm guns.

While we were moving north on November 13, the Germans used two companies to hit Sanry at around 14:00 hours. It was a counterattack the likes of which we had not seen since Verneville the previous September. These were SS troops from the 21st SS Panzergrenadier Division. They were veterans and they knew how to fight. They hit Sanry from the north and northeast simultaneously, but were driven off with heavy casualties by machine gun fire and artillery. Unfortunately, they gave as good as they got. Some of their elements had even taken some of our high ground, and had to be rooted out by one by one.

Despite all this, they came back to hit Sanry yet again. They came once more from the northeast around 19:00 hours when it was good and dark. Their mortars and artillery were awfully damn accurate and took out an anti-tank gun, a tank destroyer, and an ammo truck. They reached the outskirts of Sanry and started to enter the town proper.

Company E of our 2d Battalion had been holding Sanry, but had to fall back to an area just outside of town to establish a sound defensive position. They concentrated armor and machine gun fire on the Germans' newly acquired real estate. This then opened the door for our units to counter attack and push the Germans back to the opposite edge of town.

The battle reached its climax at around 22:30 hours. The Germans hit Sanry with every mortar they had and followed it up with a rapid infantry advance into town. Fighting in the streets was everywhere. The Germans also got fire support from Fort Sorbey, which was due west of Sanry. That night the fire from both sides was constant. Tracer bullets flew back and forth up and down the streets and lit up the place like the Fourth of July. It was literally impossible to stick your head out a door or window without losing it.

The Germans couldn't sustain their momentum, and by 02:30 hours on November 14 our side had secured the town. They nevertheless still made three lesser attempts to take Sanry or destroy its bridgehead, but all were driven back. We needed that bridgehead for the 6th Armored Division to cross the river. The Germans put up such a fierce fight against Sanry and its bridgehead because they needed to keep control of Fort Sorbey and Courcelles-Sur-Neid, a major loading area for evacuating their supplies from Metz. When I gleaned this fact from German prisoners, I knew that even the enemy realized that we had already won the battle. They were also down to using medics and service personnel to man defensive positions.

During the night of November 17 to 18, we were ordered south into reserve to an assembly area near Pontoy. Our respite didn't last long, because it was necessary to hit the enemy while he was vulnerable in retreat. At 09:00 hours on November 18, we were on the move. We jumped off against Mercy-la-Metz at 16:00 hours and went on to take the Groupe Fortifié de la Marne against light opposition. We held up in the woods just to the east of our objectives. The following day we took Lauvaliers and Fort Lauvaliers, thus completing the encirclement of Metz by American forces. All resistance in the city itself came to an end at 02:35 hours on November 22.

The 5th Division nevertheless still had almost three weeks of skirmishing ahead of it. We grappled with some 3,000 German die-hards holed up in Forts Driant, Jeanne D'Arc, Plappeville, and St. Quentin, until the last of them finally surrendered to us on December 8. The rest of Patton's forces had proceeded towards the West Wall and Germany without us. Patton had informed our divisional commander, General Irwin, on November 19 that he was not entirely pleased with the division's performance, and that it should be improved. This seemed to even things out a bit, as we in the 5th were a little less than thrilled with Patton's performance at Metz.

Patton all the same came out to commend the 5th Division and decorate some of its members on Thanksgiving Day. According to Anthony Kemp, that day Patton told the 5th Division: "I am very proud of you. Your country is proud of you. You are magnificent fighting men. Your deeds in the Battle of Metz will fill the pages of history for a thousand years."

He was a little off the mark. I don't want to lessen another unit's glory, but while the 5th Division did most of the fighting and dying at Metz, it was the 95th Infantry Division, the same outfit that relieved us in October and lost most of the hard-won ground we had taken, who were dubbed the "Iron Men of Metz." To this day, the 95th remains the only American outfit that fought at Metz to be honored with a statue erected by the city.

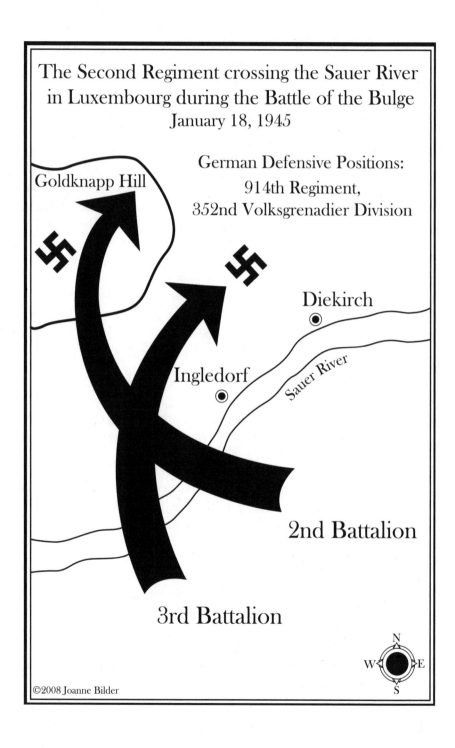

The Second Regiment crossing the Sauer River in Luxembourg during the Battle of the Bulge
January 18, 1945

German Defensive Positions:
914th Regiment,
352nd Volksgrenadier Division

Goldknapp Hill

Diekirch

Ingledorf

Sauer River

2nd Battalion

3rd Battalion

©2008 Joanne Bilder

9

THE FORGOTTEN 5TH IN THE BATTLE OF THE BULGE

Fighting and Freezing in Luxembourg

"Silent, and soft, and slow
Descends the snow."
—Henry Wadsworth Longfellow, "Snow-Flakes"

Throughout early December, we kept the German die-hards in the remaining four forts at Metz in check. Our cannon companies were gracious, and used the artillery pieces and ammo stockpiles captured from the Germans to return to the enemy the stock of shells they had previously used to bombard us. Battle damage to piping ensured that the Germans no longer had a source for water, and the fact that we had them surrounded kept them from getting additional supplies of any kind.

The German commanders in the forts ignored all broadcasts from army psychological warfare units and appeals to a sense of common decency to avoid any further and unnecessary loss of life. The German wounded, now without medicine of any kind, began to swell in number and seriously suffer inside the fortifications. It was this that finally forced their commanders to surrender. Fort St. Quentin surrendered on December 6 and Fort Plappeville followed suit the next day. Both forts surrendered to the 11th Regiment. Forts Driant and Jeanne D'Arc were still holding out, but it was nearly time for the 5th Division to move from the Metz area to join the drive against the West Wall and into Germany. The 10th Regiment had already moved east for just that purpose in late November and, with the 2d Regiment about to follow, it appeared the 5th Division was about to lose the honor of claiming the prize for which we had all sacrificed so much to win.

On the morning of December 8, the 2d Regiment was only 15 minutes away from being relieved of its duties to secure Fort Driant by the 87th Infantry Division when two German NCOs emerged from the fort to request a meeting to discuss surrender. Word went up the chain of command and General Walker, the commanding general of XX Corps, saw to it that our relief by the 87th would be delayed long enough for the 2d Regiment to claim the battle honor of Fort Driant's surrender for the 5th Division.

Word came down from 2d Battalion Headquarters that they needed me as an interpreter, and I was to get up there immediately. Most of our regiment had already been relieved by the 345th Regiment of the 87th Division. We only had headquarters people back in Metz. I had actually been on my way up to Kreutzwald on the Lorraine-German border when I got my orders to head back.

When I arrived at Battalion HQ, I saw the two German NCOs with their white flags. Major William Goethal said, "Bilder, we're going to follow these Germans up to the main entrance of Fort Driant. They're going to surrender the fort and I want you to act as my interpreter." Most of us didn't know it at the time, but we were loading up a captured German Tiger tank with ten tons of TNT, with the intent of sending it into the side of the fort's main casement if the Germans tried to hold out any longer.

We set out with some 20 MPs, all well armed, and some staff and administrative personnel. When we got to the fort we had to follow behind the Germans in single file formation to avoid their mines. They even told us to be certain to walk exactly in their footsteps, as we carefully followed their zigzag pattern to the entrance of the fort. They had already marked off most of the safe areas with white tape.

Once in the fort, I saw broken pieces from dismantled weapons everywhere strewn about, making them useless for our arsenals. The air was thick with a strange and awful combination of foul smells. There was no running water so there were no working toilets or showers, and the smell from human waste and body odor, combined with gunpowder, trench foot, and infected wounds, was enough to make the devil himself wretch. Train tracks for miniature rail cars to carry men, heavy shells, and other supplies ran throughout the fort. The German soldiers were standing without their helmets on. Some of them were crying.

We entered a vault-like room. There was one desk in the room with a single light on it. Lt. Colonel Wilhelm Richter, the commander of the fort, was sitting behind the desk and his interpreter was standing next to him. Major Goethal took one look at him and said, "Bilder, tell that kraut-head son of a bitch to stand up when I walk into a room. He doesn't sit—I do!"

My German was natural and without accent, but the English of Richter's interpreter was even better than my German. He asked me to allow him to inform his colonel of Major Goethal's words. Of course, he softened things a little, but he got the message across. Richter jumped to his feet, clicked his heels, saluted, and extended his hand, which Major Goethal refused. Richter then insisted that Major Goethal take his chair, which he did, and Goethal had me tell Richter that as long as he spoke, Richter was to stand. Both the German interpreter and I relayed this message.

Richter made it clear that he could and would have continued to fight if his wounded did not need medical attention so badly. Back on December 2, the Germans had requested permission to evacuate their wounded. Their request was denied. I did as Major Goethal instructed and asked Richter about other German outfits in the area and ahead of us, but he refused to answer any such questions. Richter did ask the Major what would happen to him and his men.

Major Goethal told Richter that he was not to move from the room. Military Police would collect him and his men and they would all be taken to prison camps. The wounded would receive medical attention. The MPs who accompanied us were posted to guard our new prisoners. There were 19 officers and 592 enlisted men. This was a far cry from the "100 old men" that we were told were defending the fort when we went up against it the previous September and October.

The same two German NCOs who escorted us into the fort also escorted us out. Colonel Richter would later go outside and meet Colonel Roffe to make an official, if not ceremonial, surrender to our regimental commander at 15:00 hours that same day. We pulled out of the area and the 87th Division got to take the surrender of Fort Jeanne D'Arc on December 13. It was the only one of the four remaining forts whose surrender was not claimed by the 5th Division.

We were assembled at Kreutzwald very near the German border on December 9 preparing for our coming assault against the Siegfried Line (West Wall), which was Germany's last line of defense. We got a refresher course in many of the things we had learned about attacking fortifications and fixed positions during the ten days we had spent at Morfontain the previous October.

Word came on December 12 from our old buddies in the 95th Division, the "Iron Men of Metz," that they could use our assistance in taking Saarlautern, the first step into Germany. The West Wall ran right through the town, and for obvious reasons, we had to hold the bridgehead at the Saar River. The Saar is one of the provinces in the Rhineland, an area so-named because it covers geography on both sides of the Rhine River. Contrary to what many people thought back then and still think now, part of Germany proper lies west of the Rhine.

To the surprise of the world, and most of all to the Allied commanders and foot soldiers in northwestern Europe, the Germans were making a major push to the north of us in the dead of winter. The Battle of the Bulge began on December 16. We had no idea at the time that the Germans had launched a major offensive, for we were still in the process of relieving elements of the 95th Division at Saarlautern on December 17. We spent four days fighting there before we were ordered north into the Bulge.

The Germans were dropping some two to three thousand shells a day on the American-held portion of Saarlautern. It really played hell on our nerves. We were battling for German soil and the enemy was not prepared to give it up without one hell of a fight. This was urban warfare: the Germans even went so far as to disguise their pillboxes as store fronts and their machine gun nests as coal piles!

We were forced to take the city house by house, a situation that allowed us to give little quarter. We had to do our fighting indoors because the Germans had placed machine guns and 20mms at their ends of virtually every street, laying down a deadly fire. Any American who appeared outside a building did so at great personal risk.

Our tankers were using the same rough tactics as their French counterparts had used back in Normandy. The houses were built one directly alongside another and shared common walls. Rather than going through doors and risk getting shot up, we used a technique known as mouse holing. A tank fired into the side wall of an end house, and the shell usually traveled through several walls. This created an opening through a number of houses and also often eliminated any enemy inside. We then advanced from house to house through these mouse holes. If no tanks were available, we made mouse holes with grenades.

We had been fighting this way for four days and nights, but the Germans were far from beaten. On the night of December 20 to 21, they launched two vicious counter attacks, both of which we beat back. We then were ordered north and west into Luxembourg to hit the southern flank of the German thrust towards the all-important port of Antwerp. The 5th Division was detached from General Walker's XX Corps on December 21 and assigned to General Eddy's XII Corps. This hasty rearrangement of XII Corps put us in with the 4th and 28th Infantry Divisions as well as the 9th and 10th Armored Divisions. Together, we had the responsibility of first blunting the German offensive, and then to regain the initiative and go over to the offensive to drive the enemy out of Luxembourg.

By 04:00 hours on December 22, the 95th Division had relieved us at Saarlautern, and we were headed for our rendezvous point in Metzervisse, France. The official records show that by the time we disengaged the enemy, we had already taken 232 buildings and five pillboxes. We rode in trucks, on tanks, in overcrowded jeeps, or anything else that would carry us. The journey was miserable and very slow going. The falling snow had reduced visibility to nearly zero. This was our last time on French soil during the war. As soon as we arrived in Metzervisse, we were ordered into Niederranven, Luxembourg. We were about to enter what is officially known as the Ardennes Offensive, which most people simply call the Battle of the Bulge. It was Hitler's last desperate gamble to try and win the war. To launch it, he had assembled the last of all of Germany's resources.

Hitler's plan was relatively simple. He wanted to repeat the success he had enjoyed in May 1940, when he had quickly routed French and British forces in Belgium. His forces had then come through the seemingly impenetrable Ardennes Forest to sweep through Belgium and Luxembourg and secure the areas to the rear of the advancing Allies, thus cutting them off from their ports and supply lines.

In 1944 Hitler attempted this same strategy again, sending his forces through the Ardennes along the same routes used in 1940 to push through a weak area in the Allied lines. His initial success created a "bulge" in the Allied lines on a map, hence creating the popular name of the battle. Hitler's objective was to cut the Allied armies off before they could enter Germany. Unlike 1940, however, sufficient Allied forces not only held out in Belgium, but there were more than enough men and supplies to the rear of the German assault to mount an Allied counter attack.

Put in simplest terms, the German forces moved from east to west, separating General Hodges' First Army from Patton's Third. Their counter-strategy was to have the Third Army hit the Germans from the south while the First Army attacked from the north. This would break the German line and render impossible any further enemy advance to the west. We infantry grunts of course had no knowledge of this at the time. We never knew the size of an operation, how many units might be involved, or the strategy behind it all. We simply went where we were told and fought for our objectives. Survivors learned the details long after the fact.

In this instance, it didn't take a West Point graduate to figure out that something big was up. When you were with Patton you didn't disengage the enemy at his own border, then travel 100 miles to fight him somewhere else without good reason. We knew that the Germans had made a big push somewhere and the situation was serious. The Germans were supposed to be beaten. Since they surprised our commanders with weapons and men that no one ever dreamed they could have, there were all kinds of nasty rumors flying around and we were all a little unnerved. We wondered what else might they be capable of doing.

Luxembourg had been liberated the previous September and now the northern half of the country was again under enemy control. Patton set up his headquarters in Luxembourg City, the capital, which was not far south of the German lines, as a clear statement that he was not about to let the enemy push any further in that direction.

Most histories of the Battle of the Bulge describe the German drive northeast through Belgium and mention the Germans' position on their southern flank as purely defensive. As a result, this area of the battle gets short shrift and commonly receives no more than a single line or paragraph of discussion in an entire book on the Bulge. The problem for those of us fighting in Luxembourg was that the Germans were totally unaware that this was the way they were supposed to be conducting themselves. Their actions on the southern flank of the Bulge were far from purely defensive. On the contrary: they were often very aggressive in their attempts to break through our lines and advance further south.

We, on the other hand, were tired. We had disengaged the enemy in the middle of a fight at Saarlautern, moved 100 miles through three countries in just 22 hours, and were now about to go into battle without any sleep, hot food, or relief of any kind in sight. To make matters worse, we were in the midst of the coldest winter Europe had experienced for a century, and we were going to spend it fighting in the snow and frigid temperatures.

On December 23 our 2d Regiment relieved the 12th Regiment of the 4th Infantry Division in a relatively open area near Berdorf. The 4th Division had been in the thick of things since they landed at Utah Beach on D-Day. They were in Luxembourg to recoup and lick their wounds after months of hard fighting. They were supposed to be getting the kind of respite we had received between Metz and Saarlautern, but instead they now were fighting in the Bulge.

We went into combat on Christmas Eve at roughly 11:00 hours, jumping off from a point a few hundred yards north of Breitweiler and Consdorf. Our 2d Battalion was on the left flank and the 3rd was on the right. The 1st Battalion was in reserve. We knew things were bad when it took a full eight hours for Company G and Company F just to advance a mere 200 yards! First there was Normandy, then Metz, and now this. When were these "beaten Germans" we kept fighting finally going to surrender as our commanders assured us they would?

By Christmas Day the fog had temporarily lifted and the skies were relatively clear. This meant that there was at least the possibility of air support. We soon were strafed by our own P-47 fighters, planes supposedly "captured" by Germans. You would have indeed thought they were manned by the enemy from all the damage they inflicted, but I have never read anything about captured American fighter planes in any of the numerous books I have read on the Bulge. I think it was most likely a case of friendly fire by an American pilot (or pilots) who mistook us for Germans.

Our immediate objective was to push the Germans back to the north side of the Sauer River into Diekirch. For us, the Battle of the Bulge then became a war of attrition fought primarily between the towns of Ettelbruck and Diekirch. We moved up to the high ground west of the Mullerthal draw, captured Doster Farm, and pushed on through the Langenbusch Woods near Mons Heibach.

It was around this time that Eugene Brinkman, the former reporter for the *Chicago Tribune*, received word from the Red Cross that his father had died. (This was one Red Cross message that I did not deliver.) Brinkman was a friend of mine from years back, when our seemingly harmless target practice during guard duty in Iceland created the unintentional illusion that German commandos were invading the island. Brinkman was an only son and the sole means of financial support for his mother; he therefore was to receive an emergency (honorable) discharge from the army and go home.

Brinkman obviously had mixed emotions. He was sorry to lose his father, but still ecstatic at the thought of going back to the States. Everyone was glad for him. Now a sergeant, he was a good soldier and a decent guy and he had earned the right to go home. As sergeant, Brinkman often had to lead patrols, and he was assigned to take us out on one the very night before he was to head back to the States! Why the hell another NCO wasn't picked for this particular duty I'll never know.

We had to move from one patch of woods to another, crossing a large open area with some small houses between the two sections of woods. The separation was not complete, however, since a large cluster of trees off to a far side connected the two wooded areas. The normal military procedure was to hug the tree line for cover and go around the long way for safety's sake. Brinkman must have been preoccupied with the thought of going home, for he proceeded to lead us right across the open ground!

A German machine gun in the first house ahead of us opened up and hit him in both legs. He went down but was still very much alive. We yelled for him to stay put as we put fire on the enemy gun. Brinkman in a state of panic began to use his arms to drag himself towards us as quickly as he could. The German on the machine gun spotted him moving and fired a line of bullets that raced across the ground and over the trunk of his body, killing him instantly. It was a huge waste of life and there was big stink about it. Just who had to answer for it was something I never discovered.

Taking patrols out at night for reconnaissance was always very dangerous. While I always refused any stripes, I was still ordered to take charge of small patrols on a number of occasions. I remember once I led a patrol into an ambush. We entered a pre-sited area and the Germans hit us with mortars and machine gun fire. There are two different types of immediate action for a soldier to choose from when this happens. He can either drop to the ground, where he's liable to become a victim of either sniper or mortar fire, or he can follow procedure and run like hell. In this instance, I ordered the latter and I thank God for it, because by some miracle we all made it out alive.

On another occasion, we went out on a recon patrol at night and probably got two or more miles behind enemy lines without finding any enemy. We all knew that if we went much further we were likely to get cut off, which would mean our capture or death. We all agreed on a story and stuck to it. We would go back and report how far we had actually gone, but say we had heard vehicle movement up ahead of us and figured we'd better get back and report it. It worked. These were the kinds of things we all did for one another. We had to trust one another and stick together if we were to stay alive. We put our lives in each other's hands almost every day. It was all built on trust.

On Christmas night the skies were lit up, and I don't mean by stars. The Germans were hitting our positions with rockets from their Nebelwerfers. They were as frightening as all hell and many a soldier needed a change of underwear when he heard those rockets being launched. We were responding with white phosphorus shells originally designed for chemical warfare, fired from heavy mortars (usually 105mm).

We jumped off around 05:00 hours on the day after Christmas to take the town of Berdorf. The Germans in the southern and central part of the town were completely surprised and we captured over 100 of them. It was one of the most bloodless actions of the war that I can ever recall. It didn't last long. Then the Germans on the north side of the Sauer River got wise to what had happened and opened up on our area of Berdorf with rockets, mortars, and heavy artillery. The Germans in the northern part of the town decided to make a real fight of it, which lasted all day and into the night. We didn't finish driving them out until 02:00 hours on December 27.

I was still often responsible for keeping a protective watch over replacements. After Metz, it became customary to pull five percent of the rear echelon people from their duties and turn them into infantrymen. We had a sergeant from the Air Corps who refused the advice to give up his stripes when he became an infantryman. He felt he had earned them and he intended to keep them. I was given the responsibility of teaching him the ropes and keeping him alive.

One day this sergeant was with us when we were in a large, block-long row of apartment complexes. I think this was in Berdorf on the day after Christmas. The complexes consisted of small, three-room apartments stacked in such a way that they resembled the public housing units later built in most large cities back home. I had kept this sergeant safe for some two to three weeks, and it now appeared that he was experienced enough to assume the duties of an infantry NCO.

We knew that the Germans were in another apartment just like ours some 600 yards or so away. We were going to assault their building the next day under the cover of smoke. With everything quiet for the moment, we were advised to wash our feet and put on clean, dry socks. I was always deathly afraid of trench foot, and we had all been trained to keep our feet clean and dry as the best way to avoid it.

Trench foot is similar to gangrene, and comes from the constant exposure to filth and moisture when feet have been confined too long in combat boots. It requires medical attention and can end in amputation. Although some men contracted it intentionally in order to get out of combat, almost everybody made it a point to do everything possible to avoid it. I always took the spare socks from Germans I captured. The POW camp provided them with plenty of new ones.

I had finished washing and was putting on fresh socks. The

sergeant was about to do the same when he spotted a pair of manicure scissors sitting right in the middle of a table. "I think I'll trim my toenails," he said. He reached for the scissors and a large bang followed as he picked them up. The blast took three fingers off the sergeant's hand. The Germans had drilled a tiny hole right through the table and used an almost invisible wire to connect the scissors to a small explosive charge. I was at the other end of the room, but the noise from the explosion kept my ears ringing for two hours. The sergeant simply sat down and started to cry. I felt awful. Even with my all experience, I knew that I could just as easily have detonated the explosive. I also got balled out big time. Apparently there were those in the army who had big plans for this guy.

We also had to be very careful about Germans impersonating Americans. A number of the enemy had been dropped behind American lines a few days before Christmas. They wore American uniforms, and had American weapons, cigarettes, pay books, and even service records. Many had lived in the United States before the war and could speak English with an American accent. Their mission was to commit acts of sabotage and cause as much confusion as possible. They were very successful at both.

We were holed up in different houses (probably in Berdorf) watching carefully for enemy movement when we saw three GIs foolishly walking down the middle of the street right toward the house occupied by Sergeant Henry Lipski. Lipski was out of Detroit. He was a good man and well liked. He opened the door and yelled to them, "Get off the street, you stupid bastards."

These troops were actually Germans. They opened fire and killed Lipski, instantly putting about 20 rounds into him. Everyone was so stunned by the sight that the Germans had time to run around the rear of the building before we could get a bead on them. Just then, Sergeant Miller and his 18-year-old runner pulled up around the back in a jeep, and came to stop right in front of the Germans. Miller was returning from HQ with our instructions, and had no clue as to what had just happened.

One of the Germans simply placed his machine gun on the hood of the jeep and pointed it at Miller. Miller had no choice but to throw his hands up. The kid ran though and the Germans opened up but only got him in the thigh. Even with his wound he continued to run and dove into a ditch filled with water. The Germans didn't chase him. They didn't have to: his wound would keep him out of the war and that accomplished the same thing as killing him. The Germans then left with the sergeant as their prisoner. I ran into him at a reunion years later and discovered that he had survived the ordeal as a prisoner of war.

The following day we captured three Germans in American uniforms. I don't think they were the same men we had encountered the day before, but one of Lipski's buddies wanted them anyway. "Go on," he told us. "Everybody just get out of here. I'll take care of things." I still don't feel right about it, but we left him alone with the prisoners knowing exactly what he was going to do.

We also lost another good man to Germans impersonating Americans. There were about a dozen of us grouped together behind our lines, huddled together for warmth and just talking. We saw four GIs were approaching, but no one thought a thing about it. Suddenly they pulled MP-40s out from behind their backs and began to fire. We all dove for cover, but Sergeant Stein was wounded. We were trying to regain our composure when Stein attempted to move to a safer location. He didn't make it. This time the German fire was fatal. Once again, the Germans had hit and run. They made it away safely, at least for the moment.

Another time, I was acting as interpreter during the interrogation of an enemy medical officer. He was wearing pants from an American uniform, but all the other parts of his uniform were German. He wasn't asked about it during the interrogation, but the major questioning him must have noticed because when the interrogation ended he told me to take the prisoner out back and shoot him.

I didn't believe this German was attempting to impersonate an American. He had probably shit his pants and the only clean pair available to him was from a dead GI. There was no way I was going to shoot this guy, but I couldn't disobey orders on the frontline in front of witnesses. I took the prisoner out back and put the barrel of my carbine near the side of his calf and pulled the trigger. The bullet passed relatively harmlessly through the soft tissue and exited on the opposite side. He fell over like a ton of bricks. I helped him to his feet and told him he had a wound that would keep him out of the war and, more importantly, alive.

I brought him up to the road and waved down an ambulance. "This man's been shot," I said. "Get him to an aid station." The medics, unaware of the circumstances involved, put him on a litter without question. I said good-bye and wished him luck. He thanked me as he was taken away. The first thing the doctors would do at the aid station would be to cut his pants off so they could treat his wound. That would take care of any evidence implicating him as a spy. Later the Major who conducted the interrogation asked me if I shot that kraut. "I took care of it sir," I said.

By 09:00 hours on December 27, we were billeted in Consdorf and being held in reserve. The next day we went out again and took up positions along the Sauer River near Stegen just south of Diekirch, where we relieved an infantry battalion from the 6th Armored Division. We observed there was a lot of activity in Diekirch, with enemy vehicles coming and going. We continued to man our outposts, patrol, and occasionally experience minor harassment from German planes and artillery. The lines stabilized and everything was relatively static over the next two weeks. Sometimes it was too cold to fight, and on those occasions both sides lit fires to stay warm, observing an unofficial truce.

Frostbite seemed likely to inflict as many casualties on us as the Germans. I was sharing a foxhole with a soldier who complained to me about one of his feet going numb and staying unresponsive. It caused a dull pain inside his foot and burned on the surface. He took off his boot and sock to take a look at it and, while I'd never had any medical training, it sure looked like everything I had ever heard about frostbite. "You'd better get that looked at," I told him. "Leave it alone. It'll be all right," he kept insisting with confidence. A week later he was repeating that line as a plea when they had to remove his foot.

Since I could speak German, the company commander wanted me to take a jeep with a driver and head south into Luxembourg City to get some whiskey for the men. There was a standing order that a quart was to be shared by three soldiers to help them keep warm (and for courage, no doubt). I was given some canned meat, cigarettes, and other such items to barter with. I had my picture taken in a photographer's studio while I was there. This assignment got me off the line for a while, which was always welcome.

A similar previous mission to Echternach had turned out more exciting. I was talking with a bartender in a pub when four GIs came in and sat down. For no apparent reason, the bartender suddenly left in the middle of our conversation, and a few moments later MPs burst simultaneously through the front and rear doors of the pub. They scooped up the four GIs sitting at the table and took them away.

"What the hell's going on?" I said with surprise. "What's this all about?" An MP put his arm out to keep me away. "Stay out of this, Yank," He said. He was American, but still referred to me as Yank.

As soon as everyone was gone, I asked the bartender what had just happened. "Those four men weren't Americans," he said. "They were Germans. Americans usually put their helmets on the floor under their chair," he explained, "but Germans usually hang their helmets on hooks. When all four of those men hung their helmets on hooks, I knew they couldn't be Americans." I heard later that the four were sentenced to death at a summary court-martial and then taken out and shot.

Around this time, after I'd been back on the line a while, I became very sick with a sore throat, sore chest, and a cough. I could also tell that I was running a fairly high fever. I was concerned because I had contracted pneumonia before in both Iceland and Northern Ireland. Luxembourg was covered by snow a foot deep and the temperatures were so low that I remember thinking that even if I did get out of there alive, I would never again be truly warm.

I asked for permission to go to the battalion aid station to see a doctor. The first sergeant took one look at me, said, "You don't look so good," and immediately granted my request. I had to walk some 600 yards back to the aid station, but when I got there all I got in the way of attention was a staff sergeant who took my temperature and gave me a funny look. The sergeant went over to the corner of the tent and spoke in hushed tones to a man I think was a doctor. The sergeant came back with an envelope with some pills in it and told me to take one every four hours. I think they were sulfa tablets, but I suppose they could have been penicillin. I was then told to go back and rejoin my company.

"Give me a straight answer," I said. "What's my temperature?" He looked at me and said, "I'm not supposed to tell you this, but it's 101 degrees." I think he was bullshitting me. I felt like I was burning up and figured it had to higher than that, but every man was needed on the line, so they weren't admitting anyone to the hospitals but the wounded.

I took the envelope of tablets and headed out, but when I got back to the frontline the first sergeant said I looked too sick to resume my post. He ordered me to turn around and get to the company command post, which was nothing more than a tiny shack, where I was allowed to lie down in the corner with a blanket and get some sleep. I slept all day and all that night, and by the next morning my fever had broken and I was feeling well enough to resume my duties.

A soldier always has to stay sharp on sentry duty, but this was especially true during the Bulge. The Germans didn't necessarily have to go to great lengths or be clever enough to impersonate Americans in order to cause casualties. Sometimes stupidity or carelessness on our part was all it took to get our own men captured or killed.

One bitterly cold morning, I was in a foxhole with two other soldiers manning a .30-caliber machine gun. I say foxhole, but in actuality the ground was so frozen that all we could do was pull snow up around us and put some foliage on top. It couldn't stop a bullet or provide any real protection, but it gave us a little cover and a psychological sense of safety. We were in a forward position along a relatively open, flat stretch of ground, facing a heavily wooded area about 100 yards ahead of us.

There was another foxhole about 50 yards to our right with three men performing the same task that we were. On our left, positioned 50 yards, and then 100 yards away, were two other outposts, each with a .30-caliber machine gun and three men. Each of these four positions had its own field of fire and area to watch. Together, acting in unison, we secured our frontline.

Just as the sun was coming up, one of our officers approached us and asked, "Where the hell are the men on the left?" We had no idea what he was talking about, so he told two of us to get up out of our position and follow him. We walked to the foxholes on our left and saw that each contained the dead body of a GI who had been bayoneted. The .30-calibers were missing, and several sets of footprints led to the woods ahead of us.

The theory was that the men in these foxholes had fallen asleep during watch the previous night, and were caught by surprise by the Germans. Those who had resisted had been killed before they could yell or get off a shot. The fact that someone had resisted, without opening fire, reinforced the theory that the Germans had taken these men by surprise and not through stealth or as part of a ruse.

Even worse, once the Germans had penetrated our lines, they went on to our rear and killed some of the wounded who were waiting for ambulances to take them to a hospital. They also captured two squads who were getting their turn in the rear to catch some sack time. The men who fell asleep during their watch not only got themselves captured or killed, but endangered others who were counting on them for protection. All in all, the enemy, probably at patrol strength or less, was able to capture or kill a number of Americans roughly equal to a full platoon! No doubt they considered this a good night's work.

To add insult to injury, the stupidity or carelessness of our own people greatly contributed to our enemy's success. Our officers were justifiably angry over these events, angrier, in fact, than I had ever seen them before. According to the Articles of War, a soldier on the frontlines can be shot if caught sleeping on guard duty. They stressed that men assigned sentry duty had to be up to the job. This was not a duty to pass around as a matter of routine so that every man got a turn, nor was it something to pawn off on new replacements. It was a life-or-death matter for everyone, and the men performing this duty damn well better be up to the job, or they could expect a bayonet up the ass. This was one time that every grunt was in complete agreement with the officers.

The American forces in Luxembourg enjoyed the benefit of tremendous air and artillery superiority. This advantage was employed to the fullest, but it was important for us to remember that our tactical advantages didn't guarantee our safety. I'll always remember a PFC from 2d Battalion Headquarters by the name of Paul Davidson. He was not normally on the frontline, but when he was, he always stayed as close as possible to a tank. It gave him a tremendous, albeit false, sense of security. One day during the Bulge as we were advancing with tank support, Davidson was right up against a tank as we moved forward. In a bizarre twist of fate, a German mortar round deflected off that very tank and landed right at Davidson's feet, killing him instantly. There was no such thing as playing it safe in combat.

The great thing about our firepower during the Bulge was that it wreaked havoc on the Germans; unfortunately, it did the same to the civilians of Luxembourg as well. The white phosphorous from our shells stuck to their homes and burned many to the ground. The P-47s dropped 500-pound bombs and napalm with the same type of effect. Many civilians were left homeless in the bitter cold, while others took refuge in cellars as best they could.

Despite this, and the possibility that German collaborators could turn them in if the enemy pushed us back, the civilians of Luxembourg courageously continued to welcome us as liberators and support us any way they could. These poor souls even offered to share their meager portions of food with us, even though they, not we, were the ones who were starving!

I first started to come across civilians who spoke German in Metz, but in Luxembourg almost everyone could speak German. Once word got out that I was fluent, I was constantly besieged by people needing food, warm clothing, medical care or shelter, or just plain searching for their relatives. Between the fierce fighting and the bitter cold, Luxembourg civilians suffered hardships that stagger the imagination. They lost their homes to shelling, were caught in the middle of firefights and sometimes killed by the crossfire, and they also died from hunger, stress, and exposure to the extreme cold. Their unburied bodies, preserved by the freezing weather, lay along the roadsides. You would have to have a heart made of stone not to feel for them.

I was not an officer, so there was little I could do for them in an official capacity, but I could inform them where to go in order to get the things they needed. The army's primary concern at the time was fighting a war, not providing humanitarian services, so it didn't really encourage or appreciate it when civilians showed up looking for help. The civilians knew this already, and they also knew that to have their requests seriously considered they needed to know exactly where to go for help and to supply the name of the person who had sent them. I would tell them what they needed to know, and told them to say that

"Karl Lootzman" sent them with the promise that the American Army would help them out.

These were the days before American soldiers had their names printed on the right chest of their uniforms, and I didn't share this alias with anyone in the army. I did, however, hear both enlisted men and officers say that headquarters was looking for some guy named Karl Lootzman, and nobody could figure out who the hell he was. I used this alias not only in Luxembourg, but also in Germany, Czechoslovakia, and even during occupation duty in Austria. I was already doing my fair share of killing, so why not save a few civilians along the way?

Throughout this relative lull, we knew that we would eventually have to cross the Sauer and take Diekirch. This was a task we dreaded, because it promised to be a nasty fight. On January 16, our 2d Battalion was pulled off the frontline and relieved by the 3rd Battalion. We were sent back towards Stegen and put in reserve while our replacements patrolled the Sauer looking for the place of least resistance to use as a crossing site in preparation for the assault. The following morning we were back on the line with the 3rd Battalion, and both outfits were placed in position to attack Diekirch and Ingeldorf. We got word that an assault across the Sauer River to capture these objectives was planned for 03:00 hours on January 18.

The 2d Regiment's plan of attack called for the 1st Battalion to cross the Sauer on the left, using footbridges the engineers would make, with the objective of taking the high ground near Goldnapp Hill. The 2d Battalion would form the right flank and cross the river with the objective of moving on Diekirch. Meanwhile, the 3rd Battalion was to lay down cover fire for our assault, then follow us across to move on their objective of Ingeldorf.

The temperature was brutally cold: some accounts report 16 degrees above zero, while others say 18 degrees below. The frozen snow crunched beneath our feet. Snow had been falling since the previous day, and a whitish fog hung in the air. These things combined to give an especially eerie and even surreal effect to everything. We were supposed to have the cover of darkness and the benefit of surprise, so there was no artillery barrage to cover our crossing. After two unsuccessful attempts to bridge the river, we only succeeded in drawing fire and alerting the Germans to our presence. German snipers picked off our engineers with ease as they tried to lay down a footbridge. It was then decided that we would have to do this the hard way, and fall back on what our officers probably regarded as Plan B.

We moved as quickly as we could down the riverbank, where our engineers were waiting for us. They had army-issued assault boats and any other kind of water craft they could find, including rubber rafts and a number of boats appropriated from civilians, to get as many men across as quickly as possible. Neither I nor any of the other certified men could possibly perform combat lifeguard duty in weather this cold. If any poor soul fell into the icy river during the assault, his fate was sealed.

As previously stated, the 5th Division was intended to cross the Sauer River in a surprise attack. Our brothers in the 10th Regiment to our right succeeded in pulling this off, but those of us in the 2d Regiment didn't have the same good fortune. The Germans on the other side of the river, the 914th Regiment, 352 Volksgrenadier Division, were not only ready, but waiting for us when we came. No sooner did we reach our own side of the riverbank than the Germans opened up on us with machine guns. The 3rd Battalion responded with everything they had to cover our crossing, and we climbed into our boats and started across.

Our boats had just left the riverbank when the Germans lit up the area with flares. The previously benign-looking landscape on the opposite bank cleared enough to reveal a full compliment of Germans, dug in and well armed. Screams of pain, shouted orders, and noises of every kind filled the air as the enemy poured down fire on us during our journey across.

The 3rd Battalion, on the south side of the riverbank, pounded away at the Germans across the Sauer, but they were restricted to clearly defined fields of fire. We were crossing in fog, darkness, and our own smoke screen, so it was imperative that everyone stay in their designated area to avoid becoming a victim of friendly fire. This was far from easy, because our visibility was as limited as the Germans'. Crossing with German fire to our front and American fire from our rear was as frightening as all hell. It was a miracle that any of us made it through alive.

The machine gun and small arms fire were bad enough, but to our horror German mortar rounds started to drop among us, some scoring direct hits on our assault boats. The unfortunate men in these crafts who weren't killed instantly by the explosion found themselves in the Sauer, wounded, weak, and weighted down with heavy equipment, as the icy water carried them downstream or they sank to the river bottom.

We blasted away at the enemy as we crossed and kept on blasting when we reached the other side. The chaos continued along the riverbank as we set off trip flares carefully hidden in foliage, which revealed our positions to the Germans. Our artillery scored some direct hits on the enemy's position, breaking them up enough to allow us to advance up the high ground immediately in front of us. By this time the engineers had a footbridge set up behind us, which allowed for additional men to come across.

The initial crossing had been costly. One officer and 16 enlisted men were killed, another 81 were wounded, and a whopping 30 missing and most probably at the bottom of the Sauer. The total roughly equaled the entirety of an infantry company. It was a heavy price to pay by anyone's standards.

The Germans continued to fight and hit us with artillery as we took the high ground and swung around to a position northwest of Diekirch. By dawn, most of Diekirch was surrounded. Street fighting was going on in and around the railroad station as the 2d Regiment closed in on all sides and started to enter the city. Our Company G blocked the only escape route out for the Germans (who were mostly from the 79th Volksgrenadier Division), but they continued to put up stiff resistance. We had to be very careful in Diekirch and all around the entire area, because mines were planted everywhere. Since we had first begun to cross the Sauer, the Germans had also constantly subjected us to screaming meemies, firing the dreaded rockets at any and every area they suspected they might find us.

On January 20 we assisted the 3rd Battalion in their assault against Kippenhauf Farm. The Germans had the advantage of holding a solid defensive position. The farm was something like a fortress with concrete walls almost two feet thick. Once again, as at Metz, sending infantry forward against such an objective proved futile and did nothing but get good men killed. A tank company was brought up to soften the middle of the German position while our company moved in from the southeast under the cover of darkness and took the farm. In the process we captured about 45 enlisted personnel and the German officer commanding the 208th Volksgrenadier Regiment.

By the end of the day, we had secured Diekirch. It was here the 2d Battalion was sent to be put in reserve. Inside Diekirch we discovered the bodies of six Americans whom the Germans had taken prisoner and shot through the back of the head, execution style. It was also in Diekirch that I first saw the results of a fair-size atrocity against civilians, the type that would later render our enemy so infamous. The Germans had shot in cold blood some 12 to 15 Luxembourg civilians who had been identified by fellow countrymen collaborating with the enemy. Their crime had been to welcome the Americans who had arrived a few hours earlier to liberate them. The victims included men, women, and children. The Germans committed this atrocity sometime in a period of just four hours, after they briefly pushed us back out of the central area of the city. The bodies were left piled in the town square as a message to others.

With the Americans back in control of the city, the tables were now turned. The men of Diekirch who had collaborated with the Germans were rounded up. The Luxembourg resistance had identified them and took them off. Some were shot immediately, but most were charged with various war crimes and imprisoned. One woman in hysterics pleaded with me to save her daughter from having her head shaved. The company commander told me that this was regarded as a local matter and outside the army's jurisdiction. I told the woman there was nothing I could do.

We were quartered in the homes of Luxembourg civilians, who couldn't be evicted due to the extreme cold. A woman in the home I was in showed me a picture of her boyfriend, who had joined the SS. She asked me what I thought would happen to him if he survived the war. "He can never come home again," I told her. "If he does, he'll be shot. You're better off trying to get into Switzerland if you two want to stay together." I even warned her to be careful with the photograph because it could be dangerous to her.

By January 21 the Germans were retreating with little reluctance.

They abandoned their vehicles and in some cases their weapons, and started walking back to Germany. It was obvious that their final push was over and it would soon be our turn to go on the offensive in full force. We could then drive into Germany and end this war, but we still had some mopping up to do in Luxembourg.

By this time, we were again getting young kids as replacements. They had never seen combat, and were not yet reliable in a fight. This was something Lieutenant Livingston, who had gone AWOL from the hospital just to get back to his unit, was about to find out. Livingston was a schoolteacher out of Effingham, Illinois, and a very brave and capable officer. He was not tall, but he had a commanding presence. He was quite patriotic and took his duties seriously. This was obvious by the fact that both his hands were still wrapped in bandages when he returned to duty.

We had to take a hill, and Lieutenant Livingston led us out to it. Starting up the hill, he turned around and discovered that only myself and three other vets were following him. He stopped immediately and shook his head in disgust. "All right you guys," he said to the four of us. "Get your safeties off and back me up on this." We followed him back to our starting point where our weak-kneed replacements were hiding in the tree line. "Any man who fails to advance up that hill will be shot for cowardice," he told them. He then threw a glance at us and we cocked our weapons to show them we'd carry out his order. The Lieutenant remained in our rear to make certain that every one those guys went up that hill. We took our objective and the replacements got their baptism of fire. That was the only way to do it.

The weakened state of the German forces had old soldiers feeling invincible, and some of us got a little careless from over confidence. I typified this kind of thinking when I got out of a foxhole quickly one morning without properly checking the area around me. A German flung a potato masher in my direction, which exploded just 12 to 15 feet away from me. The concussion picked me up off the ground and threw me down again hard.

A number of guys came scrambling to my aid, shouting things like, "Bilder's been hit!" I had a bloody nose and the wind knocked out of me, but other than that I was all right. The medics threw me onto a litter and carried me back to the aid station. I assured everyone there that I could get up and go back to my unit, but they all made a fuss and told me to stay put. The army doctor, a man named Goldberg who, like me, was from Chicago, had been with the 5th Division since our days at Fort Custer. I explained what had happened and said I was ready to rejoin my outfit. "You need to be checked out. Besides, it'll give you a break and pull you off the line for a while," he said. All of a sudden being "wounded" didn't sound half bad.

Goldberg told me that he was sending me to a hospital in Luxembourg City for shell shock and, without anything more being said, I knew I was to play the role accordingly. I was loaded into an ambulance and sent back to a hospital and a bed with clean sheets. I spent almost two weeks in that hospital sitting in a rocking chair looking out the window. On occasion I shook and quivered, just to keep up appearances. By day, I was a shell shock victim in need of rest, and by night I was a man about town in Luxembourg City enjoying good booze, fine food, and good-looking women.

The hospital staff and even Dr Goldberg all knew what was going on and they started to get pissed off. I was fine and there were real casualties who needed the bed space. It was made clear that I should get my ass the hell out of there and back to the frontlines. I got the message loud and clear and returned to my outfit before the hospital staff threw me out.

It's a funny thing, but I was told later that the bloody nose I had received would have entitled me to a Purple Heart, not that I would have accepted it. I felt an award like that should go to guys who lost limbs, sight, or other vital functions or parts. My good friend Vern Kelner told me how he and another soldier were once digging a foxhole together in a combat area. The other soldier had his helmet off and was digging with the blade end of a pick when he accidentally struck himself in the forehead with the pointed end. He wanted a Purple Heart for his injury and he got it! They should have pinned it on his head.

I didn't miss too much during my absence because the 2d Regiment had gotten lucky and been put in reserve. They had spent a week in Diekirch reorganizing, rearming, re-supplying, and replacing their losses to prepare for the next assault. The 10th and 11th Regiments had continued the advance against heavy opposition.

Word filtered into us from the 10th Regiment after they took Bastendorf on January 19 that the Germans in that town had executed American POWs from the 28th Infantry Division who'd been captured in the early days of the Bulge. Typified by the massacre at Malmedy, this kind of news caused a great deal of hard feelings among many American units, but it seemed to effect some of our men in the 5th Division particularly strongly. After word got out that American POWs had been killed, a number of our guys became a lot less likely to offer quarter to any surrendering Germans, and the enemy quickly picked up on out change of attitude. The Germans again began referring to the men of the 5th Division as the "Red Devils," just as they had referred to our predecessors in World War I.

The 2d Regiment's weeklong period in reserve ended on January 28, when it was ordered to relieve elements of the 10th and 11th Regiments overlooking the Our River at a point west of Vianden. Its assignment was to observe the enemy and patrol with the hope of capturing prisoners. A few fair-sized firefights took place, but we mostly battled the extreme cold and the elements. Units were rotated frequently and during February 4 and 5, the regiment was relieved and sent to be billeted in the areas of Altlinster, Lorentzweller and Burglinster, all of which were in Luxembourg. It was around this point that I returned to the regiment.

The Germans were falling back and we were patrolling aggressively when we came across a very old and weathered barn out in the open. The wood had become soft and flexible from age and moisture, so the barn offered little more than an opportunity for concealment. We figured there were probably Germans in the barn so we decided to take advantage of our large numbers and full supply caches to confirm our hunch the easy way. Our heavy weapons company set up a couple of .50-caliber machine guns and put a few bursts through the walls. The Germans ran out of there with their hands up like the place was on fire.

We questioned them about where their units were and how many troops they had in the area. They tried to give the appearance of cooperating with us, but it was obvious they were talking in circles and avoided giving us any information of real value. Finally, the company commander decided to send two men into the tiny village ahead of us to see if the enemy was there. I was lucky enough to be picked along with a soldier by the name of Condra.

This little village was typical of many we encountered during our trek through Europe. They were seemingly unoccupied by civilians or the military, and we were often sent out in small numbers to confirm if this was indeed the case. This particular village was very old, with streets made of cobblestone. Condra and I moved up along the main street using the buddy system, one of us on the right side of the street the other the left. I took cover in a doorway or behind an object and watched, ready to provide cover fire, as Condra moved up half a block, then he returned the favor as I moved up.

I was on the left side of the street nearing a corner when I motioned Condra to move up ahead and get behind a haystack or manure pile to cover me. Once he did this, I ran forward toward the corner of the next street. My boots were noisy against the cobblestones. There was a German around that corner, who was probably there on the same kind of mission that we were. He pressed himself up against the side of the building on the corner as he heard me approach.

We, of course, didn't know he was there. As I swung quickly around the corner, the German got the drop on me and jammed his pistol up against my forehead before I knew what was happening. I was momentarily paralyzed from shock. He stared at my forehead and I expected the worst. Without hesitation, he squeezed the trigger, but instead of the sound of gunfire there was only a harmless click.

Condra witnessed the whole thing from across the street. He fired his rifle, putting three slugs into that German. Each time the German was hit, his body jerked in a dance-like motion as he fell to the ground. Condra then ran over to make certain that I was OK.

I was still unnerved, and he pushed me into a doorway and gave me a drink of whiskey to help me get my courage back. I'll bet I drank half that bottle. I had to find out something about the soldier, who by all reason should have killed me. I saw by the stripes on his sleeve that he was a corporal. Condra had taken his papers and the pistol, a 7.65 Mauser, and now we looked them over. The corporal was a musician from Austria, and a violinist no less. It proved how desperate the Germans had to be to put a man with that kind of talent and education on the frontline.

We returned to our unit and reported on the situation in the village. Afterward Condra took the captured pistol, ejected the shell in the chamber, raised the gun into the air and pulled the trigger. This time it fired. "Now you know just how lucky you are," he said. "There's nothing wrong with the firing pin. It was the round that was no good."

Years later, I read how people the Germans used as forced labor in munitions factories did their best to sabotage the Nazi war effort by turning out substandard work whenever possible. Still, I knew this was more than pure chance. My family, Mary's family and my friends at home were praying daily for my safety, and the incident made me realize just how powerful their prayers were. Their prayers were also what enabled me to keep my humanity.

A short time later we were marching down a road when I heard someone call out, "Mike!" I turned, but couldn't see who in particular it was. Then I heard it again. "Mike, Mike Bilder!" This time I saw the call had come from one of the soldiers alongside the road. It was Bill Nielson, the soldier who'd received the head wound when we were racing to get out of Fort Driant back at Metz.

He was not only alive and well, but back on the line. I stepped out of formation and joined him on the road. "Bill, what are you doing here?" I asked. "Well," he said, "when the fire from that German tank hit me, it penetrated my helmet but obviously didn't kill me. The medics got me back to the aid station and the doctors fixed me up with a plate in my head. There's just one problem, though. They didn't get all the shrapnel out, and these little metal slivers keep coming to the surface. Can you help me?"

Bill took off his helmet and he was completely bald. He handed me a knife and I picked a few slivers from his scalp. These continued to rise to the surface for some time, especially when he ran a comb or his hand across his head. When Bill came to visit me a couple of years after the war ended, he was still picking metal slivers from his scalp, and I was still helping him. I didn't mind. It was something like family. I was just glad to have him back alive.

We were moving up one day when two Me-109 fighters strafed us, and fire from a 20mm nose cannon killed two of our men. We kept moving, but later that day an officer called me in and explained that leaving dead GIs on the road was bad for morale. "There are replacements coming up," the officer explained, "and it's bad for them to see something like that before they even get up to the line. Take a jeep and bring their bodies back," he said.

I did as I was told and got three other guys to go with me. We took a jeep with a small open trailer attached to the back and headed out. We found the two dead men lying in the road right where we had left them. One was in the ditch and had a huge hole in his side. The other was half in the ditch and had his right leg blown off at the knee.

We had put their bodies in the trailer when one of the guys asked me, "What about the leg?" To which I replied, "Why don't we just leave it? He's not gonna need it anymore." This guy didn't like my answer. "That wouldn't be right," he said. I went back to get the leg, but when I reached down to pick it up I learned to my chagrin that it had frozen to the road. I went back and got a shovel and chipped and pried until it came loose. When I brought it back to the trailer and threw it in, I felt so sick I vomited.

During another incident in the Bulge, we attempted to advance against an enemy position with some tank support, but the Germans were waiting for us and their armor was better. They hit some of our tanks, which quickly ignited, and we were ordered to fall back. We attacked a second time some four hours later, and this time we successfully took our objectives. The tanks we lost during our initial attack had been hit with incendiary shells and the bodies of the poor crewmen inside were half melted. Their facial expressions were frozen in a look of terror and agony.

Killing prisoners was never officially permitted, but sometimes a blind eye and deaf ear were turned towards it. If we had to move up quickly and had taken prisoners before we reached our final objective, those prisoners were in trouble if we couldn't spare anyone to stay behind and guard them. Someone was expected to lag behind for a moment or two in order to do the dirty work. It was never an order, or even mentioned. It was simply understood.

This was not a matter I ever had to struggle over. Someone who had just lost a close buddy or simply enjoyed killing always stepped forward to do the job. They caught up to us right after they "took care" of the prisoners.

In retrospect, somebody, including me, should have objected, but in battle, all the rules of heaven and earth become casualties of war, and it seems that everyone knows it. I stayed silent and accepted what was done because I wasn't the one doing it, and because that was how everyone else handled it. A poor benchmark to be sure, but also a circumstance that proves a crowd has no conscience.

During the Bulge, we once had two German prisoners whom we had just finished checking out at the local level. Battalion Headquarters was eager to interrogate these men and they were ordered up there immediately. Their hands were tied behind their backs and they were seated on the hood of a jeep. A lone man took off with them and that seemingly was the end of the matter.

Our company command post got a call from Battalion HQ a short time later, wanting to know why we were sending up dead Germans instead of live prisoners. When the soldier who was supposed to take the POWs up to Battalion returned, we asked him what had happened. He said that he sped up the jeep and then slammed on the breaks. The two Germans flew forward away from the jeep, so they were obviously "attempting to escape." He shot them both with a pistol.

By the end of the first week of February 1945, we had pushed the Germans completely out of Luxembourg and back onto their own soil. Our division was positioned along a five-mile front northwest of Echternach near the Sauer River. We were getting ready to cross the river and drive right on into Germany, as the enemy knew full well. They dug in and prepared for our assault. The Germans were not about to go quietly into the night. The Fatherland had to be defended at all costs, no matter who the invader. Although they realized that this would mean their death, they were equally determined to take as many of us along with them as possible.

10

THE PUSH INTO GERMANY
Breaching the Westwall and Wasting Time in the Ruhr

"You plunged me into the bottom of the pit;
Into the darkness of the abyss."
—*Psalms* 88:7

We first crossed the Sauer River just below Diekirch in the wee hours of January 18, going from south to north. Early February found us near Echternach, southeast of Diekirch, again preparing to cross the Sauer, this time from west to east into Germany. The long-term objective was the city of Bitburg, which served as a communications hub for the enemy.

This would be no cakewalk. The Germans held the high ground on the opposite bank of the river, where they had established extensive pillbox and machine gun emplacements. This was to be the cracking of the famed Siegfried Line, and it was the Germans' final opportunity for a determined last stand, a real fight to the finish.

I was with two other GIs, teaching some new replacements how to use a mortar. We were behind the safety of a stone wall some nine or ten feet high that served as fencing along the river. We had the replacements sending their practice rounds across the river at the Germans, so their training was also pragmatic.

We also had them raising the mortar tube about five degrees after every round they fired. The three of us were passing around a bottle of cognac, not paying very close attention to these green kids. The replacements continued to fire, and continued to elevate the angle of the tube. Oblivious to the obvious danger, they dropped a round into the tube, which was now pointing straight up! One of the guys with us spotted it and yelled out, "Incoming!" Everyone scattered, including the replacements, and fortunately the round arched and landed harmlessly on the other side of the stone wall.

An NCO screamed at us with good reason until he was hoarse, and I later heard him tell someone that he would have insisted we be court-martialed, except that every man was needed on the line. As punishment for our stupidity, we were sent out on a seemingly pointless patrol along the Sauer River. We knew the Germans were on the other side busily preparing their defenses for our coming assault. We heard noises in the brush on their side of the river pretty close to the shoreline, and I couldn't resist calling out sarcastically in their own language, "Are you Germans over there?"

To my complete surprise they actually answered. "Yeah, we're here," one replied in German. It was dark and I couldn't tell whether or not there was a full squad of them. There were only three of us, not much cover, and they seemed willing to talk, so considering the circumstances we didn't open fire. Neither group trusted the other enough to reveal themselves, so both sides talked crouched behind what little cover there was. I asked them what they were doing so close to American lines. They responded with a bullshit excuse that they thought they were still operating well within their own lines. Then they asked me how it was that I could speak German so well.

My German had a slight Bavarian accent to it and I told them I was of German descent. I knew they'd love that. I also told them that my folks had come from Germany before the First World War and I had learned to speak German in my own home when I was growing up. "Then what are you doing in that uniform?" one of them asked. I said I was born and raised American so that was where my loyalty was. My service was to my native land and not my ancestry. This was something they truly couldn't comprehend. They actually believed all that crap about German blood and racial superiority.

After this, our exchange took a more humorous turn as each side tried to coax the other into surrendering. "We'll give you some delicious strudel. You can finish out the war in safety," they said almost convincingly. I half thought about it for a second before yelling out in response, "Why don't you come over here and surrender to us? We'll give you some delicious lemon cream pie." I think they thought about it as well, but soldiers always worried about the treatment they'd receive once they became a POW. We entertained each other for a moment or two longer before both sides slowly backed away from the riverbank. I reported the enemy activity, but left out some of the details of our encounter.

By the grace of God, the 2d Regiment did not make the initial assault across the Sauer. That duty fell to the 10th and 11th Regiments, and they paid dearly for it. On February 7, our searchlights lit up the skies as simulated moonlight, the first such use of this type of light by the American Army in Europe. The poor souls in the 10th Regiment started across the Sauer after a 90-minute artillery barrage. It was supposed to have softened up the area, but it didn't help. Thirty-eight craft comprised of assault boats, rubber rafts, and civilian rowboats set out full of troops, but only two reached the other side. A grand total of eight men made it across and later had to be evacuated back.

The 10th Regiment took another crack at the enemy around 01:00 hours the following day. This time they crossed under the cover of smoke and with artillery and mortar support, reaching the other side to establish a bridgehead near Bollendorf, Germany. Others followed immediately to secure the area and we waited for orders to go in and relieve them. We now had 155mm self-propelled guns, and standard 105s, which rolled up and down the West Wall blowing German pillboxes and other defenses to smithereens.

Our orders to relieve the 10th Regiment came on February 15, and by late evening the 1st and 3rd Battalions had taken up positions on the frontlines; the 2d Battalion was held in reserve. This was what every one of us had been waiting for: we were now on German soil. We were all the closer to the end of the war and going home.

The 10th and 11th Regiments had made incredible progress. Crossing into Germany created a newfound energy and determination on our part, which the enemy could clearly see. There was a kind of pattern forming: our units would slug it out with the Germans, gain ground, and then resist a determined counter attack. Then a large number of Germans would approach our lines and surrender.

On February 16 we were in reserve in some woods near Shankweiler while the 1st Battalion took the town. We thought we were relatively safe when suddenly German artillery and rockets began to pound our position and sent us burrowing down into the deepest recesses of our foxholes. I think every soldier deluded himself into thinking he could fold himself small enough to fit into a matchbook, if that was what it took to avoid exposure during a barrage. It's difficult to describe how terrifying it is to have the earth all around you heave and convulse. Each incoming round sounds like it's going to drop directly into your foxhole. The Germans shelled those woods until they looked like a moonscape.

The following day we were ordered forward to take the town of Stockem. The Germans opened up on us with mortars as we approached the town, and we ran forward to get into the rubble for cover. This didn't do us too much good, as the Germans then brought up tanks for additional support. When our tanks raced forward to support us, the battle became more evenly matched. We drove the Germans back, killing a number of them and continued to advance, taking 66 enemy prisoners according to official records.

Captured German pillboxes were often turned into observation or command posts if they were in decent shape and close enough to the frontline to be of use. Vern Kelner and I were ordered to accompany a rather gutsy lieutenant colonel by the name of Leslie Ball who intended to set up a command/observation post in just such a pillbox. Two forward observers from the artillery as well as Sergeant William Henderson and Corporal Harry Folenias from Headquarters Company were also with us. Henderson and Folenias were our communications people, whose job was to set up a phone system inside the pillbox.

We knew the Germans were close by, and the Colonel picked up on our unease about the operation. In order to reassure us he got into the back of a jeep and stood up in it as it drove around over open ground, presenting itself as a clear target. There was no sign whatsoever of the enemy and so we proceeded. The pillbox was located on top of a hill. After we got situated there, the Colonel told me to go to the bottom of the slope and keep my eyes open so we wouldn't be surprised from our rear. No sooner had I reached the bottom than a German artillery shell scored a direct hit on the pillbox. The doors were wide open so the men inside could set up the phone.

I raced up the hill as fast as I could. Poor Henderson and Folenias had been killed instantly by the concussion from the blast. There wasn't a mark on either of them. The two artillerymen were badly wounded and Vern was lying on the ground with the lower half of one of his legs hanging on by a thread. He was going into shock. The Colonel had been wounded in the groin by shrapnel and lost part of a thumb.

I got help as quickly as possible. Both of the artillerymen died, either in route to the aid station or after they arrived. Vern lost his leg midway below the knee. He had been a "tree climber" working on telephone poles before the war. The phone company gave him an office job when he recovered and he worked his way up, doing quite well for himself. He deserved it. He was a hell of a nice guy and a first-rate soldier.

Colonel Ball survived his wounds and was awarded the Silver Star. To his great credit, he refused to be moved or even treated until all of the other men had been attended to. The colonel's wounds, I'm sure, were very painful, and it was clear to see that he had lost a lot of blood. He conducted himself as an officer, a real leader. Sergeant Henderson received the Silver Star posthumously.

One sergeant made two attempts to get me into Battalion HQ. He felt I would do well there, and if I had not witnessed what happened to Henderson and Folenias, I might have thought it was a good assignment. I thanked the sergeant for his effort and politely declined the offer. There simply was no way for an infantryman to guarantee his safety.

Even though we knew there was still plenty of fight left in the Germans, we could feel every aspect of the war shifting dramatically in our favor. We seemed to have unlimited amounts of tanks, planes, artillery, troops, ammunition, and even gasoline. We were also razor sharp and we knew it. We had learned from hard-won experience how to hit hard and fast. We were the ones now practicing blitzkrieg (lightning war). We had superiority over the Germans in seemingly every aspect of the war, and what's more they knew it too. They started surrendering in larger numbers.

A continuous rain in mid-February turned the roads into muddy rivers and hampered our progress. Our engineers did what they could to make them passable, using fallen trees and other materials as planking. We at least had the advantage of mechanized vehicles, but the Germans were using their remaining gasoline for their tanks. Their troops had to walk and use horses to pull supply carts.

By February 17 we were on the high ground overlooking the Prum River, gearing up for yet another river crossing. The objective was Bitburg, and this time it was our regiment's turn to make the initial river crossing. I remember sitting up there on the high ground watching our heavy guns as they shelled the hell out of that city in preparation for our assault. The 1st and 3rd Battalions started across the Prum at about 23:00 hours on February 24. This crossing was a walk in the park compared to the Sauer ten days earlier.

Our 2d Battalion followed quickly after the initial crossing and moved on Olsdorf and Bettingen. There were snipers in the woods near Birtlingen, but we took the town and its bridge intact by February 26. The 11th Regiment cleared Bitburg two days later, but we remained on its outskirts.

Our armor was like a juggernaut as it zoomed down city streets and around corners. Patton now had the new M-26 Pershing tanks, real behemoths, whose 90mm guns and thick armor were more than a match for anything the Germans had, including their Panthers and Tigers. Previously, we infantrymen had to look around corners and make certain that a street was clear of enemy tanks or anti-tank guns before our tankers proceeded. These new and improved tanks made this unnecessary: our tankers turned sharply around corners blind, and simply crushed any anti-tank guns and their crews that happened to be in their path.

Even our Sherman tanks were greatly improved. They now had high velocity 76mm turret cannons capable of piercing the armor on German tanks. The Shermans also had thicker armor on their own frames. Patton now allowed his tank crews to cannibalize knocked-out Shermans to weld on added armor for more protection. His earlier complaint that added armor hampered the maneuverability of the tanks no longer pertained. A new tread width of 23 inches (up from the previous 16.5) made the new Shermans all but unstoppable.

I was on the outer rim of Bitburg when German shells started falling all around us. I took refuge with a few other guys in an abandoned industrial building. Things were just beginning to settle down when I noticed a crooked painting half hanging off the wall with a safe behind it. I suggested we open it up.

There were three of us there: a medic, a combat engineer, and myself. I asked the engineer if he had any TNT. He did indeed, so I suggested we blow the safe and see what was inside. We followed his suggestion to carve out a hole in the wall under the safe to plant the TNT. The explosive charge blew the safe out of the wall and opened it wide. It had some really interesting and valuable booty including jewelry and 100,000 German marks.

Since I was the one to first notice the safe, the guys gave me first choice of its contents. There were two diamond rings, and I claimed them both. One was a full carrot and the other had a half carrot with a quarter carrot mounted on each side. The engineer took the remaining jewelry, which consisted of some modest bracelets and necklaces.

The medic hit what turned out to be pay dirt. A bartender from Chicago, he was left with the 100,000 German marks, whose value seemed very dubious at the time. He learned later that marks printed up to 1930 retained their value; it just so happened that all of his money was good. I found out from him years later that he had an attorney friend invest the money for him in various South American stocks. The return on the investment was $10,000, of which the attorney got ten percent and the medic got the rest. This kind of money was an absolute fortune by 1945 standards.

During one of our advances in Germany, we came to an approach that was sloped on each side with a low point in between. This was to be our jump off point for an advance in the morning. Three patrols were sent out that night to check the area out, one on the right flank, one on the left, and one up the center. I led the patrol on the right. We had gone about halfway down the area and had started back when the Germans let us have it. We were right in the middle of a pre-sited zone. I immediately ordered everybody back to our lines as fast as they could run, but we lost six or seven men in the process. The other patrols had fared the same. This obviously wasn't merely a kill zone, but an absolute meat grinder.

As a patrol leader, I had to report to our captain, and so I was present as he evaluated our circumstances. He came to the conclusion that our outfit would suffer some 60 percent casualties if our advance jumped off through this area. He said it would be quite a show in the morning if things went forward as planned, but he stressed that he intended to object. It would be murder to send men into such an inferno.

"Do you realize what you're saying?" asked the lieutenant next to him. Our captain must have thought about it carefully, because shortly before zero hour the next morning he called the executive officer and requested permission to move to another area for jump off. This captain was a good officer and a capable man. He believed it would literally be murder to send men into such an obvious ambush. I remember I even felt a sense of kinship for him because he was from Evergreen Park, which was then a rural suburb along the western boundary of Chicago.

Our captain was then given the direct order to proceed through the jump off area as planned. He still insisted that he couldn't in good conscience obey such an order. I was told later that the voice on the other end of the line said, "You're relieved. Stay right there. I'm sending another man to replace you immediately." A new captain showed up and ordered us forward as planned.

Our particular outfit was assigned to move along the same portion of the right flank where I had led the patrol the previous night. We were the lucky ones. No sooner did we reach the halfway point than all hell broke loose. The Germans opened up on us with machine guns and mortars. We ran forward with GIs dropping like flies all around us and seized our objective on the other end. We looked back to see the area we had just come through littered with the bodies of our own men. Our advance through this area had resulted in 60 percent casualties: an unacceptable number even by Patton's standards. The captain had been right.

Aside from all the men we lost, four BARs were unaccounted for. That night we had to go back to the scene of the carnage in the pitch dark and crawl on our hands and knees over the ground we had taken to find the weapons. I remember crawling over bodies, but it was too dark for me to identify any of them. We found two of the BARs, but we never did find the other ones.

A short time later at Battalion Headquarters, I ran into the captain who had refused to make the advance. He was standing outside warming himself near a fire burning in an empty 50-gallon drum. He had been busted and had no rank on his uniform. He needed a shave so badly that I almost didn't recognize him.

He was being reassigned as a private to another outfit, although one of our officers told me that he would be promoted to a sergeant's rank almost immediately. They probably had been forced to let him off relatively easy, in light of the fact witnesses had heard him warn in advance what would happen. His courage and leadership abilities resulted in his becoming a different type of casualty.

As February closed, we were well inside Germany and enemy resistance was becoming more and more disorganized. Records for the month show we took about 1,000 German prisoners. The Germans continued to fall back in confusion. There were fewer and fewer concrete fortifications; instead we now found hastily constructed trenches and wooden pillboxes. The Germans also had their own form of psychological warfare. They were shooting containers that sprinkled leaflets down on us. The pictures were almost pornographic and mostly consisted of women sitting on men's laps. A caption reminded us that there were eight men in the rear echelon for every man at the front, and that didn't include all the men back home. The message was that all these men were out screwing our women while we were busy fighting the war for them. We used the leaflets as toilet paper.

Hitler had recruited teenagers and children into an organization known as the "Werewolves." Many were too young for military service even by Nazi standards. Their mission was to carry out guerilla war tactics. They were great at scrawling slogans in white paint that were intended to demoralize us. "See the Reich and die," "Death awaits you," "Leave your skull at the Rhine" and other such slogans were painted on bridges, barns, and walls, usually accompanied by a skull and crossbones or a swastika. They harassed us with minor actions like destroying footbridges, but they never stood and fought us, and I don't remember them ever inflicting any casualties on our outfit.

The Germans not only developed V (vengeance) rockets and jets; they were also geniuses at modifying everyday vehicles, mostly trucks, to run on steam. I saw one that had a small stove-like contraption in the rear that burned wood. The wood in turn provided steam, which generated enough power to drive the vehicle. It was amazing!

We were out on a patrol led by a lieutenant when we heard from our first scout over the walkie-talkie that a single truck flying numerous German flags was headed our way. It was either lost or unaware of our rapid advance into the area. The lieutenant ordered us off to the side of the road and into cover. Soldiers always stay on one side of a road when attacking a vehicle, lest they unintentionally hit each other with crossfire.

When the vehicle came into view, we saw that it was nothing but a simple box van like an Opel-Blitz or a Pritsche. The flags it was flying signaled it was a military vehicle, and so we all poured fire on it as it drove past. I was near the front of our column and one of the first to shoot at it. That van must have been hit a thousand times and even its tires exploded. It did not burn, crash, or even go off the road. It just slowed very eerily to a dead stop, its occupants all killed.

Even after it stopped, the guys kept pouring lead into it, and the Lieutenant had to order them to knock it off. GIs immediately started to crowd around the car, but I didn't want to go and look. I had already seen enough dead bodies. I just continued forward and I thank God I did. We had hit a German military payroll in the midst of its delivery and there were mountains of cash inside that van. Many of the men who looked inside the vehicle grabbed the cash and stuffed their pockets and packs with it. I might have been tempted to do the same if I had been with them.

This van had written receipts and record books in it, and our officers soon got wind of what happened. The next day they had us all line up in formation and stand at attention. They checked our pockets and packs and anybody with German money from that vehicle was put into a labor battalion as punishment for looting. The lieutenant who led the patrol had also grabbed some loot and was cashiered out of the army for it.

The 2d Regiment spent the first week of March along the Kyll River. We were moved from the division's left flank over to the right in preparation for the drive on the Rhine River. The plan was to cross the Kyll, Mosel, and Rhine Rivers in quick succession, which would open the floodgates for the famed 4th Armored Division.

The Germans had retreated across the Kyll and blown the bridges after them. The 5th Division, ahead of the outfits on our flanks, mopped up what remained of the scattered enemy units, including the renowned 2d Panzer Division. The Germans had the high ground on the opposite side of the river and shelled our positions. We responded with artillery and air attacks delivered by P-47s and P-51s of the Ninth Air Force. The 11th Regiment crossed successfully on March 2.

While the 2d Regiment was in reserve during the first week of March, we had to dump any equipment or other items that were not strictly necessary. We were to move ahead as far and as fast as possible and resupply ourselves with captured enemy equipment. Anything we couldn't take with us was to be destroyed. We were then put under a security blackout. This would be a European version of Sherman's March to the Sea. Unfortunately, the blackout not only kept the 5th Division out of the news, but out of most historical accounts as well.

The 2d Battalion moved out on March 7 towards the Salm River and the town of Eisenschmitt. The 1st and 3rd Battalions saw most of the action and took most of the casualties. Assigned to 2d Battalion, I was lucky yet again. On March 8 our battalion was combined with light and medium tanks and assault guns, as well as some artillery, to form Task Force Graham. Walter Graham, the executive officer of the 2d Regiment, was assigned to lead the task force over the Mosel River and towards the Rhine. We jumped off from Oberkail at 08:00 hours.

Graham led us in a flanking movement that bypassed the enemy's main line of defense and came in from their rear to take the town of Manderscheid by surprise. By March 10 we had completed a movement that went first east and then south to take Kochem, and put us right on the north bank of the Mosel River. We waited for three days in Kochem to prepare to cross the Mosel, and the Germans hit us with mortars the entire time. Our nerves remained steady through it all because we were holding a city that contained one of the largest stockpiles of wine in all of Germany. I avoided all champagne, but the other wines did nicely.

It was also in March that Rolland Dysinger, our BAR man, asked if he could borrow my Lugar to take with him out on a patrol. This Lugar was beautiful. It had a barrel so long that there was a hole in the bottom of the holster that went along with it. A Lugar of this type was initially issued to forward observers in the German artillery. It was easy to see why—it looked like a cannon.

I guarded that Lugar jealously and was reluctant to give it to Dysinger that night. I had received it from a German officer right after his capture. I had to question him and, since I could speak German and he couldn't keep the gun any longer, he told me to keep it. I imagine it was intended to be an act of kindness. No one wanted to lose a prize like that, even though the Germans would probably use it on any GI they captured who was unfortunate enough to be carrying it.

My instincts were right. That night Dysinger and the others walked into a German ambush. When mortar rounds started to land around them, Dysinger threw himself onto the ground, and a round landed directly on his back. No traces were left of him from the waist up. He was not a close friend, but I was still sorry about what happened to him. The medics told me my Lugar was nowhere to be found, which was also disappointing but hardly a surprise.

Task Force Graham tried to cross the Mosel into Triers on March 12, but German rear guard elements fought very well and slowed our advance. Some reconnaissance elements were working their way across the bridge just as the Germans blew it. I can't imagine anybody made it off that bridge alive. I saw the bodies of some of those men floating down the Mosel.

The 1st and 2d Battalions of the 2d Regiment jumped off to cross the Mosel at 02:00 hours on March 13. We secured a bridgehead within three hours. The 11th Regiment followed across on pontoon bridges and quickly advanced. The 5th Infantry Division was partnered with the 4th Armored Division and together they punched holes everywhere in the German lines. It was becoming a free-for-all. The Germans were having a tougher and tougher time organizing any serious resistance, and we were taking large numbers of prisoners. They ran at us with their hands up and we waved them on to our rear and told them to keep going. Sometimes we threw stones at them as they ran by.

As one of the seasoned veterans, I was allowed to wear an Eisenhower jacket. It zippered instead of buttoned and ended at the waist. Normally only officers wore them, but they were also given out as a kind of perk to survivors. Even though I never wore any type of rank or insignia on the jacket, people who saw me in it naturally assumed I was an officer. This assumption helped me with two groups. First, the new replacements were quicker to listen to me, which helped me to keep them alive. Second, German officers, who often insisted on surrendering to an American officer, would see me in that coat, hear me speak German, and just naturally assume that I was a career soldier and an officer. I never actually misrepresented myself. I simply let people follow their natural assumptions.

It's possible that jacket may have sometimes made me think like an officer as well. Another soldier and I were ordered to take up a position on the second floor of a particular building to spot for the artillery. When we got there, I decided another building would serve us better. We went up to the second floor in the building I selected and started to set up our field phone.

The Germans were firing shells at troops and artillery well to our rear. As fate would have it, we took a hit from a tumbler. The defective shell rolled end over end instead of spinning round and round, and fell well short of its intended target, landing directly in the first floor of the building we were in. The floor collapsed beneath us and we dropped down, landing hard against the concrete slab on the ground level. We were covered with dirt, sawdust, and other debris.

We were not seriously hurt, but had lost our phone, so we obviously had to scrub our mission and return for further orders. The lieutenant who sent us out was furious with me, and I had to listen to the usual rant of how I would be court-martialed, if not for the serious shortage of manpower.

Patton wanted to cross the Rhine before Britain's General Montgomery. These two had been archrivals since the Allied campaign in North Africa. We may not have cared for Patton, but we liked Montgomery even less. Patton could at least justify his prima donna attitude with results, but Montgomery was far too cautious and seemed to plod along. He was like George McClellan, whose famed inaction during the civil war prompted Lincoln to write: "If you're not going to use the army, do you mind if I borrow it for a while." Monty would not attack until he had overwhelming superiority, and even then he advanced in inches. Most of us felt that he, like McCellen, should also have been fired.

Patton told General Eddy to get one of the outfits in XII Corps over the Rhine before Monty. The 5th Division was the only outfit even close to the Rhine, so we got the order to cross it for the Third Army and the United States. We weren't exactly in the immediate vicinity, so we had to race at breakneck speed for a full day to meet Patton's deadline. The division reached Oppenheim on the west side of the Rhine on March 21·

We continued to push aside all opposition before us. The division took Worms that same day, although my outfit was not involved in any fighting there. Worms was the city where Martin Luther organized his new religious faith, and statues of Luther were in abundance. I climbed into the outstretched arms of one, reclined casually, and had my picture taken.

The 11th Regiment started to cross the Rhine into Nierstein at 22:00 hours on March 22. The area was very lightly defended and the crossing was carried out with little incident. Patton had won his race with Montgomery by a full 24 hours.

Immediately after we crossed the Rhine, the Germans regained their fighting spirit. German fighters and bombers hit the engineers working to set up a bridge, and their infantry attacked our bridgehead with tank support. Despite this, we advanced and expanded the bridgehead some eight miles wide and five miles deep. Heavy fighting continued until March 24. Once we crossed the river, our command advanced us any way they could. We rode any type of vehicle available, and if none were available, we marched on foot. The idea was to keep moving. We had to keep the Germans off balance and prevent them from setting up a stable defense or counter attacking.

Around this time I was among some twelve or fourteen men selected to go out on a commando-type raid behind German lines. We knew they were assembling armor to hit us in what they hoped would be a surprise attack, and we wanted to shake them up. Our reconnaissance pilots had complete control of the air, and it was almost impossible for the enemy to do anything at this time without our knowing about it.

We wore fatigues with no insignia and each man tied a white cloth around his arm so we could identify one another. We were all issued four hand grenades and a trench knife. That was it. If we were captured, our commanders didn't want the Germans to know which outfit we were from. I suppose they weren't worried about any of us talking, because if we were captured, the Germans would probably just shoot us in retribution.

Our mission was to hit an enemy supply depot and cause pain and confusion, as quickly and on as large a scale, as possible. We moved at night, benefiting from trees and foliage for cover. We crept up towards our objective, surrounded it, then flung our grenades into the perimeter and ran like hell. We could hear the explosions and scrambling that followed.

I was running back towards our lines alone, using the moon for navigation, when I heard footsteps running behind me. I knew from the sound that my follower was not American, because we had rubber soles on our boots, but the Germans used leather, which made more noise. My pursuer would overtake me unless I did something. I turned off the road and ran into some bushes. I gripped my trench knife, intending to stab him when he caught up to me. It's a truly gruesome act to stab a man. In an instant, I decided to use the brass knuckles on the knife handle instead of the blade.

When my pursuer reached my position, I jumped out from the bushes right in front of him and thrust my right fist forward. I hit him on the rim of his helmet and he fell backwards like a ton of bricks. He was out cold. I had avoided stabbing him, but my awkward move had jammed my thumb up into my right hand.

I initially thought I had broken my hand, but quickly realized that wouldn't be such a bad thing. It would put me out of action for a while. When I got back to camp, the first sergeant saw my hand. "That's not so bad," he said. "I can fix that." He took my right hand with his left, grabbed my thumb with this other hand, and gave it a yank. It wasn't painful, but the thumb never healed correctly, giving me a strange bump at the joint that has stayed with me all my life. It was a small price to pay: about half the men sent out on that mission never returned.

Our battalion took the town of Bischofsheim as the entire division drove north to the Main River. By March 26 we were at the banks of the Main overlooking our next objective: Frankfurt, the ninth largest city in Germany. An estimated 20 percent of its 500,000 residents were still in the city. The Germans had already blown two of the three bridges across the Main River. We were ordered to secure the left flank of the remaining bridge; this we did, and elements of the 11th Regiment, followed by elements of the 10th, started across under heavy artillery fire.

They were facing SS men with light tanks on the other side, and the entire crossing turned into a real slugfest. We went over on the following morning and got the same welcome from German artillery that our sister regiments had received. The Germans put up quite a fight: even civilians and city police units joined in the fray. Not until March 29 did we have the city under control.

I remember advancing up a street in Frankfurt, fairly far ahead of anyone else. It was dusk but not yet dark. The street forked into a Y, and I hugged the walls behind me and proceeded forward along the street to my right. Suddenly a shot rang out and a bullet snapped against the concrete just an inch or two above my head. I immediately ran forward towards the safety of a doorway, when a second shot hit the concrete about my head, just as the first had done. I was fortunate that this sniper was shooting high. He had had two chances and he blew them. I was alive and my fears were now replaced with anger. I wanted to dispense a little payback. This is a common reaction when people try to kill you.

I had seen the flash from the second shot come from an upper window across the way at the corner where the street had forked. I ducked around the back of the closest building and worked my way across the street. I went down an alley and up some yards until I reached the back of the building where the shot had come from. Inside were two separate staircases. I chose one and hoped that I guessed right. I quietly and slowly advanced up the stairs, knowing that if they creaked I was a dead man. On the second floor there was no one to be seen. I slowly and quietly continued up the stairs to the third floor.

Once on the third floor, I peered around the corner and saw a silhouetted figure scanning the field of fire out the window, looking for a target. The shooter was probably still looking for me. My Tommy gun was already cocked, so I flipped the switch from fully to semi-automatic fire. There was no sense in wasting an entire burst on this character. I quietly rested my weapon against the doorframe and took deliberate aim at this obscure outline of semi-shadows. I slowly squeezed the trigger and he collapsed before the shot finished ringing out.

I approached cautiously, holding my weapon forward in case he had anything in his hand like a pistol. He was moaning and obviously in great pain. As I turned him over, a feeling of dread swept over me. It was plain to see that he was only a kid in his mid-teens!

I asked him in German how badly he was hit. He answered me in broken German but I understood him. He told me that he was a 16-year-old Pole who had been put in uniform and left there by the Germans with the promise that they would return for him. They assured him that the Americans took no prisoners and that he was as good as dead if he surrendered.

My shot had hit him high near the left shoulder. It was a million-dollar wound with the bullet going clear through him, but I could tell he was going into shock. I patched him up as best I could, put his coat over him, and assured him that he would be all right.

By this time, I could see out the window that our men had caught up to me. I called down, "Hey medic, get up here right away! I need your help badly!" The medic quickly ran up the three flights of stairs and I explained what had happened. He bandaged the kid up and I then carried him down to the street, where I placed him on a litter secured on a waiting jeep. I told the kid again that he would be all right, and then the jeep sped away. I inquired about him a few days later when I was in the rear and I was told that he was going to make it. I was glad to hear it.

A GI could occasionally get away with looting items left behind by fleeing civilians, but murdering a civilian was something the army simply would not tolerate, as we were all about to see. We had moved quickly into the Frankfurt Excelsior Hotel when it appeared to be unoccupied by enemy troops. We were on the forward end of an advance, and knew the Germans couldn't be far off. We separated and began to search the hotel, but one GI went into the bar and helped himself to a drink. The hotel manager screamed that this was looting, and insisted that he stop immediately. The rest of us were oblivious as we had more important things to do. The hotel had eight or nine floors, which meant we had a lot of work ahead of us.

I was on the third floor when I was startled to hear three shots from an M-1 ring out in rapid succession in front of the hotel. I figured a skirmish had started and bolted down the stairs, expecting to find an assault under way. Instead, I learned that the soldier in the bar had taken the hotel manager into the street and murdered him.

The next day our entire company, some 150 men, was ordered to stand in formation in a courtyard as an eyewitness to the crime walked among our open ranks and correctly picked out the man responsible. The identified man was then moved to another spot in the ranks and a second eyewitness, who had been kept out of sight and sound from the first, went on to correctly identify the same GI. This process was repeated yet a third time, with a third eyewitness, and again the correct man was identified. The GI responsible was appropriately court-martialed and sentenced to death. I have no idea whether his sentence was carried out or if it was commuted. I never saw him again.

While the Germans were retreating out of Frankfurt, I was selected with three other men to occupy a tower for sniper duty against the fleeing foe. The Germans were racing to evacuate the city and the surrounding area, but were slowed by the civilian foot traffic that clogged the roads. Our mission was to shoot as many German soldiers as possible, using Springfield bolt action rifles equipped with telescopic sights. It didn't matter whether we killed or wounded them, just so long as we hit them. In either case our victims would be out of the war. Our actions left a number of Wehrmacht bodies littered about.

The others knew that I was aiming at the trunk of my targets. I didn't want to shoot anybody in the head or see their faces in my sight. The next morning, I awoke on the floor of that tower to find myself staring into the opened-mouthed, wide-eyed expression of a dead German soldier, whom my buddies had placed right alongside me as I slept. I let out a shriek and jumped to my feet as my comrades roared with laughter.

I was glad to get the hell out of Frankfurt. The city had given me the creeps. I came closer to, and delivered, more death in Frankfurt than I was accustomed to even as a frontline soldier.

The historian Max Hastings accurately describes how Hitler's propaganda minister, Joseph Goebbels, began to complain about this time that German civilians were greeting Americans as liberators rather than as conquerors. Germans, whether civilian or military, knew they were licked. We were a far better alternative than the Russians, and German civilians treated us accordingly. It was not uncommon for German women to offer GIs shelter in their homes, a warm bed, and the willingness to share it with them. Americans had become the new protectors for the women of the Reich.

Opportunities were so abundant that I was even called on once to pimp for an officer. He didn't want to stay in a town we had just taken, and he asked me to find him a place outside the area where he could spend the night. It was understood that he also wanted female companionship included in the accommodations. I had to make a number of stops, but I finally found a home with adult daughters who were not only willing, but actually eager to put out.

The oldest girl was twenty-one and good-looking. Both she and her parents were clear about what the deal entailed. None of them spoke any English, so I decided to have some fun. I carefully coached the girl to say to the officer after sex "(So and so), you can't perform worth a shit." I assured her it was a compliment, but reminded her to wait until after the act.

This officer and I were on good terms, so I knew I could get away this. The next day, he caught up with me and said sarcastically, "Thanks a lot Bilder, you really made that experience memorable." I smiled and said, "Next time, do your own pimping, sir." We both laughed.

One of the many enemy units melting out of existence at this time was the 6th SS Mountain Division of the German 89th Corps. The sudden advances of the American armies had cut them off and they were trying to get back to their own lines. Like many Germans in the west, they had been battle-hardened from years of fighting the Russians. They captured one of our field hospitals and had their fill of American rations and cigarettes. The next morning they took whatever remained, and even carted their booty away on American trucks. You could almost admire such pure audacity.

They were only interested in materials and supplies, and they left the doctors and nurses alone and unharmed. Despite this, the rumor spread throughout our ranks that they killed the doctors in cold blood and gang raped the nurses. On March 31 the 3rd Battalion got the assignment to go and round them up out of the woods near Erbstadt.

The rest of the 2d Regiment joined them the following day. Most everyone had payback on their minds and venom in their hearts as they set out. This operation lasted until April 5. An estimated half of these 1,300 SS men were killed after they surrendered or were in the process of doing so.

I personally witnessed one incident. A soldier with a BAR was escorting about a dozen of these men when he suddenly open fired on them without provocation, killing them all in cold blood in front of numerous witnesses. Then he yelled, "I'll kill myself, I'll kill myself!" over and over again. He wanted out of combat any way possible and he must have figured that a Section 8 (insanity) was as good a way as any. We all knew he was sane, but he still got his Section 8 and out of combat at the price of a dozen lives. Most of us, however, preferred to leave executions up to the proper authorities. We already had enough moral burdens weighing us down.

I was getting tired of war. While I had never killed in cold blood or bothered civilians, the war was taking a toll on me. I was tired, dirty, underfed, and homesick, just like millions of other GIs. Death almost has a physical presence. I saw it and delivered it almost daily and never grew accustomed to it. It was only the certainty that it was all winding down that pushed me on. Just a short while longer and it would all be over. I was so looking forward to the end that I almost didn't care whether or not I made it through alive. I just wanted it to be done.

Around this time I slipped away and really had a good cry. I was beginning to wonder how much more of this shit I could take. A combat soldier normally doesn't cry around anyone else. In my case, I hid my feelings partly because of the expectations and attitudes of the era, but also because of the circumstances of war. War creates the necessity to always portray yourself as a tough guy. You have to view yourself as tough enough to do your duty in combat and the enemy needs to see you as someone tough enough to fear.

There was also a more practical reason. Crying is one of the symptoms that precedes combat fatigue. Once other guys see you cry, they worry you might be losing your nerve and on the verge of a breakdown. They may avoid you, fearing you might no longer be reliable in combat. This can end up leaving you alone, vulnerable, and dead.

I had written Mary a letter dated April 5, her birthday, and while I tried to be upbeat, my depression still came through. I told her that I could even accept death, if only I could see her just once more. Thoughts of the future and marriage were the only bright areas in my life, and my sole reason for survival. I was again starting to think of things beyond the present moment. Maybe, just maybe, there was light at the end of the tunnel.

After the incidents with the 6th SS Mountain Division, we were ordered to make certain that all enemy soldiers who wanted to surrender were given quarter. The Germans had sent word to our command that if we didn't take prisoners, they would return the favor when any of our men fell into their hands.

Surrender, however, could be a tricky thing. One town in Germany had all white flags out as we approached. They hung from every window in every building. It was an historic town, and the burgermiester had persuaded the German army to leave it to us without a fight. Despite the obvious lack of resistance, we moved into the town cautiously, hugging the sides of the buildings on both sides of the street.

The lieutenant leading us nevertheless walked right down the middle of the main drag. He was gutsy and exemplified real qualities of leadership and command. A shot rang out from a high point and he fell over, wounded in the groin. About eight of us rushed the house where the shot had originated, freely throwing grenades into the window. When the smoke cleared, we found the body of a girl in her mid-teens. She may once have even been pretty, but now she looked like she had been fed through a meat grinder. I could only think she had been a committed Nazi. Her action was a near guarantee of suicide, and she was wearing numerous swastika armbands. She was determined to die for her cause, and she did. Fortunately, our officer survived.

The other Germans in the town were far more sincere about surrendering. We gave orders for everyone to turn in their weapons and all Nazi paraphernalia. I was one of several GIs ordered to remain behind in town to check for snipers, fanatics, or any other signs of trouble. The civilians turned in their contraband, and later that night I was approached by a woman who saw and heard that I could speak German. She told me a friend of her family was hiding in her cellar.

He had stayed behind (in other words, deserted) after the German retreat in order to surrender, but he was afraid to come out. I knew this could be an ambush, but for some reason I trusted the woman and went with her.

When we reached her place she pointed to the cellar where he was hiding. I asked her why he simply didn't come up out of there and surrender. "He's afraid you'll shoot him," she said. "But if I go with you, he thinks you will be more likely to take him prisoner." I accepted the proposition and told her to lead the way.

We went down into the cellar with her in the lead. The angle of the stairs was such that by simply holding my Tommy gun at my waist, I pointed its barrel right at the nape of her neck. If this was an ambush, she'd be the first to get it. The cellar was lit and there, seated at a small table, was indeed a German soldier. His rifle was off to the side well away from him, leaning up against the wall.

I asked him who he was and why he wanted to surrender. He told me his name and that he had been in the army for six years. He was 43 years old, had extensive combat experience on the Russian front, and had had enough. He just wanted to surrender and make it through the war alive. He also sang like a canary. There wasn't anything he wouldn't answer, and he answered thoroughly and without hesitation.

I told him to go outside and I'd see to it that he was handed over to people who would ensure he made it to a prison camp alive. By this time the outfit behind us had come up and our men were marching through the town. I told him to put his hands behind his head in order to make this look official, and he immediately complied. I took him outside and got hold of a sergeant and explained the situation. I told him that this German was frightened and very willing to cooperate. There was no need to threaten him or rough him up.

This was something I might have otherwise seen to myself, but I explained that I was already far behind my unit and had to get back to it as quickly as possible. As it was, I'd probably have to hitch a ride just to catch up. The sergeant understood and assured me that he would see to it that the prisoner got back safely to a holding area. My prisoner smiled at me and nodded as he was escorted away. The woman told me that if I wanted to spend the night, she'd be willing to share her bed with me. I thanked her for the offer but told her that I had to rejoin my outfit.

Both the 2d and 10th Regiments were detached from XII Corps and held in reserve until April 8, when they were attached to III Corps of the First Army. A large concentration of German forces were surrounded in their industrial heartland, some 160 miles to the northwest of us along the Ruhr River. Historians now refer to this area as the "Ruhr Pocket." Sometimes it is also called the "Rose Pocket" after General Maurice Rose, who commanded American forces there.

General Rose, who was Jewish, was killed under what some consider mysterious circumstances. He was in a jeep patrolling the perimeter area of the pocket when his group encountered three heavy German tanks and were forced to surrender. The more probable version of the story is that General Rose made a move to unfasten his sidearm that the Germans misinterpreted as a hostile act, and shot and killed him as a result. The other version is that the Germans killed the General in cold blood because he was Jewish. It's unlikely the truth will ever be proven beyond all debate.

It is my personal belief that most of the action in the Ruhr was unnecessary. It was nothing than a waste of time intended to keep American forces busy so the Russians could capture Berlin. I know that apologists for Roosevelt and the Russians talk about the terrible cost of the Battle of Berlin, but I saw how demoralized the Germans were and I believe that instead of fighting to the end, as they did in the face of Russian occupation, they would have surrendered to Americans after token resistance, just as they did later in Austria and Czechoslovakia.

Eisenhower originally expected to take Berlin, but his superiors in Washington decided that the ultimate prize should go to the Russians. Leo Kessler quotes Eisenhower as saying in September 1944, "Clearly Berlin is the main prize. There is no doubt whatsoever in my mind that we should concentrate our energies and resources on a rapid thrust to Berlin." Kessler goes on to document Eisenhower's change of heart with a quote from March 1945: "That place (Berlin) has become, so far as I am concerned, nothing but a geographical location, and I have never been interested in these."

The Germans in the Ruhr Pocket were trapped and unable to break out. They probably had little desire to break out anyway, and could have easily been contained and allowed to wither on the vine, like they did at the fortresses at Metz, while Patton took Berlin. I, along with countless historians, can only guess the rational for our government's decision, but as a soldier who was there I can honestly say that I thought even at the time that it was a mistake not to take Berlin. The U.S. Army was owed that prize and it should have been ours.

We reached the Ruhr area on April 10 and established ourselves in the vicinity of Kalle. Our tank support came from the 737th Tank Battalion. The Germans in most cases were eager to surrender and the division's official history estimates that we took some 500 prisoners a day. Among these was German General Richard Wirtz, the chief engineer officer for Army Group B, who was captured in the town of Stemel.

A news bulletin originating in England came over the radio in our halftrack announcing that Roosevelt had died on April 12. None of us were really moved. We knew the end of the war was very near, and we were all preoccupied with making it through alive. At the risk of sounding cynical, I say that most of us regarded Roosevelt as simply another politician, with the difference that he happened to occupy the White House. We knew that his death wouldn't have any effect on the conduct or outcome of the war.

Aside from the loss of life, it was sickening to see the complete and utter destruction of an entire landscape. To be sure, the Germans brought destruction on themselves with their belief in racial superiority and their desire for conquest, but it was still disheartening to me to see every last factory, school, and house leveled to the ground in twisted wrecks.

Everyone was starving, German soldiers, German civilians, and their slave labor. We had to protect warehouses with food stores lest the mobs of hungry people loot them. We were the only order there was. We encountered some of the many teenagers that Hitler was putting into uniform. We were rounding up boys as young as 15 years old. I did my best not to look them in the eye. They reminded me too much of the younger brothers of guys I had hung around with back in my old neighborhood. Sometimes I swore I was looking right into the face of one of those kids back home.

I was with a captain checking out a private residence when we encountered a German man of military age. He showed us his papers and a medical discharge from the army. We were outside near the cellar door, and the captain asked him what was inside. He told us it was full of personal items and none of our affair. It would be looting for us to take anything in there.

For all we knew, he could have been hiding anything from an arms cache to a squad of enemy soldiers, so the captain said to me, "Bilder, show him we mean business." I hauled off and belted that German right in the jaw, and he tumbled down the three steps leading into the cellar. He got up, immediately unlocked the door, and ran off. The place was loaded with booze.

The captain and I were checking the place out and salivating over our find when the German returned with an American lieutenant. "Captain," the lieutenant said, "this man claims that you're looting." The captain looked up from what he was doing and calmly replied, "He's a liar." The lieutenant looked taken aback and added, "He also claims that he was struck." The captain stepped forward and looked the lieutenant squarely in the eye. "Now look, Lieutenant," he said firmly. "I've already told you that he's a liar. I'm carrying out my duties and I've got the situation well in hand. Have you got anything further?" The lieutenant could clearly see that there was no point in pursuing the matter any longer. He snapped to attention and said in a solid military tone, "No, sir!" He then departed and the captain and I helped ourselves to a couple of bottles before we left.

We continued to clean up isolated pockets of resistance and to process prisoners. We literally gave these prisoners a kick in the pants or a slap in the face. "Are you gonna start any more wars?" we'd ask, or "How many Americans did you kill?" To which they would invariably reply, "None!" as they had always just come from the Russian front. With all these Germans on the Russian front, we couldn't figure out who it was that had been killing so many of our guys over the last ten months.

By this time, I was one of the few enlisted men invited to sit with officers as they relaxed during our quiet times. The fact that I spoke

German and often assisted them with prisoners and civilians, coupled with the fact that I was one of only a few old soldiers who had been around since Normandy all served to make me an interesting commodity.

We were in a town in Germany when a field kitchen arrived and set up shop to give us a hot meal. This was a rare treat and everyone grabbed their mess kits and started lining up as quickly as possible. I was sitting under a tree with some officers when one lieutenant took his mess kit and went right to the head of the line. The captain watched him go without saying a word and waited until he had taken his position in front of everyone else.

The captain then got up, walked up to the lieutenant, and asked him in front of everyone present, "Lieutenant, what's the first thing you learned at Officer's Candidate School?" To which the lieutenant replied, "Always take care of your men first." The captain just grinned. "That's right," he said. "So get your ass to the back of this line, right now!" Everyone, officers and enlisted men alike, cheered.

General Eddy, commander of XII Corps, was relieved due to severe hypertension, and Patton selected our own 5th Division Commander, Major General S. Leroy Irwin, to replace General Eddy on April 21. Command of the 5th Division now went to Major General Albert E. Brown, a veteran of World War I who had served in the campaign to retake the Aleutian Islands (Alaska) from the Japanese in 1943.

The rapid Allied drive in Germany kept our division bouncing around between organizations like a rubber ball. We were assigned to XVI Corps of the Ninth Army from April 22 to 24, when we got orders to move out for southern Germany (Bavaria). We used captured German trucks for transportation and I even drove one. The trucks didn't last the journey and we had to hitch a ride on whatever we could find, or just plain walk. We were back in Patton's Third Army again on April 25, but the division continued to swing back and forth between corps assignments. We were with General Walker's XX Corps for five days (at least on paper) before going back to XII Corps and its new commander, General Irwin, on April 29.

Units of the 2d and 10th Regiments were scattered as we scrambled for rides with anyone who would take us on anything that would carry us. As we hurried southeast to reunite with the rest of the division, our route from the Ruhr Pocket brought us near Weimar. Our group was some five miles northwest of the city when we saw Buchenwald Concentration Camp. It had just been liberated on April 11 by the 6th Armored Division. It was a horror beyond words. The camp had been designed for slave labor, not mass extermination, but we never would have known that from the looks of it. More than two weeks after the liberation, bodies were still stacked in the open as attempts to identify the dead were made. Others were being exhumed from shallow graves. Those inmates who survived bore a closer resemblance to the dead than to the living. The inhumanity almost defies description.

The 80th Infantry Division had been assigned to oversee the camp on April 12, and we lent them a hand in making the Germans properly bury the dead, even if they had to use their bare hands to do it. I advised one NCO to get every German-speaking GI he had to make the rounds and be certain that every German who was physically up to the task was busy properly burying the victims. Despite those who claim the holocaust never happened, or that it was not as bad as reported, I can say definitively that it did indeed happen, and that it was every bit as bad as it has been described!

The Germans had now become very frightened about surrendering and tried to do so cautiously. I was on point patrolling some woods in Bavaria when three Germans suddenly jumped up in front of me from behind a log with their hands up. "Kamerad!" they shouted in unison. They startled me, and although my carbine was pointing down, I had my finger on the trigger and unintentionally pulled it. The shot frightened them and they started to run. A soldier came up from behind me, dropped to one knee, and shot them in the back as they ran. He fired three shots and each one was fatal. I've always felt strangely responsible for their deaths and still wish I could have taken them prisoner.

The German 7th Army, loosely estimated at 150,000 to 450,000 troops, was holed up in Czechoslovakia and supposedly waiting to go out in a blaze of glory by taking as many Americans and Russians with them as possible. On May 1 Patton relayed an ultimatum from Eisenhower for them to surrender, and they were said to be considering it. Word went around the world that Hitler was now dead, and we hoped that this might finally bring the curtain down on the war.

We were billeted in Altreichenau, Germany near the Tepla (or Templa) Vlatva River, which formed the border between Germany and Czechoslovakia. We were waiting to hear if the war was going to end the easy or the hard way. We saw peace planes flying overhead and of course the orders were that no one fire on them. They were painted all white and had no insignia. They carried German negotiators back and forth but the discussions apparently went nowhere.

Time was up for the Germans on May 4. When they didn't agree to surrender, Patton was ordered to send his Third Army into Czechoslovakia the following day. Patton had 18 divisions, more than 500,000 troops, under his command to get the job done. It was, and still remains, the largest force the United States has ever fielded for an offensive. In retrospect, I've often wondered if this was because Patton expected trouble from our Russian allies once the Germans were beaten.

Our Company G was sent out that night to patrol the river for the best place to cross east into Czechoslovakia the following morning. Just before midnight we found a bridge slightly to the east of Hill 746, but enemy resistance was enough to drive us off. Our platoon then found a busted-up bridge that we still could use for a crossing in the morning. Amazingly, the Germans were still putting up firm resistance.

At dawn (06:00 hours) on May 5, we were ready to go, but the Germans now had a tank blocking our way across the footbridge. Everyone was pinned down by enemy machine gun fire from two pill-boxes and the ground was too soft and muddy to get our tank destroyers up. We used another footbridge further downstream, crossed the Tepla, and cleared the woods out to the north. A number of our men received the Bronze Star Medal for their heroic actions that day when they charged across the Tepla River under heavy enemy fire.

Then we moved forward and took the towns of Milesice and Mullerschlag. We advanced another two miles or so along a front roughly three-quarters of a mile wide. This was the Sudetenland, occupied by ethnic Germans. Their sympathies were with Germany and they had no love for us. They stayed in their homes and glared at us with unforgiving eyes from behind lace curtains as we advanced.

Later, as we moved deeper into the country, past the Sudetenland, we saw beautiful rich farm fields. It was some of the most beautiful and productive land in all of Europe, and it was easy to see why the Germans had wanted it for themselves. It was like France all over again as the people ran out to greet us, welcoming their liberators with food and drink of every kind.

Just before 07:00 hours on May 6, we moved out under rainy conditions in a northeasterly direction. The 5th and 90th Infantry Divisions were advancing parallel to one another. Together, we had initially opened a path that the 4th Armored Division could have blazed all the way into Prague. They could have come to the aid of the Czech partisans who were now in revolt against their German occupiers and sending pleas for help over the radio. Alas, Prague, like Berlin, was yet another capital promised to the Russians, and once again the U.S. Army was forced to halt in its tracks.

Part of our 2d Battalion captured Pech B, just two miles west of Volary, a town the Germans had renamed Wallern. We here exchanged some mortar and artillery rounds with the enemy. We were ordered to crawl up some nearby wooded high ground in search of some SS men who refused to quit. As we advanced, a replacement was dragging his carbine along the ground instead of laying it flat across his arms as we were trained to do. Sure enough, the trigger caught on some foliage and the gun discharged, sending an armor-piercing round right through the stomach of Charles McGuire, who had made it through with us all the way from Normandy. I watched in great sadness as he lay with his head in the lap of another soldier, and his life slipped away in 15 minutes. At this point, everyone knew that any more killing and dying was just bullshit. The war was essentially over. This irony was not lost on McGuire. "What a hell of a way to get it, what a hell of a way to go," he said before dying.

Our officers could see how ridiculous it was to lose any more men in infantry advances, so they simply called in the artillery to clear the high ground before us. Our divisional field artillery opened up and got the job done the easy way. We knew it couldn't last much longer. The Germans were in sad shape and approaching our lines in mass to surrender. Long columns of enemy vehicles and foot soldiers advanced on us, flying not swastikas, but white flags. They were no longer willing to die and desperately wanted to avoid falling into the hands of the Russians.

On May 7 we were ready to continue our sweeping advance to the northeast. At approximately 08:20 hours, elements of the German 11th Panzer Division, hidden in the nearby woods, zapped the forward section of one of our columns in a nasty ambush. There was a brief, but intense, skirmish before both sides were told to cease fire. Private Charles Havlat of the 5th Division's 803rd Tank Destroyer Battalion became the last known American to be killed in action in the European Theater. (The 2d Regiment's records show him as a Warrant Officer.) The war was to end officially at midnight and no further actions were to be taken by either side. An armistice was now in effect. That last skirmish had been totally unnecessary.

The 5th Infantry Division fired some of the last shots of the war in Europe. We had also advanced some 10 miles beyond the Karlovy Vary-Plzen-Ceska Budejovice demarcation (halt) line into territory promised to the Russians. On May 7, 1945, the Germans surrendered unconditionally at Reims, France, a city our 2d Regiment had liberated on August 30, 1944.

Our trek across northwestern Europe had lasted ten months and taken us across roughly 2,000 miles of terrain. We participated in all five of Third Army's campaigns. Our division accumulated 300 days of combat time and captured more than 71,000 of the enemy.

It had been a costly venture. The 5th Infantry Division had arrived in France with roughly 14,000 men. Almost 2,700 of our GIs were killed in action or died from wounds. Casualties included more than 9,000 wounded, 1,000 missing, and 100 captured. Hardly anyone who began with us was still with the unit at the end of the war. I felt very much alone.

The fighting was officially over but we knew we couldn't let our guard down. There were still die-hard SS out there. We also had Hitler's teenage Werewolves to contend with, and land mines were planted everywhere. No one wanted to do anything risky, much less die, now that the war was over and we were on the verge of going home.

There was no cheering and there were no celebrations at the news of the war's end. Everyone just felt kind of numb. All we had to do now was make it through the occupation. It wouldn't be as easy as it sounded, and unfortunately there were still some among us who wouldn't make it home alive.

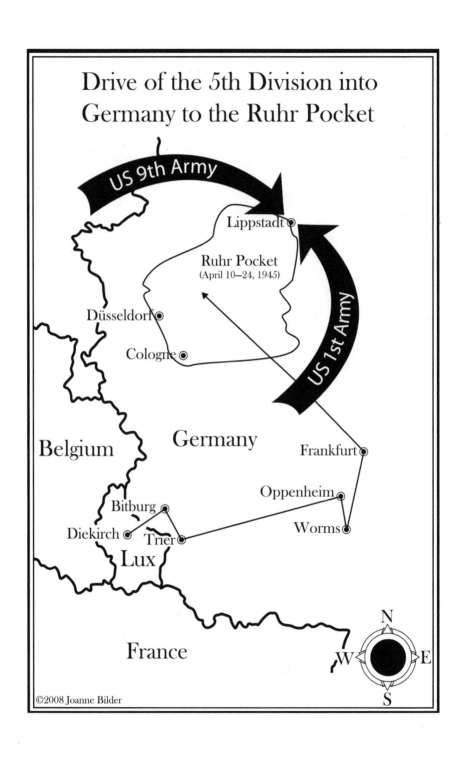

Drive of the 5th Division into
Germany to the Ruhr Pocket

US 9th Army

Lippstadt

Ruhr Pocket
(April 10–24, 1945)

US 1st Army

Düsseldorf

Cologne

Belgium

Germany

Frankfurt

Oppenheim

Bitburg

Worms

Diekirch   Trier

Lux

France

N

W   E

S

©2008 Joanne Bilder

11

WAR'S END
Adding Points and Avoiding Final Opportunities for Getting Killed

"There, above noise and danger,
Sweet Peace sits crown'd with smiles."
—Henry Vaughan, "Peace"

The 5th Division was in Volary, Czechoslovakia, when all hostilities came to an end at midnight on May 8, 1945. This date is best known to the world as VE (Victory in Europe) Day. Volary was only two miles from Pech B, and it appears the division got there just in time.

According to historical record, the 5th Division saved the lives of 118 Jewish girls by its timely liberation of the area. The previous January, these girls had been forced on a 700-kilometer death march from Poland to Czechoslovakia. Unfortunately, we unable to save 93 of their unfortunate companions, most of whom had been shot by the Nazis because they had been uncooperative enough to survive the exposure, exhaustion, and starvation of their trek from Poland, and their brief internment at Volary. We got there before the enemy could finish their grisly work. One of the survivors, Gerda Weismann Klein, describes this experience in *All But My Life*, which was made into the Academy Award-winning documentary *One Survivor Remembers*. She married one of her liberators, Kurt Klein, a lieutenant in the 5th Division.

Word went out to the civilian population that they would be granted a form of general amnesty, provided that they turned in every last weapon, military or not, to city hall. This also included all Nazi paraphernalia from civilians and military alike. As long as civilians followed the rules, would be no questions asked, but if they were found with any weapons or Nazi emblems, after their window of opportunity closed, they would be in real trouble. The meeting room in city hall soon was completely filled with guns, flags, rings, lapel pins, and countless other items. Our guys were visibly salivating at the chance to get in there at all those souvenirs.

Our boys began gobbling up souvenirs the moment the war ended. Everybody wanted something to take home. The Germans looted their POWs, we looted the Germans, and on occasion our officers looted us. An officer told me to take another GI and have him drive a jeep slowly up and down the formations of enemy prisoners in the disarming fields, while I directed them in German to put all their small arms (pistols and knives) into the back of the jeep. My instructions (at that point they were no longer orders) were to sell the small arms we collected to any of our boys who wanted them, and believe me there was no shortage of demand. "Take care of it Bilder, you know what to do," he said.

We opened up shop in the back of the jeep, charging $50 for the larger and better quality pistols and $25 for the smaller ones as well as for knives and daggers. We had no trouble quickly selling all our wares, and I turned the money over to the officer, who then divided it up with us. My share was a couple of hundred dollars. I did well with the side arms, but the rifles were entrusted to someone else who wheeled and dealed less than I did. I had a good friend, an ammunition sergeant, who acquired a Czech pistol. He forgot to unload it or put the safety on. He was showing off his booty when it discharged in his hand, and the bullet took the top of one of his fingers with it. He got busted for being so careless.

I was also present when a German colonel and his entourage came in to surrender. Their staff car was a beautiful Mercedes Benz. I saw that the colonel in charge had a Lugar, and thought this might be my chance to recoup the one lost I'd lost when Dysinger was killed. The German colonel refused my request for the pistol, which he was determined to surrender to an American officer, but when I asked about the car, he told me to take it. He even had his men pull it off the road near some trees where it would be out of clear view. I knew I could use this car for some private touring during the occupation.

There was still plenty of business to take care of in Volary. Our officers' first concern was the dead bodies of the Jewish prisoners for whom rescue had arrived too late. We got the usual story from the ethnic Germans, who acted completely surprised that such horrible things could have gone on under their very noses, and claimed they never had a clue that the crimes were occurring.

Now that the war was over, we no longer had to race to take the next town. We hence could remain long enough in Volary to see that justice was served. The corpses, including those exhumed from shallow graves, were laid out for public viewing, and the German locals were forced to walk past the bodies and take a good look at the victims. I was ordered to get the civilians busy building coffins so the dead could be given a fitting burial. I instructed them what to do, including how to dig graves. If they lacked the proper digging tools, then they had to use their hands. On May 11, Herman Dicker, a Jewish chaplain from our division, conducted a ceremony for the victims as they were laid to rest.

I was assigned to one of the many motorized patrols sent out to make certain the Germans had ceased all hostile activity. Some enemy soldiers out in the woods and farm fields still had not surrendered. This was due to several different reasons. A few had not yet heard that the war was officially over. For others, it didn't matter if the war was over or not. Finally, others still were trying to work their way through the Russian lines in order to surrender to the Americans. If our patrol encountered any Germans, we informed them the war was over and they had to turn themselves in. If they refused to surrender, we engaged them in a fight. Our mission was standard patrol activity in a clearly defined and limited area.

There were about six of us in my group. We piled into a scout car (a half track with wheels instead of treads) and headed out. At their furthest point, the American lines extended to Pilsen. After that, an undefined area or no man's land stretched to the Russian zone of occupation. We were to patrol a part of this no man's land, an area about five miles wide, just southeast of Pilsen. When we reached the outskirts of the city, we were to radio in to our command post for further instructions. Ours was a conventional patrol, unlike certain American "white flag" operations that had orders to go all the way over to the

Russian lines. Such operations not only got the word out that the war had ended, but picked up American POWs from their German captors or Russian liberators.

Our starting point was already east of where it was supposed to be, according to the map. This was because our division was already ten miles into the area designated for the Russians. We drove for quite a while without encountering any problems or signs of German activity, so we assumed we were well within our lines and sure to reach the Pilsen area shortly. The map-related navigational screw-up caused us to miss our objective completely. We continued east for about 40 miles looking for Pilsen, but did not realize just how lost we were until we saw a sign that read "Prague." No one had to tell us that we had far exceeded our assigned area.

Now on the outer edges of the Czech capital, we saw bodies hanging from lampposts. Some were in German uniforms and others in civilian clothes, but there seemed to be a body on just about every post. There were green military vehicles and uniforms up ahead of us: tanks, jeeps, trucks, and others. They were all American vehicles, except they had a red star instead of a white one painted on them. We also saw troops looting shops and rounding up civilians.

We stopped dead in our tracks and radioed for instructions. Our radio operator called our command post, explained our situation, then turned to us and said, "We're in the Russian zone. They said to get the hell out of here, NOW, before we cause an international incident." We were under the command of an NCO who ordered us to keep our hands off our weapons and turn around as quickly and quietly as possible. The Russians either didn't notice us or thought we were part of their group, because no one approached or attempted to stop us.

We wandered around the suburbs of Prague until we finally found a local who could speak some German. He gave me directions that allowed us to get back to our own lines. We figured that the civilians hanging from the lampposts included both German collaborators and Czech partisans opposed to communism. We had already heard that lynching might be occurring. As witnesses to these events, we thought we might have conveniently "disappeared," had we been caught. The Russians would never have sent our commanders a word about our fate.

The cold war had not yet started officially, but we had all heard stories about the Russians. We had taken Poles prisoner who had started off as soldiers in their own army only to be captured by the Russians and impressed into service in the Russian army. They were then captured by the Germans and impressed into service for Germany before we finally captured them ourselves. They said that the Russians were every bit as bad, if not worse, than the Germans. The Germans we took prisoner all throughout the war kept assuring us that while we were enemies for the moment, we would soon be allies in a war against the Russians. I thought about this and everything we had just seen as our scout car headed back to our own lines, and wondered how the Czechs or anyone else "liberated" by the Red Army was any better off than they had been under the Nazis.

Patton told interviewers that he could have easily taken Prague instead of the thin 3,500 square-mile slice of western Bohemia that he had captured. When reporters asked him what had stopped him from going all the way to Prague, he simply replied, "Orders!" His orders must have been very specific, because we got chewed out big time for our screw-up once we got back.

There must have been a camp for Russian POWs near Volary, because freed Russian prisoners were now roaming all over our area. They took refuge in barns on local farms and ate whatever they could dig out of the ground. Their stomachs were distended and paper thin from years of starvation in German captivity. Some of them literally ate themselves to death simply by consuming a few raw vegetables. Their foraging activities and use of the barns were shaking up the locals, and one old German woman in particular raised a real ruckus. The captain called me in and told me to get a jeep and go out to see what I could do to restore order.

I found about 50 Russians holed up in her barn. They had been digging up potatoes, beets, and anything else that grew in the ground. They had also killed and eaten some chickens and the bones were strewn around the barn floor. There were half a dozen bodies of men who had already eaten themselves to death. They did not realize that their stomachs had shrunk from prolonged starvation and couldn't handle even the small amounts of food they consumed.

None of them could speak English, but they did have an officer who had picked up some German during captivity. I explained that order had to be maintained among the civilians and that he and his men could not continue to use local barns as barracks. I also told him that they needed to get medical attention and to be careful what they ate. I informed him about a camp some five miles down the road where he and his men would get everything they needed.

He understood and thanked me for my kindness. He told me that he and the others would comply with the U.S. directives and that we would have no further problems from them. True to his word, he and his men set off for the camp. I don't know if they ever made it, but I hope they did. The old woman did not thank me, but groused instead that it was high time that something had been done about the matter.

The Russian prisoners I saw were truly a pathetic lot. They had long been living in filth, squalor and disease. Their toilets were nothing more than zigzagged slit trenches with logs placed alongside the edges. These men most fervently did not want to be repatriated back to the Soviet Union. They knew it would mean their death because Stalin regarded them as traitors for surrendering. We on the other hand had no choice in the matter. Our political leaders had made agreements with Stalin: the Russian internees were to be boarded onto trains, by force if necessary, and returned to their own immediate area of occupation in Vodnany.

This process began on May 16. I saw these men scream, cry, and drop to their knees and beg not to be sent back, but it was all to no avail. We got them on the trains and sent them back to their own army. I personally witnessed a number of these men jump from fast moving train cars to their deaths rather than return voluntarily for execution.

We also had to deal with German POWs. We had no fenced-in area to keep them in. We parked our tanks and half-tracks side by side in a square formation, and kept the Germans within the perimeters. Every tenth German soldier was given a Mauser rifle and ten rounds of ammunition to police and maintain order amongst their own. We simply couldn't spare the manpower to do it ourselves. The tanks and half-tracks were equipped with machine guns, so we did not worry about unrest. Besides, escape to the Russian-occupied areas was hardly an option.

The SS prisoners were a different story. They were held in a separate area. While many had thrown away part or all of their uniforms, the lightning bolt tattoos on their arms easily gave them away. Some had tried to burn off their tattoos with acid, but it only smeared the markings a little. They often asked me what was going to happen to them. Their faces drooped when I told them they were either going to be hanged or imprisoned for life.

We had very strict orders against fraternizing with enemy civilians, but we were on the edge of the Sudetenland, where the population was a mixture of ethnic Germans, who were pro-Hitler, and Czech nationals, who were not. As a German-speaking American, I was constantly called on to serve as an interpreter or perform policing tasks. I stopped at one home in the course of my duties one day to ask for directions, and met a very pleasant and attractive woman about ten years older than myself. During our conversation, I asked her if she could make a particular German dish that my mother and grandmother had made for me back home. She could, and did, and we quickly became friends.

She had a daughter about fourteen years old, and I would bring her chocolate when I came by on occasion for a home-cooked meal. I paid the woman in fresh food and army rations. There was nothing romantic between us, and she even asked if I could help her obtain information about her missing husband. He had been impressed into military service by the Germans and sent to fight on the Russian front. She had not received word from him for over two years. I explained that he had probably been killed in action, and that even if the Russians had taken him prisoner, he was unlikely ever to return. It was better she forget him and get on with her life as best as possible.

We couldn't stay in Czechoslovakia for too long: Roosevelt and Truman had promised it to the Russians. They and their advisors regarded "good 'ole Uncle Joe" Stalin as a stabilizing force for the continent, and political agreements gave the communists reign over Eastern Europe. As we now know, this intolerable situation lasted for 45 years. Czechoslovakia, like her Russian-occupied neighbors, saw the non-communist members of its coalition government murdered in 1948, and the nation reduced to a mere puppet of the U.S.S.R. Czech monuments built immediately after the war to honor their American liberators were all torn down in 1950 after the start of the Korean

War. The Czechs, however, eventually got their liberty, and had the last laugh. The Czech Republic officially dedicated the George Patton Museum in Pilsen in May 2005 at ceremonies celebrating the 60th anniversary of the end of the war and their now authentic liberation.

I was not impressed by the Russians. Their equipment was all American, they used horse-drawn carts like the Germans, and all the women in their military service were homely and dumpy. There were nevertheless no problems between us and the Russian troops. On the contrary, our interactions were cordial, almost friendly. I remember one of their soldiers taking a big bite out of a sausage, then handing it to me to do the same. He washed it down with some of my whiskey, and I did the same with his vodka. It almost knocked me flat.

The orders to turn over our areas of occupation to our Russian allies finally arrived, and we began to move out on May 21. We were sent to Bavaria in southeast Germany to the area of Passau, a city tucked in along the borders of Czechoslovakia and Austria. The 2d Battalion had its headquarters up and running in Eggleham by May 25. I was stationed nearby in the small town of Bambeth. Our duties were to maintain order, help to process German prisoners, and wait for orders. The war in the Pacific was still raging, and we knew the 5th Division was slated to participate in the invasion of Japan.

We all were interested in the number of points we had earned for military service. Those with 85 or more points would be discharged and spared any further fighting. The point system had been established to avoid the type of inequities that arose when Americans were discharged from service at the end of World War I. Men were then sent home by units: newly arrived replacements lucky enough to be assigned to units scheduled to return home got to leave ahead of long-term veterans whose outfits were still assigned to perform occupation duty.

The new point system was designed to avoid this problem, but it, too, had its shortcomings. For starters, it made no distinctions among soldiers who had earned beyond the necessary 85 points for discharge. It simply determined who qualified for discharge and who did not. A soldier who had earned 100 points had no more priority for discharge than one who had the bare minimum of 85. We also felt it failed to give enough points for combat duty, which allowed many long-serving rear echelon people to go home ahead of some combat vets who had not been in service for as long.

The system worked like this: a soldier was given one point for every month spent in service between September 1940 and May 1945, and an additional point for every month spent overseas during that same period. Every campaign or battle star earned was worth five points, as were any American awards for valor (Bronze Star, Silver Star, and so forth). Each dependent child a soldier had was worth 12 points.

I had been in the army since April 1941, which earned me 48 points. I had been overseas since February of 1942 and had another 40 points for that. My service time alone thus qualified me to go home, giving me 88 points. I had also been in five of the six campaigns fought in Northwest Europe: Normandy, Northern France, the Ardennes, the Rhineland, and Central Europe. The only campaign I had not been a part of was Southern France, where America's most highly decorated veteran of World War II, Audie Murphy of the 3rd Infantry Division, had landed in August 1944. My combat service in five campaigns was worth an additional 25 points.

The pie was sweetened by another 5 points on June 4, when General Orders 52 came down from 5th Division Headquarters, specifying that I was among those awarded the Bronze Star Medal. I knew from certain officers that I had been put in for the medal, but had had to wait for word of its approval.

The orders stated that I had earned it for "Distinctive Service in connection with military operations against the enemy during the period 15 October 1944 to 1 May 1945 in Europe." I can only guess, but I suppose this meant that aside from fighting for ten months as an infantryman in a rifle company where I also oversaw new replacements, I had often been called upon as an interpreter to assist in the interrogation of enemy prisoners. In addition, there was my service in combat as a lifeguard during contested river crossings and my work as a messenger for the American Red Cross. My superior officers must have viewed the culmination of these actions as worth more than an Army Commendation Medal, but not enough for the American Legion of Merit. The Bronze Star Medal falls right between these two awards.

Those awarded the Combat Infantry Badge or Combat Medical

Badge were entitled to receive either their first Bronze Star Medal, or a cluster to their original medal, after the award modifications made in 1962. Army Chief of Staff George Marshall had made that recommendation in 1947, in the belief that any American military personnel who participated in combat should be decorated.

I went down to the adjutant's office with some other soldiers and was handed the Bronze Star Medal in a case. They joked with us that they were sorry there wouldn't be any parades or ceremony. There wasn't even an award certificate with it. There was only a small strip cut from ordinary white paper, on which someone had typed that I had crawled from foxhole to foxhole under enemy shell fire (presumably at Metz) to save others, risking my life in the process. I wasn't told anything more than that. I now had a total of 118 points and was more than qualified and ready to go home.

Along with the Bronze Star Medal, just about every junior officer I served with came on the line to tell me that he had put me in for the Good Conduct Ribbon (later medal). I did receive the ribbon, but I was amazed after all the years of my shenanigans that I would even be considered, much less awarded, such a decoration. Most guys prided themselves on not having this ribbon, especially those of us who had earned the combat infantry badge. Oh well, this was one time the army's reverse logic worked out for me.

I had a beautiful little portable typewriter of German make that I used to write letters to Mary. I mentioned to her in a letter dated May 25 that I had recently received her letters from 14 and 15 May and was cheered by them. Reading between the lines, I could tell she wanted to make certain that I was all right, still wanted to get married, and that war hadn't significantly changed me. I was able to reassure her that I was indeed well, still very much in love with her, and wanted to get married as soon as I returned home, which I thought could be as early as six weeks away. I was able to tell her truthfully that war had not significantly changed me. My religious faith and psyche were still intact, and I was eager to return to civilian life. I even thanked her for the can of popcorn she had sent me. I was now signing my letters to Mary as "your husband, Mike."

On May 19 I celebrated my 26th birthday. Mary sent me a new shaving kit as a present and I was glad to get it. My old kit was beat to hell and needed to be replaced. I was so happy and thankful to be alive that I can't do my feelings justice through mere words. I remember thinking long and hard that day about how fortunate and blessed I truly was. I also couldn't help but think about all the fine men I knew who had died since my last birthday. On balance, it was a great day.

My letter to Mary was dated May 25 and written in Birnbach, Germany. It described the type of destruction I'd seen all over Germany. I explained to Mary that while the Germans brought this on themselves, it was impossible not to feel for the civilians and especially for young children, many of whom were orphaned and homeless. We gave these kids our chocolate, our ration kits, and any extra food our kitchens could spare. I was able to speak with these children in their own language, and the saddest thing was that so many of them had been orphaned for so long that they could not even remember what it was like to have a parent's love. All they knew was war, death, and destruction.

A great many Hungarian refugees had fled to Bavaria to avoid their Russian liberators. In my area most of the young orphans were German, but there was this one young boy from Hungary that I took under my wing. The other children shunned him since he was not German, and tried to muscle him out when we brought food from the kitchen for them. This young boy told me that his father was a high-ranking officer in the Hungarian Army, which prevented his parents from fleeing the country as the Russians approached. His family sent him out of the country with some other Hungarians of influence, but now he had to fend for himself and was essentially orphaned. He and some other Hungarian refugees were housed in a church atop a near-by hill.

I clued the other GIs in on the situation. I told them to feed the German kids, but that I would look after the Hungarian boy. I also told the German kids not to bother him any more if they wanted to continue to receive food from us. I would come from the mess area with a large plate of warm food prepared especially for him by a terrific mess sergeant. I then told the German kids to hit the road until the other GIs brought their food later on.

In mid-June, when I got orders to leave Bavaria for further occupation duties in Austria, this kid knew in advance that I was leaving.

The morning we moved out, he was waiting for me near our trucks. He thanked me and I could tell he was doing everything he could not to cry. He wasn't doing this for himself, but for me. Despite his bravery, he finally broke down and began crying. As I said good-bye to him, I hugged him and assured him that he would be all right. We waved to each other as my truck drove away until he finally faded from sight. It was yet another one of those heart-felt separations caused by war.

We also left behind a young Italian refugee around 19 years old. He was a nice kid. He liked Americans and even cooked for us, but he put garlic in everything, right down to the scrambled eggs! That was something I didn't care for. He wanted to come with us when we pulled out, but the brass said no.

The adults in occupied Germany were a different matter. Their problems were often much larger and far more numerous than those of the children. They almost always approached us with their heads hung low and began with the word "please." I had no official assignment as an interpreter, but I nevertheless interpreted all day long for our officers as they worked with the local populations. I grew weary of spending day after day translating stories of pain and misery: missing relatives, accusations of rape against GIs, malnutrition, illness, stories that finger pointed this one or that one who had been a Nazi Party member and so on. I now had an idea how psychiatrists and priests in the confessional felt.

I needed a break and that Mercedes I had could provide it. A sergeant in the motor pool helped me out by painting some white stars and a phony set of serial numbers on it, making it road-ready. I got three other guys and we decided to drive into Vienna to do some sightseeing. I sat in the passenger seat with a map acting as navigator.

At Lintz we reached a Russian checkpoint. There were machine guns set in fixed positions on each side of the road and a wooden gate manned by numerous soldiers, all of whom were carrying submachine guns. We stopped the car in front of the gate in response to their hand signals and Russians approached us from all sides. They rested the barrels of their guns on the bottom sections of our open windows, clearly demonstrating that they meant business.

Communication was initially a problem until a Russian who could speak broken German finally came forward. He asked us why we were there and what our business was. I explained that we wanted to go into Vienna to do some sightseeing. He responded that the city was off limits and we could not enter it without written authorization. We had no such thing, so we were instructed to turn the car around and head back in the direction we came. We complied immediately.

We then decided to go up to Burgess Garden, Hitler's Bavarian lair. There wasn't much to see other than the scenic view. The men from the 101st Airborne had been there first and picked it clean. There were no souvenirs to be had and nothing of interest to look at. That was about all the touring I got to do in that Mercedes. It wasn't long before the upper echelon got wind of it and, before a GI could find time enough to utter an obscenity, it was appropriated and gone.

I had one more close brush with death before I left Germany and I didn't even realize at the time how much danger I was in. A Polish refugee came to us one day and told us of a house hidden deep in the woods as a seeming hideout. I got another soldier to accompany me and we took the Pole with us to investigate. When we got there we saw how well the place had been camouflaged. A person had to be almost on top of it to be able even to see it. I told the other soldier to stay out front with the Pole and cover me. I went up to the door, which was opened by a civilian woman. I identified myself in German and asked about her situation.

She invited me in and I entered to find a house full of people. There were women and children as well as men in civilian clothes who carried themselves with a military bearing. The man seemingly in charge was in bed under some blankets and looked to be in his mid-fifties. He assured me they were all civilians, and since our only other interest could be souvenirs we would find them buried outside. I don't know why, but for some reason I accepted their story. I went outside and the other soldier and I found the buried stuff and we left feeling we had made a pretty good haul.

The Pole assured us all the way back that we had made a mistake and that the people were German military, maybe even SS, and their families on the lam. I thought about it and returned shortly thereafter with a lot more men and firepower. The hideout was now dark and empty and there was no trace of any of its former occupants. We found wagon wheel tracks that we followed to a nearby farm, but there the trail went cold and so we forgot the matter.

The hideout was probably a depot on an underground railroad, and I had stupidly accepted things there at face value. On the other hand, the man in bed was probably a colonel or even a general. It was also likely that he had a gun under those blankets and would have started blasting if I had gotten too nosey or too close. The "souvenirs" we found buried outside were simply their own military equipment. Maybe my survival instincts came through my subconscious that day. Whatever the reason, I ignored the obvious and walked away from the hideout and what could well have been a fatal situation.

The women in Germany practically threw themselves at Americans and I didn't always decline. We had food, cigarettes, and the possibility of American citizenship through marriage. To the truly needy women, I would simply give food and other items, but declined their offers of sex. Exchanging food or cigarettes for sexual favors, especially with women who were starving, struck me as nothing more than prostitution, and that was something I never wanted no matter how strong my urges got.

I did get involved with one woman in Germany whose family had money before the war and managed to keep it once the fighting was over. Her husband had been killed on the Russian front and she most probably had marriage to an American on her mind. She was naked when she got into my bed and crawled up on top of me. I had no prophylactic and told her to get off of me before she got pregnant. "I want to have your baby," she said. I jumped up and she flew off of me. I told her that I didn't intend to leave any children behind in Europe.

It seemed that everybody wanted to get in on the sexual action in Bavaria and I was often called on to serve as an interpreter. One sergeant who had a wife back home had been treated twice for venereal disease. He brought a young German woman to me so I could translate his intentions, which boiled down to a great dinner and a stockpile of food in exchange for sex.

I was far from sainthood myself, but I didn't have a wife or VD. I told this girl in German that the sergeant had both, and advised her not to go to his sleeping quarters or allow him into hers. She turned white when she heard the news, and came up with some flimsy excuse to avoid the entire evening. The sergeant figured that I said something to nix the deal and was mad as hell, but I didn't care. There was nothing he could do to me, and conditions in Germany being what they were, I figured the girl already had enough to deal with.

We also spent time on the beautiful Bavarian lakes. They were clear, crisp, and filled with delicious fish. We fished the lazy way by simply lobbing captured German hand grenades in the water. There was a huge blast under the water followed by numerous dead fish floating up to the surface. One man in our outfit was a self-taught armaments expert. He was so knowledgeable about weapons that he could hold court on the subject. Men, especially the young new arrivals, loved to watch and listen to this guy expound. I swear he could jump start a car with a machine gun.

He said that throwing a single hand grenade into a lake didn't produce a large enough catch when we went "fishing," and putting two grenades together would give us a bigger haul. He decided one day to put his theory into practice, but things didn't work out for him. The last I heard, they couldn't find enough of his remains to send home. Unfortunately, the end of war didn't mean the end of men getting killed.

We were all approached about volunteering to fight in the Pacific but I don't recall a single man taking the army up on the offer. This meant the army would have to start getting us back home. Arrangements began around June 15.and required some transferring to get the more seasoned combat vets back. The 5th Division was returning to the United States, but this was intended only to be a stop on its way to the Pacific. Meanwhile, the 103rd Infantry (Cactus) Division, which arrived at the front after the American campaigns in Europe were already well underway, was scheduled to go back to the States to be deactivated.

Soldiers in the 103rd Division who had fewer than 85 points were transferred into the 5th Division for eventual service in the Pacific, while high point men in the 5th Division were transferred into the 103rd so they could go home and be discharged. This involved a swap of around 4,000 men. I changed the 5th Division Red Diamond insignia on my sleeve for the Cactus of the 103rd, boarded a truck with other high point men, and headed for Innsbruck, Austria. The initial rumor was that we would be put on C-47s from there and sent home. It was a bunch of crap. There were no planes and no discharges waiting for us in Austria. The scenic views, however, were breathtaking. Austria has some of the most beautiful landscapes in the world, and it was relatively untouched by the war.

We detrucked and formed up in companies to hear our new assignments read out to us. When it was over, everyone had an assignment but me. The first sergeant came up and told me that I was being assigned to the Headquarters Company of the 409th Regiment. I would have my own little office (a desk separated from the rest of the room by a wooden partition) where I would serve the company commander as an interpreter. I couldn't believe my good fortune. I was being assigned a cushy job in a beautiful land. It wasn't as good as going home, but it would suffice for the moment.

My company commander, Captain Smith, wanted to have as little trouble with civilians as possible, and so I was given a considerably broad range of authority. In fact, it was probably more authority than an enlisted man should have had. Captain Smith decided that I was going to wear stripes whether I liked it or not. I was working in headquarters now, and he was not about to have me there, or allow me to leave his company after almost a year in combat, without rank. I was made a technician 5th grade (a more prestigious form of corporal), and since the war was over, I no longer had any objections to wearing stripes. I probably could have requested, and received, a sergeant's rank if I had been present when the promotion was decided.

Captain Smith was a first-rate officer and we got along very well. There were no tech 5 stripes available, so I sewed a regular pair of gold corporal stripes on my sleeve. The captain still needed an excuse for having a soldier of lower rank spending so much time at headquarters, so he told me to put a bazooka in the corner near my desk and to tell anyone who asked me about my duties that I was a bazooka man. No one from the army ever bothered me in Austria.

The club for enlisted men was every bit as nice as the officers' club. The Austrians were very friendly and I even got a chance to go up into the mountains and put to use the ski training I had received in Iceland. We nevertheless didn't enjoy it all that much. All we tended to do was talk about going home.

I was called in one day in July to see Captain Smith, who had a lieutenant with him from G-2 (Intelligence). The captain said that the army planned to classify me as essential and keep me in service for further duties. "Why?" I asked with some degree of incredulity. "Because of your knowledge of German," he replied. I was stunned to say the least. Mary was making wedding plans, and I had anticipated being discharged in a matter of weeks.

"Look, Captain," I said. "There's nothing in my service record that says I can speak German and, as far as I'm concerned, I picked up the language while I was over here and I can forget it just as quickly." The G-2 lieutenant piped in and said, "We'll make you a warrant officer in six months!" I turned to him and pointed to my shoulders. "Lieutenant," I said, "I wouldn't care if you put eagles up there. I'm getting married next month and I want out of this man's army."

They both smiled and the Captain Smith gave a look to the G-2 man as if to say, "I told you so." He then said, "OK Bilder, we get the message. You're not essential; you can go home." I saluted and left knowing that I was soon to be a civilian again.

It was in Austria that I truly bested the bureaucrats. I was given two requisitions (trip tickets) and told to get a three-quarter-ton truck from the motor pool to pick up the liquor ration for both the officers' and the enlisted men's clubs. I decided to do a little creative editing and put the top copy of the liquor order for the enlisted personnel into my soft roll typewriter. There was a large space between the specified quantity of items and their description to the right. I used this space to type in a zero after every quantity so that "1" became "10" and "2" became "20" and so forth.

I got three other men and we went down to the motor pool, where the sergeant in charge looked at the order and said, "You're going to need a bigger truck." The sergeant was a bright guy, and I figured he suspected right away what I was up to. He then supplied me with a two-and-a-half-ton truck.

I drove to the brewery in Innsbruck and handed the order to the brewmiester. He looked at it quizzically and started to balk. It was obviously much larger than usual. He seemed to imply that he wanted it confirmed from a higher authority. I, of course, couldn't let that happen, and immediately started to ball him out in German. I told him we were busy and had other duties to perform. "Get to work and fill that order," I told him. The booze, seemingly an endless supply, came down the chutes and we loaded it onto the trucks. I told the men to put the officers' portion up front so we could unload that immediately. I had to sign for the shipment, and I signed the receipt as "Captain Patrick Henry."

We got the liquor back to camp and had it hidden before anyone could see it. For the following few weeks, I was the most popular dogface in all of Innsbruck. Our officers couldn't figure out how their men could be so drunk every night when there wasn't that great a liquor supply. The sergeant from the motor pool was so grateful that he gave me a jeep so I could take a joy ride down the Brenner Pass and cross over into Italy, just to be able to say I had been there. I did it simply as a lark.

Word came down around mid-July that we were going home. There would be no planes to take us and, due to the repatriation of refugees, there weren't even any real trains. We would have to ride in the famed forty and eight railroad cars used by the doughboys in the First World War. These were boxcars so-named because they could hold forty soldiers and eight horses. They stank and moved at a painfully slow pace, never exceeding twenty miles an hour.

I had to dump the two diamond rings I picked up in Bitburg. The authorities would be conducting "shake downs" at every stop we made between Europe and America, and since these included cavity searches there was no point in having the rings needlessly confiscated. I got $500.00 for the two of them.

I got other military souvenirs like weapons, medals, and even a helmet home through a friend in Regimental Headquarters. He had been wounded in action and the army was going to assign him to a different unit that was performing some kind of non-combat duty. He was adamant about returning to the 5th Division so that was where he got his assignment. We had been friends since Fort Custer, so I knew he would pack up my spoils and send them back home to my mother's house.

During the train journey to the Channel, I stopped in Fontainebleau, France, and visited Tom Spain's grave. It was painful to realize yet once again that he would not be coming home with me.

I attended a dance, and a paratrooper and I kept bumping into one another on the crowded floor until it erupted into a fistfight. It didn't last very long because everyone jumped in to break it up.

Our departure area was Camp Tophat in Antwerp, Belgium. Most of the so-called "cigarette camps" were in the Le Havre area in France. They included Camps Lucky Strike, Pall Mall, Chesterfield, Philip Morris, and numerous others. During the war, they served as staging areas for new arrivals and had been code named after American cigarettes to confuse the Germans about their location. Now at war's end, they became departure areas to ship us home.

Camp Tophat was a tent city. Black tents housed as many as twenty men each. By the time I got there in late July 1945, it was in pretty good shape. There were five movie theaters, an ice cream bar, an enlisted men's club, a penny arcade, and as many of the comforts of home that the army could reasonably supply. The camp had been named for the military unit that built it, which had a top hat for its symbol, but since a brand of cigarettes called Tophat was actually produced in Belgium, it also qualified as a cigarette camp.

I soon learned that the Red Cross had been looking for me ever since I left Austria. It turned out they had missed me in Innsbruck by only a few hours. There was a message waiting for me from them when I arrived at Camp Tophat, so I got in touch with them immediately, and discovered that they wanted to offer me a full-time job as an assistant field director. I informed them I was going home to get married, and asked if I could return as a civilian with a new bride. They assured me I could, and told me to contact them once I was situated back home. I wasn't even a civilian yet, and already I had a job lined up! I could even bring Mary with me and show her Europe. It was an exciting time, when every opportunity and good thing seemed possible.

I can't remember the name of the ship I sailed on, but like all troop ships at that time, it was loaded from stem to stern with GIs going home. We sailed from Antwerp on July 22, and I got seasick yet again. During the journey, I got into a card game and lost $100 before I realized that the men I was playing with were a team of con artists. They didn't fix the deals but their plays were phony. These three men would sucker a fourth player in and take turns bumping up the pot with the expectation that one of the three of them would win. They could then split the winnings later amongst themselves.

Dirty dealing would have gotten men thrown overboard, but this type of cheating was all but impossible to prove. I decided to bow out and simply consider myself wiser for the experience. I saw one poor dogface up on deck crying his eyes out. He had lost everything he had to these cheats.

I was amazed to meet a soldier on board who I was certain had been killed in combat. I had seen him sustain a serious gut wound and we left him to the medics, not wanting to watch yet another GI die. We obviously missed witnessing a man beat incredible odds. He explained how the medics patched him up and said he kept himself alive by sheer force of will until he arrived at an army hospital. I warned him not to take his luck to the card table.

We disembarked at Newport News, Virginia, on August 4. After taking a train to the station we marched to Camp Patrick Henry, where we were brought into an auditorium to be briefed on the discharge process. I was now a corporal and in a group of some 450 NCOs. Our outfit was composed of men from several different units and we all felt we had earned the right to become civilians. Most of us had chips on our shoulders and at this point were barely tolerant of military discipline. For this reason we were pegged as troublemakers and a potential problem. We would soon prove this evaluation correct.

In the mess hall we ate alongside several German POWs who had been there for some time. They looked better groomed, better fed, and better rested than any of us. Comments like "dirty Nazis," and "lousy krauts" were flying freely, so when one of the Germans told one of our guys what he could do with himself, we pounced on them. Every one of us selected a POW and started swinging. The Germans were smart enough not to punch back and merely held up their arms to block our blows. Military Police soon swooped down on us, and the whole thing broke up fairly quickly without any heads getting busted.

We were then strip-searched again, just like when we had first arrived at Camp Tophat. We were given the green light and they quickly got us the hell out of there to continue on to our final destinations. It reminded me of the bum's rush we received in England right after the racial fight at Andover.

My final stop was Fort Sheridan in Lake County, Illinois, where it had all started for me back in April 1941. When we arrived we were strip-searched yet again. An officer ordered someone to confiscate a twelve power pair of German binoculars that I had had with me ever since Austria. These were probably the most beautiful set of field glasses I had ever seen, and the officer who ordered them confiscated must have thought so too.

The phony two-week hospitalization (vacation) for "shell shock" that I took back in Luxembourg City during the Battle of the Bulge came back to haunt me now at Fort Sheridan. The day before my scheduled discharge, a sergeant came into the barracks and told me that I had to report immediately to Doctor so and so in such and such a building. When I arrived, I noticed the wide hallways, swinging doors, and blank stares. I knew without reading any signage that I was in a psychiatric ward with battle fatigue cases. The doctor (either a captain or a major, I can't remember which) was all business. He talked in generalities about the delayed effects of shell shock and how it took time before the related symptoms manifested themselves. He then floored me with the news that he and the other doctors would need to observe me for the next 30 days.

I couldn't believe it! Here I was, one day away from discharge, and the army wanted to hold me for a month's observation in the loony bin. I had to level with him if I wanted to be discharged in time to make my wedding. I didn't give him the full extent of what a con the whole thing had been, but I spoke in a clear and coherent manner, and told him enough to convince him that I was well and able to be discharged. I had to sign a release waiving my right to make any claim against the army for any possible mental harm I might have suffered due to combat. Only then would they approve an honorable discharge. I signed without even reading it.

Word went out that no one would be discharged unless their uniform had the appropriate insignia, rank, service stripe, overseas service bars, and so forth. I could sew, which meant I had nothing to worry about, but men who couldn't were paying women clerks, fellow GIs, or anybody who could use a needle and thread.

All GIs being discharged were seated in front of an officer (mine was a Captain M.R. McCormick) with a typewriter whose job was to type in information to complete the Army Qualification Separation Record or Form 100. This basically served as an army verification of job skills acquired in the service that were now transferable to the civilian job market. For most infantrymen it was nothing but a compilation of bull, the beginning of puffed-up resumes.

I had spent ten months as a rifleman (Army Code #745), and 33 months as a lineman (grunt) in the field (Army Code #641). This wouldn't mean much to civilian employers. I could hardly list being able to throw a hand grenade further than anyone else in the neighborhood, or knowing how to lead a moving target as job skills for civilian life. The captain at the typewriter therefore edited my experiences accordingly.

He asked, for example, if I ever had anything to do with stringing communication wire. This was normally a job for the Signal Corps, but I explained that I had cut communication wire and unwound wire that was connected to explosives. That was translated into, "LINEMAN FIELD: As member of crew of men erected poles, strung wire and cables, connected and operated field switchboards, installed communication systems. Used climbing iron and electrician hand tools. CIVILIAN CONVERSIONS: Lineman, Line Inspector." The only truth in all this was my work as a switchboard operator for a very brief time in Iceland.

Questioning me further, he then asked if I had ever driven any heavy military equipment. I explained how I had driven a German truck during our movement from the Ruhr Pocket down to southern Germany. This experience was adjusted to read, "TRUCK DRIVE HEAVY: Drove all types of military vehicles both semi-trailers and straight body truck. Hauled military personnel and supplies over all types of roads and under all conditions. CIVILIAN CONVERSIONS: Truck Driver Heavy; or Light; Bus Driver." The captain creatively listed me as having performed eight months as a driver of heavy trucks (Army Code # 931). There was no truth to it, but if it got me out of the army, it all sounded good to me.

There were about ten tables with personnel processing us. I saw several ambulances outside and at first I was puzzled why they were there. I didn't yet know that soldiers from the Pacific Theater were being processed for discharge along with us. Some of these men suffered malaria attacks during the discharge process and had to be rushed by ambulance to the fort hospital. They had to be admitted to the hospital and their discharges were postponed. They had desperately tried to hide their symptoms, and were yelling how they were all right and wanted to continue their processing, even as they were rushed out on stretchers to the ambulances. I could appreciate their feelings.

With the exception of my Bronze Star, I remember I was issued only ribbons and no medals for my service. Brass was still being used in munitions production, some medals were still being designed, and others were yet to be authorized and produced. It would take years, even decades, before the United States and the countries we liberated finally got around to issuing medals or certificates to the vets who fought the Second World War.

I had earned the Combat Infantry Badge, the Bronze Star Medal, the Good Conduct Ribbon (later medal), and a ribbon (later medal) for the European-African-Middle Eastern Theater Campaign with a Silver Battle Star (representing five campaigns). Years later when the army sent me my medals, they authorized an arrowhead (representing amphibious landings) for that campaign medal and its ribbon. I was also issued a ribbon (later a medal) for American Defense Service (given for being in the U.S. military during World War II, before the United States was an active participant). I had my corporal stripes, a three-year service stripe, seven overseas service bars (one for every six months overseas), and the famed "ruptured duck" lapel pin for Honorable Discharge. The American Campaign Medal, World War II Victory Medal, and Army Occupation Medal would all be sent to me forty years later. Thanks to the efforts of my youngest son, I would even be awarded the French Legion of Honor (France's highest decoration for a non-citizen) in 2006.

My discharge day was August 9, 1945. My discharge record showed that I had been in service for four years and four months. This entitled me to an additional $300 pay. First Lieutenant W. S. Risendorph of the Woman's Army Corps (WAC) signed the document, as did I. That was it. I was now officially a civilian in uniform.

I took my duffle bag and walked the mile or so to the front gate along with three or four other guys in the same circumstance as myself. The new recruits, inducted for the invasion of Japan, leaned out of their barracks windows and hooted and hollered, "You lucky dogs," and other such things as we went by. I could see that many of them were wide-eyed when they saw those seven overseas service stripes on my sleeve. I wanted to tell them something encouraging so I said, "Don't worry fellas, it goes by quick. We started the job, now you finish it."

As I walked through the front gate, I took one look back and said to the guards, "You can take this man's army and shove it up your ass." They laughed as I turned around and walked out into the world, ecstatic to be thought of as simply a citizen and no longer a soldier.

EPILOGUE

Mary was waiting for me as I stepped off the train in Chicago. I dropped my duffle bag and we ran into each other's arms and kissed. Nothing seemed to have changed. Mary was just as beautiful as when we said our tearful good-byes at Fort Dix in early 1942, and our feelings for one another were still the same. The streets and buildings looked almost as if they had been frozen in time. The wartime limits on construction materials had kept the city neighborhoods looking much as they did when I had left, and for a moment it was almost as if the whole war had been just a bad dream.

Mary had waited for me for more than three and a half years. I couldn't imagine any other unmarried woman in the whole country would have done that, especially one that had so much to offer. I loved her all the more for it. When I arrived, she had already made all the wedding arrangements for the church, the hall, and everything else. There had literally been no margin for error. You have to be young to plan such an important event with the assumption that everything will work out simply because you want it to do so.

We headed downtown to pick up a few things for our wedding, which was a mere two days away. I needed a new pair of shoes, and we had to pick up the wedding license and then go to confession. I spent over an hour in the confessional, and every time I confessed some details about men I'd killed in combat, the priest would say, "Damn those son of a bitchin' politicians who make you young men have to do such things." He was so loud that even Mary could hear him outside the confessional.

After I came out, Mary joked that she was none too sure she wanted to go through with it. "It's over," she said. "It's all behind you now. From this moment on we start fresh." I didn't have to tell her about the women in Europe. She was smart enough to know.

We were married at Saint Felicitas Church in Chicago on August 11, 1945. It was a beautiful summer day. I think my mother and siblings were put out that I wouldn't be living back home for a while before marrying, but what would I do? Sleep on the daybed? My mother also wanted me to get married in uniform, but I absolutely refused. I went to the alter wearing a tux. My poor grandmother was downhearted about me not marrying a German girl, but in the year of life she had left to live, she grew to love Mary.

We had an afternoon reception and everything went well. Our honeymoon, however, was like a storyline out of a Hollywood comedy. We spent it at a little resort in Schaefer Lake, Indiana, which turned out to be anything but romantic. The chain on the tandem bike we rented kept coming off, we ate in a greasy spoon where the pork I ordered turned out to be nothing but K-rations, and Mary got trench mouth from dirty utensils. It was awful, but we didn't really mind all that much because we were finally together.

We heard about the surrender of Japan during our honeymoon. I was glad that the killing was finally over and that all those young boys I had seen while leaving Fort Sheridan wouldn't have to go into combat after all. I was horrified when I saw the newsreels depicting the damage done by the atomic bombs dropped on Japan.

Mary and I went to the veterans' hospital up in Michigan where Vern Kelner was recuperating. It was full of amputees. I was accustomed to seeing such suffering, but it I could tell it was difficult on Mary. Fortunately, Vern was in great spirits and even joked a little about his situation. He showed us his stump, which was about midway between the knee and ankle. After his recovery, he had a very successful career and a good life. I have always liked and admired Vern a great deal.

I had some occasional nightmares the first year or so, but the war left no permanent scars on me. It nevertheless still took me a little while to adjust to civilian living. I had difficulty sleeping in a bed at first, so I slept on the floor before I finally transitioned back to a real mattress. I also dove for the ground when I heard a train approach, and I thought I would go nuts during the Fourth of July celebrations in 1946. Every house in the neighborhood seemed to have its own fireworks arsenal, and I discovered that my reactions hadn't slowed much even after a year in civilian life.

Mary and I had our fair share of life's problems, but things were mostly good. I decided against the offer from the Red Cross to return to Europe as a civilian employee. They were unwilling to pay for any of Mary's expenses, and I couldn't accept a hand-to-mouth existence to see a continent that was largely rubble. I instead took a job as a security guard at Midway Airport in Chicago. I needed to do something that allowed me to carry a gun. It was an old man's job though, and I soon tired of it. A local priest connected with the Chicago Police Department approached me about going to work for them, but Mary didn't want me to have any part of it. Aside from the danger inherent in such work, the Chicago PD did not have a stellar reputation in those days, and she worried that I'd become lazy, overweight, and possibly even corrupt.

I not only needed a career, but some help in finding one. Mary's father used his business connections with an architectural firm to get me an apprenticeship with the Carpenters' Union. I joined Local 141 in April 1946. After having done my share of demolishing farms, houses, and factories all across Western and Central Europe, I always got a real kick out of building and construction. Mary used to say with pride that if carpentry was good enough for Saint Joseph, then it was good enough for her husband. I spent the next 25 years in the field as a carpenter, mostly as a foreman.

I am happy to say that my stepfather and I reconciled. When I returned from the service he was supporting his family by working two jobs, both of them seasonal. In the spring and summer, he worked at Wrigley Field cleaning and servicing the players' locker rooms. He'd have my admission fee waived and together we'd watch the Cubs play. In the fall and winter, he worked the furnace at a movie theatre at 63rd and Kedzie, and we sometimes caught a flick together when I came at night to give him a lift home. These were some of the few times I could ever recall seeing him enjoy himself.

He had severe pulmonary problems and his health began to go

downhill rather rapidly in 1950. Toward the end, when he was too sick to get out of bed, I shaved his beard almost daily. I was with him when he died on December 18. It was the exact same day my biological father had died 32 years earlier.

In the 1960s I used my GI benefits to go to night school and earn a teaching certificate. My years in the infantry and as a carpenter were taking their toll physically, and I knew my health could turn for the worse if I continued to work outside. In 1971 I began teaching carpentry at Washburne Trade School in Chicago, where I remained until I retired in November 1984.

Mary and I were blessed with five children: Michael (1948), Jeff (1949), Marianne (1951), Joe (1954) and Jim (1958). In 1955 we moved to Chicago Ridge, which was then a small village in the country, to raise our family. Coincidently, Tom Spain's family had his remains exhumed from Fontainebleau in 1947 and reentered in Holy Sepulcher Cemetery just three blocks from my home. I visited Tom's grave almost every Memorial Day.

Mary stayed home to raise the kids, as most women did then. I earned extra money working evenings and weekends as a part-time policeman in the village from 1957 until 1961. I was also the village building inspector from 1959 to 1961, and made my building inspections while patrolling in the squad car! In a special election in 1961, the village elected me as their Police Magistrate (Justice of the Peace). I was re-elected two years later with 85% of the vote, but the State of Illinois did away with the office just weeks before the election, so the victory was meaningless.

I continued on in local politics and was appointed to fill a vacancy on the village board of trustees just three days before President Kennedy's assassination. It was an omen of political turbulence to come. I was elected to a full four-year term 18 months later, but already it was losing its luster. I was the only person on my local party's ticket to win election, and this combined with the political unrest of the 1960s served to make the whole thing a rather unpleasant experience.

I made a half-hearted run for mayor in 1969 and felt a little disappointment in losing, but Mary and I bowed out gracefully, never to return to politics. It turned out to be for the best, and it was obvious that I was still an incredibly lucky individual. My service in local government was a lot like my time in the army: I was no thief, but I was never hailed for adhering to rules and regulations. The U.S. Attorney for Northern Illinois (and future governor of the state) assumed his duties a few years after I left office, and he indicted countless Chicago and suburban politicians on corruption and other various charges. I never heard of one that beat the rap.

Mary died unexpectedly in her sleep just one week after our 59th wedding anniversary in 2004. She had battled Crohn's Disease since 1962. She had numerous surgeries and took prednisone non-stop to control the internal inflammation, but she still lived a full life and seldom showed signs of ill health to those outside the family. It was simply inevitable that age and illness would take their toll. Together, Mary and I lived to see 15 grandchildren and 5 great grandchildren, and more have been born since she passed away, or are currently on the way.

Mary and I were very proud of each of our children. More important than any monetary success or worldly recognition, they kept their faith, their marriages, and their families intact. Our oldest son, Michael, earned his MBA and then become wealthy running a midsize company dedicated to producing product packaging. He and his wife married in 1970 and have three children and two grandchildren, with another on the way. Jeff enlisted in the Air Force, specializing in maintaining aircraft environmental systems, and served for a year in Vietnam and the Philippines. Following his discharge in 1972, he pursued a career in graphics and document reproduction technologies. He and his wife were married in 1972 and have three children and two grandchildren, with a third on the way.

Marianne earned not one, but two, graduate degrees and teaches the subjects she loves, English and literature, as an adjunct instructor at a local community college. She and her husband, a retired federal agent, were married in 1970 and have five children and four grandchildren.

Joseph has had mental limitations since birth. He lives with me, but still holds down a full time job in food produce, and arranges (and pays for) his own vacation packages, traveling all around the country.

My youngest, Jim, earned both a college and a graduate degree, and served eight years as the mayor of the Village of Worth, next door to my own community. He carried out the responsibilities of this and various other public offices at night and on weekends, while devoting his daytime hours to a successful career in pharmaceutical marketing that has so far spanned 26 years. He and his wife were married in 1981 and have four children.

When he finished with politics in 2002, Jim co-authored this book, helping me to put my experiences into words and taking the time to research seemingly everything written on my outfit and its related battles and campaigns. True to his youthful zeal for my minis-cule part in the war, he also set out to demonstrate to me that my mil-itary service was somehow important and appreciated. In summer 2003, he started to make requests for official as well as commemora-tive awards on my behalf to various European embassies, towns and provinces. To my great surprise, they all responded in the affirmative.

The Czech Republic sent a beautiful medal commemorating the 60th anniversary of the end of the war and their liberation, along with a very gracious letter from their Ambassador to the United States. A historical museum and society in Luxembourg sent a large medallion commemorating the 60th anniversary of the Battle of the Bulge. Jim also obtained a Luxembourg War Cross or Croix de Guerre for me. All Allied or Luxembourg nationals who served in combat in that nation are entitled to the Croix de Guerre, but Luxembourg ceased producing and issuing the World War II version of the medal in the late 1970s, so Jim obtained one through a company that handles such items for collectors.

The French responded most enthusiastically of all. The city of Verdun sent me a medal and certificate commemorating their libera-tion. The city of Metz discontinued their commemorative medal of lib-eration in January 1981, so we obtained a reproduction. The Regional Council of Lower Normandy sent a commemorative chest badge engraved with my name and an award number for the 60th anniver-sary of the Normandy campaign. Jim also obtained for me the Medal of Liberated France and the Jubilee of Liberty Medal, which com-memorates the 50th anniversary of the Normandy campaign.

He didn't settle simply for the certificate of gratitude from the French Consulate that every GI who fought in France is entitled to receive. In fall 2005, he did all the paperwork to request I be considered for the Legion of Honor, France's highest decoration for a non-French national. I was both moved and amazed when he showed me letters from the French ambassador to the United States and the French Consul General in Chicago informing me that I had been named a Chevalier (Knight) of the Legion of Honor on February 15, 2006 by French President Jacques Chirac.

Attending an official award ceremony was more than I was up to, so the medal was sent by special delivery with a beautiful letter and certificate. The decoration is not awarded for personal heroics, but more for surviving the campaigns I fought in France and making it through the six following decades. The honor cannot be awarded posthumously. I regard it as intended for all those who served in the 5th Division in France: I'm merely a caretaker who has physical possession of a medal earned by those who starting sleeping in 1944 and were joined by others over the sixty years that followed.

At 89, I am now in what Mary always referred to as "God's waiting room." My days are filled with prayer, the newspaper, a little television, some quiet reflection, and frequent visits from my kids. I am fortunate in that they all live close by. I'm proud to have done my duty during the war and to have had the privilege to do so in the company of so many exceptional men who were fine soldiers and heroes.

I am still saddened when I think of all the potential husbands and fathers lost to the world because of the war. I realize how blessed I was to have been given the opportunity to be a husband and father, and now a grandfather and even great-grandfather myself, and some six decades to work on being the best I could at it. I hope I used my time well and I trust in God's mercy. Mary and almost everyone else I knew from that era are gone now, but my mind and my heart are at peace and I look forward to seeing them all again.

ACKNOWLEDGMENTS

It's a near impossible task even to begin to try and thank everyone who helped in this project, but I still have to try. First, my sincere thanks to my father who endured painful memories over again while telling his story, as well as my never-ending list of questions and requests for additional detail. By recounting his experiences, he and others who have recorded their accounts of World War II are preventing the Greatest Generation from becoming the Forgotten Generation.

Authors and journalists Flint Whitlock, Stephen Koepp, and Roland Gaul all provided information, insight, and encouragement. Roland, who is also Curator of the National Museum of Military History in Diekirch, Luxemburg, was especially instrumental in helping me with historical questions, as well as photos, and graciously agreed to write a foreword to this book. Stephen, my cousin and the Executive Editor at *Fortune Magazine*, assured me that I had a worthy manuscript and helped me to navigate the publishing world. Flint, an author whose books on World War II have been both widely read and recognized with awards, was the person who recommended Casemate Publishers.

I also need to thank the historians past and present of the Society of the 5th Division. Past Historian Joe Rahie, who served in combat with the 5th Division in World War II, and current historian Keith Short, who is a 5th Division combat veteran from the Vietnam War, made archival photographs readily available. They did so with the type of promptness worthy of first-rate soldiers.

My sister, Marianne Grisolano, helped me edit the first draft of the first several chapters, and my daughter, Joanne, a graduate of

Chicago's School of the Arts Institute, helped with the graphics on the maps.

I have been fortunate to have so capable a publisher as David Farnsworth at Casemate. He and Chief Editor Steven Smith did much to facilitate this project and make the story of a truly worthy, but until now unrecognized, military unit available to the world. Hopefully, the "Forgotten 5th" will no longer be so easy to forget. Gayle Wurst, of Princeton International Agency for the Arts, is a person of phenomenal talent and ability whom Casemate assigned as my editor. A gem to work with, she treated the information in my manuscript with tenderness and care, as she helped put it into its final form.

Last, but by no means least, my beautiful wife Bernie (Bernadette) became a "writer's widow" who put up with numerous weeknights and weekends alone as I combed through military histories or huddled with my father. She never stopped encouraging me, and assured me from the first day I started this project that it would be published.

To these people, my profound and eternal gratitude.

THE 2ND INFANTRY ROLL OF HONOR

My father received the following pages in the summer of 1945, just before he shipped home from Germany. It was given to him by a clerk at 5th Division HQ (the same guy who helped him ship his German booty back home to Chicago). This soldier had been a combat infantryman, but after being wounded was redesignated a clerk. He insisted on returning to the 5th Infantry so he was assigned to HQ.

Afterward my father pored closely over the list, putting the pages in his own typewriter and marking an "X" next to the KIAs he was well acquainted with and a double "X" next to those who were his really good buddies.

For those of us who did not participate in the war, it is worth noting that this long list of KIAs is only from a single U.S. regiment. The 5th Division as a whole suffered many hundreds more, as did the other units that were quickly formed from citizen soldiers to fight for their country in World War II.

As the usual image of General Patton's operations conjures up fast armored drives, happily liberated civilians, and a record of unbroken success, it may be helpful to take a look at the fallen soldiers of simply one regiment of the U.S. Third Army in the ETO.

Why a list of courts martial was also attached to this "Roll of Honor" is a mystery, but it is included here just as it was handed to my father by that clerk at HQ. After all, even the most glorious history is never without its blemishes.

—James Bilder

THE 2ND INFANTRY ROLL OF HONOR

THE FOLLOWING OFFICERS AND MEN WERE KILLED IN ACTION
WITH THE 2ND INFANTRY

KILLED IN ACTION DURING JULY, 1944

X	S/Sgt. Robert C. Bass, 36017416	Serv. Co.
	Captain Warren Wooden	Co."E"
	Sgt. Richard H. Hendrickson, 37272927	
	T/Sgt. L.C. McAllan, 16007513	
	R.L. Clyburn, 33647282	Med. Det.
	Thomas A. Sellers, 34760512	Co."I"
X	George G. Guit, 31293722	Hq. 2nd Bn.
X	Tech. Cpl. Joseph T. Tracey, 15013935	Hq. 2nd Bn.
	Ray J. Zogrocki, 33677799	
	Lee L. Smith	Co."M"
X	Pfc Patrick J. Dwyer, 35130735	Co."A"
	William C. Zell, 35230873	Med. Det.
	Pfc Russell Schwenberger, 35651914	
	Gordon J. Valentine	
X	Robert A. Guy	Co."E"
	Luther E. Hickman	
	Danial M. Vaughn	
	Raymond C. Owen	
	Lavane Luhman	
	Blanton McDanial, 34784149	
	Howard Pohannon, 34760472	
	Sgt. Orville J. Fultz, 35153205	
X	Madio A. Muratord, 35009692	
	Michael Yarkosky	
	Pfc Arnold H. Nelson, 16005895	
	S/Sgt Joseph L. Ludban, 35009861	
	Pfc John A. Towsend, 38323665	
	J.A. Worm, 160126282	
X	Andrew Treccia, 20610884	
X	S/Sgt. Verne L. Overdeer, 6667666	Co."A"
	Robert Diehl, 36107387	
	Pfc Donald A. Dern, 36206208	
	James A. Tomter, 16021299	
	Jack Marshell, 7082288	
	Clarence A. Hoff, 37141749	
	S/Sgt. Walter Piontkowski, 36107280	
	Eugene Stroupe, 34592484	
X	Joseph Varonovitch, 36018352	

THE 2ND INFANTRY ROLL OF HONOR

KILLED IN ACTION DURING JULY, 1944

```
  2nd Lt. James F. Dixon, O-1316632
  Pfc Vincent Giavanni, 32805337
  Calvin Simmers, 6910691
  Iven L. Hankins, 38450955
  Joseph M.Bizzell, 34508136
  S.C. Scott Jr., 6286856
  William J. Cantrill, 16011302
  Richard H. Wakefield, 33501805
  Wade Wilkens, 35248939
  Edward Reynolds, 32807697
  Earl George
X Benjamin Dumka, T/Sgt. 6910963
  A.F. Stranger, 36016268
  Harold J. Geerholdt, 32748342
  John T. Sieratowiez, 16012639
  Lawrence Mauser, 35009874
  Graydon D. Little, 34771873
  Ernest E. Schad
  Marvo Gonzales
X 1st. Lt. Savage                            Co."F"
  LaVerne L. Allard, 39199482
  T/Sgt. Ernest V. Griffin, 6955246
X Pfc Charles E. Lathrop, 35542002           Co."F"
  Bruno T. Zbiegien, 36019254
X Pfc George T. Polazzi, 36051942            Co."E"
  John Baptist, 36051754
  Sgt. R.W. Graham, 32157338                 Co."E"
  C.B. McGuinis, 15304531
  Robert T. George, 35130681
  John J. Guiney Jr. 31225721
  Lester Nemchick, 39180607
X Pfc Peter W. Kurlick, 36018828             Co."E"
  Robert C. DeLong, 32854866
  Vincent Schimdt, 32055144
  Rupert L. Thompson
  Henry B. Mason
```

THE 2ND INFANTRY ROLL OF HONOR

KILLED IN ACTION DURING AUGUST, 1944

B. Debellies, 11050661
Jack Gill, 51157666
Joseph Garner
Esau R. Olaque, 38125057
Arthur C. Yougren, 36017208
E.W. Kleneno, 36019622
X Sgt. Martin A. Kuhn, 36018612   Co"F"
Richard Easterlin, 36017224
Herbert Romans, 15064746
Edward Reynolds, 32807697
George Brinkly, 33638372
Charles Thuth, 36025729
Lynn Bailey, 33573423
Lloyd W. Holcombe, 34653784
Aubery German,
Leo Korppas, 36206453
Pfc Lacy E. Wallser, 35654184
William V. Malczewski, 33557008
Benjamin F. Seidel, 36051764
Harold G. Miller
Manual Ramirez, 39849373
Jacob R. Visgak, 35009636
D.V. McPherson, 36107487
Richard P. Coyle, 36052169
Michael P. Shaw, 38431435
X Sgt. Roger Whitney   Hq. 2nd Bn.
David B. Browing, 42120484
Pfc Orville L.R. Wickizer, 39315360
William G. Loew, 33113313
David King, 38D52098   ·   Hq. 3rd Bn.

THE 2ND INFANTRY ROLL OF HONOR

KILLED IN ACTION DURING AUGUST, 1944

```
   1st Lt. Leonard Harness, O-1292108
   Lawrence Ganson, 16021209
   Andrew L. Sabol, 33694649
   Stanley J. Gibus, 33351994
   R.L. Murray, 15014085
   Burley C. Wallace, 34162453
   Robert H. Richardson
   Wallace W. Simmons
   Alvin A. Berg, 3665719                         Co."G"
   Donald L. Richwine, 3350448
   Sgt. Leo O. Freeman, 38098017                  Co."B"
   Douglas Perry, 31428958                        Co."B"
   Pfc Elmer L. Dorman, 35100901                  Co.D"
   Fredrick C. Kalael              735 Tk.Bn.  )M&T
   Leland J. Rathe                 735 Tk.Bn.
X  Frank W. Jennings, 20610296                    Co."F"
X  Pfc Joseph Svoboda                             Co."F"
   Herbert Dunn, 33533020                         Co."F"
X  Sgt. Wilson Brandt, 6910990                    Co."G"
   Captain Robert A. Cranaan                      Hdqtrs.
   2nd Lt. Albert S. Batora, O-1299841            Co."B"
   Pfc Armise Shadd, 15064887                     Co."B"
   Thomas V. Hastings, 36614784                   Co.B"
   Henry Bosch
```

THE 2ND INFANTRY ROLL OF HONOR

KILLED IN ACTION DURING SEPTEMBER, 1944

X	John T. Lampel, 36781638	Co. "A"
	Edwin Chalupniczale, 36109097	Co. "A"
XX	S/Sgt. Thomas Spain	Co. "A"
X	2nd Lt. John M. Bennett, 0-491560	Co. "G"
X	T/Sgt. Bruno V. Mankus, 20607271	Co. "G"
	James C. White, 70820063	Co. "B"
	Bernard Fritzinger, 33835323	Co. "B"
	Sgt. E.F. Kropidlowski, 36109002	Co. "C"
X	Pfc Robert J. Collins, 35130778	Co. "G"
	Joseph Gervasi, 32802244	Co. "G"
X	Sheldon D. Brunner, 36107074	Co. "F"
	Arnold P. Robertson, 34608037	Co. "F"
	Captain Richard (Rocky) Stone	Co. "F"
	Kenneth S. Pease, 35130775	
	Edward Foltz, 36051822	Co. "F"
X	Sgt. Victor R. Weaver, 36052032	Co. "F"
	George W. Hale, 37623483	
	Pfc Sylverian Kuharski, 36206200	Hq. 3rd Bn.
	John E. Bennett Jr., 6761599	
	Reino J. Korpi, 36211734	
	Herman J. Singer, 36786003	
	Day L. Selph, 38233776	
X	Robert E. Fransisco, 35009786	Co. "G"
	Irvin Hansen, 36016101	Co. "F"
	Kelley R. Brahic, 36040399	
	Joseph Hernandez, 39849158	
	Chester E. Stabenow, 36255883	
	Edwin R. Noyes, 32214844	
	Blain S. Eakelison, 39923487	
	Ralph G. Newcomer, 33845266	
	Frank Masar, 36583020	
X	Sgt. Joseph F. Russo, 16002541	Co. "K"
	Sgt. Henry T. Johnson, 36119350	Co. "K"
	Horace E. Himmel, 35694374	
	Glenn R. Johnson, 36830822	
	Gerard Beaudoin, 31322983	

THE 2ND INFANTRY ROLL OF HONOR

KILLED IN ACTION DURING SEPTEMBER, 1944

```
        Thomas J. Egan, 36015702
        Rudolph H. Klaasen, 36051785
        Donald P. Troendly, 35295364
        Koert Stulp, 35303137
        Frank A. Schan, 37301094                    Co."F"
        Hubert R. McCauley, 36226188                 Co."K"
        Earl D. Hager, 35213765
        Hoyt H. Payne, 34500001
        Marshell Faulkner, 37667783
   XX   Sgt. Alfred H. Carslake, 36225797           Co."G"
        Leonard F. Swenor, 36457275                  Co."I"
        John J. Lemieux, 31440335
        Joseph M. Uram, 32771519
        Charles L. Howard, 34833400
        Raymond L. Krejca, 36015617
        Cpl. Harold R. Best, 35217927
        Pfc Harold H. Schultz, 36013010
        Pfc Paul L. Pederson, 36033194               Hq. 2nd Bn
        Ace Francuski, 35009891                      Co."I"
        Charles J. Kabela, 36019154                  Co."I"
        Edward J. Elvers, 42022002
        Leep Forest, 37629933
        William H. Cardwell, 33797991
        Henry B. Dewey, 35880177
    X   Sgt. George Copps, 36018340                  Co."C"
        Conrad Cooper, 39864880
        Arlind Loden, 34875166
        William Placantini, 33599599
        Louis Hines, 33765367
        Andrew B. Candelaria, 33747599
        James R. Barbour, 34851143
        Wayne N. Housewirth, 36773047
        Walter S. Nolan, 6573042
        1st Lt. Steyrl C. Bilger, 0-1822318
        Robert R. McCall, 34896507
```

THE 2ND INFANTRY ROLL OF HONOR

KILLED IN ACTION DURING SEPTEMBER, 1944

Clyde M. Reddish, 36784487
Charles D. Tidholm, 36700151
Walter Glaskey, 42061354
Ralph C. Leonard, 31371359
Gordon E. Mudd, 35709495
David L. Jenks, 19119646
Arthur R. Aitken, 37503703
Forest W. McHenry, 35760577
Cecil H. Williams, 36107368
Steve G. Stathopulos, 36016720
A.D. Edwards, 38449889
Thomas A. Deller, 33234989
Joe A. Rosprim, 38203347
Carl S. Freundlick, 0-01016923
Joseph R. Ruszavick, 32703167

	Sgt. Shelby Givens, 15046879	Co."C"
X	Pfc Clavin W. Wills, 34465754	Co."E"
	Sgt. Carl J. Pitts, 15060042	Co."F"
	2nd Lt. Robert J. Green, 0-1312842	Co."L"
	Michael Vukovich, 36018115	Co."H"
	Harold Bedell, 32798554	Co."H"
	Pfc Ottis W. Vaughn, 36018973	Co."H"
	Sgt. Archie W. Vaughn, 36051926	Co."H"
	Pfc Warren H. Quigley, 32948860	Co."C"
	Pfc Elmer He. Welsen, 36107364	Co."C"
X	Pfc Rudolph S. Wodarski, 36018830	Co."G"
	Pfc John Shedlock, 33465073	Co."G"

THE 2ND INFANTRY ROLL OF HONOR

KILLED IN ACTION DURING SEPTEMBER, 1944

X	Pfc John H. Lambert, 35631745	Co."G"
	Joseph P. Hull, 32948890	Co."E"
	Pfc Alberto B. Valenzuela, 39849224	Co."K"
	1st Lt. Enos Lloyd-Jones, O-1420750	
	Pfc Isidro G. Baca, 39649203	Co."F"
	Pfc Lawrence G. Forsythe, 36003125	Co."F"
	Pfc Harold W. Higgins, 35213833	Co."F"
	Alfred Landau, 31416685	Co."E"
X	Pfc William E. Kratzke, 32877316	Co."E"
X	Pfc Carl R. Sajec, 36206442	Co."H"
	Pfc Charles G. Iavomiai, 36016801	Co."L"
	Pfc Truemon Cool, 35213695	Co."F"
	Alfred Arbour, 35072559	Co."M"
	Orvall A. Fanver, 39213697	Co."G"
	Russell F. Sheatles, 33614530	Co."L"
	1st Lt. Marvin A. King, O-382511	Co."A"
	Anthony E.Dipace, 42101862	Co."D"
	Cpl. Clifford R. Mooney, 36206495	Co."M"
	Pfc Vincent W. Gengler, 35024965	Co."K"
	2nd Lt. John R. Brown Jr., O-516903	Co."E"
X	Sgt. John A. Beeson, 35130660	Co."E"
	Robert W. Keenan, 42061457	Co."E"
	S/Sgt. Eugene A. Busch, 36103261	Co."E"
	Michael P. Olsyewski, 42064635	Co."E"
	S/Sgt. Edward F. Stone, 33133335	Co."E"
	Robert D. McDanial, 35243915	Co."B"
	Harry Frelich, 36226032	Co."M"
	Pfc Leo H. Zaiki, 16024365	Co."M"
	Pfc James E. Van Dorn, 36206179	Co."L"
	Pfc Dell G. Kainz, 36203303	Co."L"
	Pfc Joseph J. Maizie, 36034462	Co."L"
	Roy E. Campbell, 34814202	Co."D"

THE 2ND INFANTRY ROLL OF HONOR

KILLED IN ACTION DURING OCTOBER, 1944

Constantine J. Iannacon, 12085047
William L. Uherek, 13088233
James H. Sullivan, 34887094
John W. Tingle, 35582075
William L. Dickerson, 34263093
Harry M. Alger, 36598423
Leo O. Garson, 34254747
Norris O. Olson, 37268731
Ernest Timiue, 6834731
James W. Bradford, 33846336
Joseph A. Brown, 34884405
Frederick R. Sayles, 32138625
Ernest E. Mills, 31267880
Floyd W. Snider, 34185558
Gaylard D. Sell, 36822623
2nd Lt. Charles F. Quick, O-1319334
X   Sgt. Silas I. Elliott,   Co."G"
Clarence G. Smith, 35070934

THE 2ND INFANTRY ROLL OF HONOR

KILLED IN ACTION DURING NOVEMBER, 1944

Charles W. Mayes, 36459624
Joseph Stark, 32860606
Joseph Parnell, 42010452
Robert B. Baird, 37538086
Wade M. Horn, 1st Lt., O- 1887355
Michael A. Raubas, 36018271
Danial A. Altier, 36019620
Herbert J. Werren, 2nd Lt. O-540033
W.P. Soboczinski, 31416431
Joseph J. Davis, 38651214
Robert L. Richmond, 36025320
Clarence N. Allgood, 14039063
Marcus C. Holbrook, 34689219
Vernon P. Thomas, 15055732
Edward J. Craven, 36151182
Norren H. Baubom, 38602358
Michael J. Takacs, 35530654
Robert E. Ensmieger, 37373717
Lawrence Church, 35650106
Robert Hintz, 36205358
John W. Phelan, 32948939
Gerald Fast, 37241012
E.W. Wegrzunowiez, 36107389
Alvin J. Drescher, 4222909
Vincent N. Giglio, 31307945
2nd Lt. Leroy B. Sather, O-1287070
Cleo L. Turner, 38343477
Raphael S. Boghosiaa, 36017398

THE 2ND INFANTRY ROLL OF HONOR

KILLED IN ACTION DURING NOVEMBER, 1944

J.J. Purczynski, 36105651
Nick Utchel, 33670887
David L. Goddwin, Jr. 33525824
Bernard J. Sullivan, 36663695
Donald C. Leach, 39216314
Harry Schnert, 42061015
Ralph V. Ridgeway, 37709353
Ralph V. Nickolas, 36018822
Ralph W. Dustin, 35603439
George F. Newbold, 36018621
Lawrence R. Simpson, 36524697
John T. Merchant, 31370903
William E. Miller, 36070993
Ralph T. Roper, 35722770
Gordon B. Pilgrim, 36814289
John P. Jones, 34784103
Edwaed J. Stroz, 42103285
Harry E. Haarman, 39531442
Leo M. Van Offerman, 36825786
Jesus F. Escabar, 39863993
Howard A. Wade, 39919381
Victor E. Claussen, 37204113
Ralph D. Sims Jr. 18169673
John C. Stevens, 31399928
Raymond L. Avery, 6594453
Glenn D. Baxder, 37361268
Michael Baden, 13122861
Albert J. Kahout, 36604562
Raymond M. Montoya, 39715608
Eugene J. Storm, 33774685
Robert E. Ludwig, 39129060
Mariano Fiumara, 31461947

THE 2ND INFANTRY ROLL OF HONOR

KILLED IN ACTION DURING NOVEMBER, 1944

Bruce W. Smith, 31378744
1st Lt. Ray H. Smith, O-451763
J.I. McGinnis, 16007238
David S. Richman, 20361306
Albert J. Terrell, 34832463
Charley Dingess, 15064755
William Schedel, 15014395
X Nickolas Russo, 32911647
Gerhardt W. Reinke, 36214539
Alton Vincent, 37106887
Raymond W. Jones,   Co. "G"
Cecil Bryant, 39722798
Thomas G. Rose, 35808684
Fred J. Doster Jr., 421010092
Sgt. Norman F. Birens, 36248089
Harold R. Albrecht, 36247878
William R. Landsman, 37212779
M.J. Degiralamo, 31193223
Harold A. Huns, 313754070

THE 2ND INFANTRY ROLL OF HONOR

KILLED IN ACTION DURING DECEMBER, 1944

(The Battle of the Bulge)

Elmore Kouba, 37293288
David T. Miner, 13141646
Buran D. Rakes, 33881537
Cecil B. Hardy, 35709206
Orvall A. Fauver, 39213497
Owen Huston, 35901285
Richard T. Bykeny, 35009875
Roy Largon Jr., 35617759
Walter F. Hock, 36150988
Bernard C. Anthony, 33674144
Alfred Smith, 34898094
Edward J. Holian, 32322010
K.W. Peters, 36606404
Howard F. Sockup, 35275897
John H. Lambert, 35631743
Theodore J. Sickinger, 33455417
John J. Hines, 33071901
Chester L. Chapman, 34707538
Burnard R. Hoorman, 69008700
John Shedlock, 33455073
2nd Lt. Woodrow A. Lewis, O-1312177
Joseph P. Hull, 32948890
X Pfc Franklin C. Nothohm, 36205365   Co. "G"
Leo W. Hobson, 34897478
Stephen Headsky, 36019153
Forrest J. Boswell, 34734601
Albert Johnson, 6285680
Henry J. Trese, 36206223
William Stein, 36016852
Walter J. Debow, 32270509
2nd Lt. Edgar Heist, O-1014273

THE 2ND INFANTRY ROLL OF HONOR

KILLED IN ACTION DURING DECEMBER, 1944
(The Battle of the Bulge)

Crey P. Kuksey, 2nd Lt., O-532097
Amando J. Flore, 32802934
Charles M. Wilkinson, 42119293
Alvin Kuek, 36206187
Charles G. Winkle, 36694778
John F. Reynolds, 31392386
James S. Norton, 35876550
Greo K. Piper, 34890300
William T. Ditz, 36973969
Forrest A. Trantham, 36842545
John D. Gasparetti, 3133089
Arthur C. Ward, 35897509
Clay A. Hosmer, 37742210
Chester S. NaPierala, 32027243
Carol Cantrell, 35973071
William A. Luciano, 32856101
X Leo P. Walsh, 36018669
X Frank H. Wright, 36018669
Walter M. Burnbough, 35243761
S/Sgt. Lewis W. Radecap, 35152853
Victor C. Gower, 37240837
1st Lt. Klas L. Hefner, O-1323695
Harold E. Smith, 35438130
Jay R. Blaines, 35144725
Waldo W. Wolgenbach, 37693780
Grover A. Sell, 36359145
Thomas W. Horinka, 5629393
Albert J. Ferrucci,
X Sgt. Eugene Brinkman,   Co."G"
X Sgt. Lipski   Co."G"
Earl I. Miller, 35627162
Harold F. Nelson, 33845265
Paul J. Berres, 3524346
William F. Taylor Jr., 35234530
Edward C. Fagan, 32905749
Paul Dockery,Jr. 34438576

THE 2ND INFANTRY ROLL OF HONOR

KILLED IN ACTION DURING DECEMBER, 1944
        (The Battle of the Bulge)

Robert Crook, 35800408
Robert T. Burgoon, 35925533
2nd Lt. Allen E. Ewing, O-1315046
Cleo F. Drake, 37742201
Harold A. Webb, 37606726
John J. Franklin, 32863189
Jerome L. Haft, 32706205
Albert A. Dengel, 36257462
Everett, M. Gorman, 29253368 -
Edward J. Handzel, 36270136
Richard N. Ryan, 33752848
Willie T. Nelson, 34831673
Samuel D. Hanley, 36056584
Herman J. Harms, 38671204
Leland A. Peterson, 39618642
Carl C. McCallis, 34917523
Henry Brice Elliott, 35899412
Joseph C. Neteja, 36019181
William Pachan, 35241500
Marvin Baker, 34971393
Albert A. Herkommer, 42045265
2nd Lt. Ervin Kvech, O-1054300
William D. Sheehan, 39583476
Charles E. Cole, 31468355
Robert J.(S) Davis, 38664074
William C. Fleming, 31446566
Louson W. Fish, 20202943
Samuel M. Bowers, 34924613
Martinez Gregory, 39722496
Fred H. Pucci, 31198466
Maurice N. Cheadle, 35130782
William N. Norman, 42102990
Everett B. Bell, 35213723
Harold D. Beldridge, 36977225
Pfc Paul Davidson,   Hq. 2nd Bn.
1st Sgt. Stien(Stein)   Co."A"
T/4 Thaddeus Peltz   Hq. 1st Bn.

THE 2ND INFANTRY ROLL OF HONOR

KILLED IN ACTION DURING FEBRUARY, 1945

	Pfc H. Bringman, 15015089	Hq. 1st Bn.
	Pfc William Gritzer, 33887017	Co."K"
	Pfc H. Sapa, 42017285	Co."L"
	Pfc L. Church, 13014254	Co."L"
	2nd Lt. R. Dolby,	Co."M"
	R.W.Sargent, 31434670	Co."A"
	Pfc Orris L. Haines, 37644723	
	Pfc W. Hart,	Co."C"
	Pfc N. Cushman,	Co."C"
	Pfc M. Stockmaster,	
X	S/Sgt. William H. Henderson,33081753	Hq. 2nd Bn.
X	T/5 Harry E. Folenias, 20507858	Hq. 2nd Bn.
	Charles C. Rehmer, 37749545	Co."I"
	Herbert Salmanowitz, 42179267	Co."I"
	Alexander Edlestein, 36978222	
	John O. Haralson, 34839472	
	Charles T. Harris, 38582246	
	Robert H. Perry, 39557238	
	2nd Lt. Lowell F. Baker, 0-306668	
	William F. Bausher, 35931480	Co."D"
	Ruben B. Hartman, 6835339	Hq. 3rd Bn.
	Bernard C. Rosenberg, 12231901	Co."I"
	Charles R. Rezeau, 37736719	Co."I"
	George V. Longdean, 31461873	Co."I"
	Joseph P. Mendonca, 31227744	
	Edward A. Wilson, 31452088	
	William L. Downing, 15012409	
	Mario Gioia, 32811810	
	T/5 John A. Adams, 42051956	Med. Det.

THE 2ND INFANTRY ROLL OF HONOR

KILLED IN ACTION DURING MARCH, 1945

Pfc Sam Kuric, 36018880	Hq. 3rd Bn.
Ruben C. Kelley, 33846008	Hq. 3rd Bn.
Danial P. Hawkins, 37752687	Co."B"
Earl C. Fanning, 36918965	Co."B"
H. Mossman, 33782187	Med. Det.
J.M. Courchesne, 31403312	
R.L. Jones, 32805416	Co."A"
H.D. Terzago, 32771373	Co."A"
Harry Mazo, 36522899	Co."A"
John W. Angwin, 31377261	Co."A"
Charles E. Paxton, 2o726560	Co."A"
Forrest E. Archibald, 42165725	Co."A"
Richard Artlieb, 67050700	Co."A"
John E. Koski,	
S/Sgt. Martin A.Stipcak, 36109084	Co."I"
Joseph Schildkraut, 42179269	Co."I"
Sgt. Howard L. Taylor, 36457873	Co."K"
James B. Murphy, 33823458	Co."K"
Pfc W. Olson, 36206447	Co."H"
Sgt, Ernest E. LoFrieniere	
Pfc Glen A. Perkins, 37256746	Co."B"
Pfc Robert L. Self, 44036005	Co."B"
Pfc Sulmon Harris, 33180927	Co."B"
Pfc Richard King, 36433184	Co."B"
T/5 Roy B. Schull, 34190067	Co."B"
Pfc Bernard T. Lewandowskim	Med. Det.
2nd Lt. Edwin M. Eberling, O-538189	Co."D"
Pfc James N. Asher, 35239717	Co."D"
Pfc Charles C. Davin, 35142141	Co."E"
Calvin V. Carter, 33855105	
Dial Hicks, 35080803	
Lucian E. Rice Jr., 388i6547	
Paul S. Spaide, 33765943	
2nd Lt. Carl E. Wilson, O-527188	
Raymond E. Wall, 34603658	
Verlin M. Carlock, 37344961	

```
            THE 2ND INFANTRY ROLL OF HONOR
            ────────────────────────────


            KILLED IN ACTION DURING MARCH, 1945
            ───────────────────────────────────
```

```
      James A. Long, 54701705
      Ernest D. Mullis, 44015632
      J.C. Keith, 18008852
      Orris C. Haines, 37644973
      Christopher C. Farner, 34985488        Co."M"
      Clifford Morningstar, 36989656         Co."M"
   X  Robert H. Perry, 39557238              Co."G"
      Clarence E. Bruce, 37594184            Co."K"
      Eldridge B. Christison, 35816498
      William J. Fulghum, 34058545           Co."A"
      Donald J. Brady, 160260988             7th Eng.
      Lewis M. Kloker, 36052744              Co."L"
      Dinsmore Knepp Jr., 33764603
      Casey J. Rodgers, 2nd Lt., 0-1017756
      David Afoa, 39578358
      Edward J. Dluzniewski, 42144365
      Vance L. Banta, 35815006
      Rufus L. Bell, 33091090
      F.R. Borman, 33950398                  Co."A"
      V.R. Clinkenbeard, 38573717            Co."A"
      Henry Costelein, 36598970
      Jessie W. Yeates, 34837298             Co."C"
      Ervin Wilkerson, 44032596              Co."C"
      Paul B. Darnell, 20600437              Hq. Co.
      Paul W. Bonewitz, 37698104
      William R. Homfeldt, 37644804          Co."E"
      Charles R. Holmes Jr., 35782802        Co."E"
      2nd Lt. William A. Burns, 0-1328113    Co."E"
```

THE 2ND INFANTRY ROLL OF HONOR

KILLED IN ACTION DURING MARCH, 1945

```
     Jessie C. Cox, 37655531              Co."E"
     Thomas G. Peters, 7006929            Co."K"
     Marshall S. Folsom, 34820264         Co."E"
     Henry W. Stanton, 42178923
 XX  Rolland L. Dysinger, 36109056        Co."K"
     Joseph A. Speck, 36018286            Co."F"
     Harold D. West, 31448412             Co."F"
     Anthony C. Straker, 13185714         Co."F"
     Fraser E. Davis, 33845997            Co."F"
     Clarence M. Coffey, 33573211         Co."F"
     Don P. Moore, 34312822
     William A. Hesson, 34360680
     John J. Zerilli, 32701184
     Doyle W. Frysinger, 15100752
     Benny C. Korsak, 36649641
     W.W. Botts Jr., 34836201
     James F. Whitworth, 34684679
     John J. Osness, 36206355
     1st Lt. Michael M. Towey, 0-1315875
     Thomas B. Terrell, 34851195
     Elsworth F. Shaffer, 35782806
     Carlo J. Bangie, 31414223            Co."K"
     Joseph A. Piwonski, 31428391
```

THE 2ND INFANTRY ROLL OF HONOR

KILLED IN ACTION DURING APRIL, 1945

Martin D. Sweeney, 36730065
Norbert J. Wauzl, 3773676
William D. McMauly, 33582206
Chris C. Speaker, 39321629
Donald J. Kolinski
Samuel H. Diehl, 33664380
Thomas F. Dixon, 339447159
Daniel R. Connell, 44006337
Walter S. Zawalich, 31436066
Arthur H. Thompson, 37481887
John J. Mackey, 32528106
William C. Williams, 34820066
Gerald Laftis, 1214565
Francis D. Lawler, 33587576
Clarence J. Niecum, 20602964
Nicholas A. Samaros, 33060205
Kenneth D. Smith, 39285112
Richard C. Marine, 38580814
James E. Calvert, 17007301
Elmer Reese, 33715529
Albert B. Carley, 37035663
James Robertson, 36592858   (Col)
James E. Ried, 33281910   (Col)
Warrant Floyd R. Willis, W-2131791
Officer
Allen Richard, 38409096   (Col)
2nd Lt. Frederick C. Jacob, O-1175470
Henry N. Kope, 12137778
Clarence B. Young, 38505970   (Col)

THE 2ND INFANTRY ROLL OF HONOR

KILLED IN ACTION DURING MAY, 1945
GERMANY SURRENDERS

    Warrant Officer Charley Havlat, W-37153423
X   Pfc John C. Wright, 33814885   Co."G"
X   Pfc Charles B. McGuire, 32639643   Co."G"
    Sgt. F. Canatsey, 36051979   Co."H"
    Frank J. Luza, 31332659
    Ernest W. Fryer, 35018222

R E S T R I C T E D

Headquarters 5th Infantry Division

6 Bebuary 1945

MEMORANDUM

The following extracts of General Court Martial sentences promulgated by Headquarters, ETOUSA, will be brought to the attention of all men of this command.

1. Cpl.--------- was tried by General Court Martial on the
following charges: (1) Murder, (2) Rape of a girl less than 16 years
of age, (3) Aiding and abetting another soldier to rape a girl less
than 16 years of age. He was sentenced and found guilty and to be hanged by the neck until dead. The sentence was approved and ordered carried into execution on January 8, 1945.

2. Captain---------- was found guilty of being drunk on duty
as a liaison officer in violation of AW 85. He was sentenced to be dismissed from the service. The sentence was approved and confirmed.

3. Pfc ---------- and Pvt.---------- committed the felony of
rape. Each was sentenced to be hanged by the neck until dead. The sentence was approved and ordered executed on January 9, 1945.

4. Second Lieutenant ---------- wilfully disobeyed the command of a superior officer and did apply to his own use and benefit,
without authority, a government vehicle. He was found guilty and sentenced to be dismissed from the service. The sentence was approved and
confirmed.

5. First Lieutenant ---------- in violation of AW 96 was
found guilty of (1) being drunk and disorderly in uniform, (2) drinking with enlisted men, (3) discharging fire arms without authority.
He was sentenced to be dismissed from the service. The sentence was
approved and confirmed.

6. Second Lieutenant ---------- was found guilty of viola-
tionof AW 64, in that he wilfully disobeyed the command of a superior officer. He was sentenced to be dismissed from the service, total
forfeitures, and confinement for 20 years. The sentence was approved
and confimed.

HEADQUARTERS
THIRD UNITED STATES ARMY
OFFICE OF THE COMMANDING GENERAL

APO 403
28 November 1944

SUBJECT: Discipline

     The following digest of significant courts-martial sentences will be brought to the attention of all personal by posting on Bulletin boards pursuant to the provisions of Circular 13, section 1b, Headquarters, European Theater of Operations, U.S.Army.

     First Lieutenant ----------- was sentenced to be dismissed from the service for being drunk and disorderly in a public place and drinking with enlisted men. (November 15, 1944) (Hqtrs.3rd Army)

     First Lieutenant---------- was sentenced to be dismissed from the service, to suffer total forfeitures, and to be confined at hard labor for six years(6), for being absent without leave for three days(3) and for wrongfully taking and withholding a government vehicle. (November 1, 1944) Hqtrs. 3rd Army)

     Second Lieutenant---------- was sentenced to forfeit fifty dollars($50.00) per month of his pay for the period of twelve(12) months for writing and mailing a post card revealing that his ship would sail unescorted, the date of sailing and the location of pier from which it would sail.

     Private----------and Private---------- were each sentenced to be hanged by the neck until dead for rape of French civilians. (November 9, 1944) (Hqtrs. 3rd Army)

     Private---------- was sentenced to dishonorable discharge, total forfeitures, and confinement at hard labor for ten years(10) for drawing a bayonet against his superior officer and failing to obey an order of a commissioned officer.(November 2, 1944) (90th Infantry Division)

     Pvt.---------- was sentenced to dishonorable discharge, total forfeitures, and confinement at hard labor for eight years(8) for being absent without leave from his organization for six(6) days . (October 16, 1944) (6th Armored Division)

<u>By command of Lieutenant General Patton</u>

R E S T R I C T E D

Headquarters 5th Infantry Division

6 Febuary 1945

MEMORANDUM

      7. First Lieutenant ---------- was found guilty of Being AWOL for three days and of embezzlement of various amounts of money. He was sentenced to be dismissed from the service, total forfeitures and confinement for six years(6). The sentence was approved and confirmed.

      8. Second Lieutenant ---------- was found guilty of abandoming his platoon while it was engaged with the emeny in violation of AW 75. He was sentenced to be dismissed from the service, total forfeitures and confinement for 20 years. The sentence was approved and confirmed.

      9. First Lieutenant ---------- was found guilty of (1) permitting an enlisted man to dispose of a service rifle by trading it away,(2) ascertaining that an enlisted man could conceal the fact that Lt.-------- had given permission to dispose of a service rifle, (3) False official statement while under oath. He was sentenced to be dismissed from the service. The sentence was approved and confirmed.

      10. Pvt.----------- was found guilty of (1) AWOL for five days (5), (2) Murder, (3) Assault with intent to commit murder by shooting a commissioned officer. He was sentenced to be hanged by the neck until dead. The sentence was approved and ordered executed January 15,1945

      11. Pvt.--------------was found guilty of rape. He was sentenced to be hanged by the neck until dead. The sentence was approved and ordered executed January 15, 1945

      12. Captain ---------- was found guilty of (1) Using morphine, a narcotic drug, (2) failure to record receipt of morphine in narcotic register. He was sentenced to be dismissed from the service. The sentence was approved and confirmed.

      13. Sgt.----------- was found guilty of rape and using without authority a government vehicle. He was sentenced to be hanged by the neck until dead. The sentence was approved and commuted to dishonorable discharge, total forfeitures, and confinement for life.

      14. Pvt.---------- was found guilty of rape on two occasions. He was sentenced to be hanged by the neck until dead. The sentence was confimmed and ordered executed on January 22, 1945.

R E S T R I C T E D

Headquarters 5th Infantry Division

6 Febuary 1945

MEMORANDUM

15. Pvt. ---------- was found guilty of murder. He was sentenced to be hanged by the neck until dead. The sentence was approved and ordered executed on January 22, 1945.

16. Pvt. ---------- was found guilty of desertion in the violation of AW 58. He was sentenced to be shot to death with musketry. The sentence was confirmed and commited to dishonorable discharge and confinement for his natural life.

17. Second Lieutenant ---------- was found guilty of wilfully disobeying the command of his superior officer and desertion. He was sentenced to be shot to death with musketry. The sentence was confirmed and commuted to dismissal from the service and confinement for life.

18. Pvt. ---------- was found guilty of rape and assault and and threatening to do bodily harm with a dangerous weapon. He was sentenced to be hanged by the neck until dead. The sentence was confirm and ordered executed on January 30, 1945

19. Second Lieutenant ---------- was found guilty of misbehavior before the enemy by failing to advance with his command and which he had been ordered forward. He was sentenced to be dismissed from the service, total forfeitures and confinement for 50 years. The sentence was approved and confirmed.

20. Captain ---------- was found guilty of being drunk on duty. He was sentenced to be dismissed from the service. The sentence was approved and confirmed.

21. Sgt. ---------- was found guilty of (1) Deserting the service of the U.S. with the intent to avoid hazardous duty and to shirk important service and did remain absent until apprehended. He was sentenced to be shot to death with musketry. The sentence was approved and ordered executed January 25, 1945.

22. Second Lieutenant ---------- was found guilty of (1) Failing to properly classify typed extracts of battle formations and for proper safe guarding of such extracts.(2) For wrongfully carrying upon or about his possessions documents cotaining battle information, locations and moves affecting the armed forces of the United States, he being a person not required to carry such information. He was sentenced to be dismissed from the service. The sentence was approved and confirmed.